"*Taking on the Big Boys* is feminism at its butt-kicking best—an exposé, a manifesto, and a spirited, delightful read. I thought I knew a lot about women's economic status before I read this book, but I had barely scratched the surface. Bravo for Bravo!" **—Barbara Ehrenreich, author of bestselling *Nickel and Dimed***

"Please, please, please. All working women must read this book! Not only does Ellen Bravo vividly expose workplace inequities, she lays out real life solutions—picking up just where my film, *Nine to Five* left off." **—Jane Fonda**

Taking on the Big Boys is an autobiographical, practical, realistic, compelling, humorous *and* carefully crafted discussion of contemporary workplace issues for women from the vantage point of a committed, veteran feminist activist/writer. Ellen Bravo believes *still* that the goals of the women's movement in the United States are reachable and she tells us—clearly and simply—what we must do. Her reflections on pay equity, sexual harassment, welfare reform, balancing work and family, and a broad range of other issues are heart-felt and compel us to action. Let's get moving!!! **—Beverly Guy-Sheftall, founding director of the Women's Research & Resource Center, Spelman College, and coauthor of *Gender Talk: The Struggle for Women's Equality in African American Communities***

Ellen Bravo "is a powerful advocate for fair treatment of women, and she makes clear in this excellent book that more needs to be done to achieve real equality, eliminate glass ceilings, reward work fairly, and strengthen families. Her proposals for reform will be of value to policymakers, activists, and caring citizens alike." **—Senator Edward M. Kennedy**

"If there is any hint of unfairness or power imbalance in your world, Ellen Bravo is your friend. Smart, kind, funny and very effective, she has at last put her lifetime of organizing skills into *Taking on the Big Boys*. She shows us how to fulfill hopes." **—Gloria Steinem**

"Stop whatever you are doing and read this book! *Taking on the Big Boys* has it all—analysis of how many problems are rooted in gender inequality, fascinating first-person accounts of the struggle for equity, and a call to arms no thinking person can refuse. Ellen Bravo makes a compelling case that feminism is not only relevant but is a key to broader political and personal issues of our time." —**Congresswoman Gwen Moore, member Committee on Small Business**

"Feminism is alive and well as long as working women and men read Ellen Bravo's compelling call to action." —**Robert B. Reich, Former U.S. Secretary of Labor, professor of public policy, University of California at Berkeley**

"This book reclaims 'feminism' by redefining it, reinvesting it with a sense of promise for a broader constituency—the family. This smart diagnosis . . . becomes a prescription for action . . . and catalyst to change the prognosis for women in the 21st century." —**Lieutenant Governor Barbara Lawton, Wisconsin**

"Finally, an answer to the Mommy Wars and opting-out myth! *Taking on the Big Boys* changes the conversation, showing the price we all have to pay when society fails to support parents' dual responsibilities. Happily, fixing the problem is not only the right thing to do, but good for everyone. Time to take on the Big Boys!" —**Joan Blades, cofounder of MoveOn! and coauthor of *The Motherhood Manifesto***

"In this eloquent and bold book, Ellen Bravo brings feminism back into the national spotlight. She enlarges our understanding of feminism by connecting it to the domination of our culture by the rich and powerful. She may spur us to challenge that domination." —**Howard Zinn, author of *People's History of the United States***

"The writing is enchanting, the information helpful and the stories accessible. By the end, Ellen Bravo convinces us that change is possible—how refreshing to end on a high note." —**Amy Richards, coauthor of *Manifesta: Young Women, Feminism and the Future***

"I love this book! It's a myth-buster and an eye-opener with an easy-to-read, compelling new take. Whether you're a policy specialist or a single mom, it's a must read. 'Dream the world you want,' it urges—and provides a valuable blueprint to do just that. What an important contribution to building the world we all need and deserve." **—Linda Chavez-Thompson, executive vice president, AFL-CIO**

"Thanks to Bravo for a book filled with well-told lessons about what feminism is: ordinary women making extraordinary changes that benefit women, men and our democracy. As she says, they aren't just smashing the glass ceiling, they are redesigning the buildings. Read it and you'll want to strap on your tool belt." **—Marie Wilson, executive director, The White House Project**

"*Taking on the Big Boys* is an unusually effective blend of scholarly research and personal experience, of humor and outrage. Ellen Bravo is a good storyteller who provides us with an insightful and compelling analysis. This is a book that is well-grounded in academic literature and practical experiences, and will make both students and advocates of social justice smarter and wiser." **—Dennis Dresang, founding director, LaFollette Public Policies Institute, University of Wisconsin**

"Ellen Bravo has written an elegant, inspiring book that should put Big Boys everywhere on notice. Read this book to see how other women did it, and then prepare to do it yourself." **—Rinku Sen, publisher, *ColorLines* Magazine**

"*Taking on the Big Boys* is more than a book about women in the work-place. It defines a lifetime of courage, dedication, and activism by its author. Ellen Bravo's name has justly become synonymous with women's rights. Her influence found in organizing efforts, testimony, courses in women's studies, books and essays, and especially advice and friendship have left indelible marks on the lives of countless women, and yes, men just like me. This book reminds us that there is still work to do when it comes to eliminating gender inequality." **—Herb Kohl, United States Senator**

TAKING ON THE BIG BOYS

Mariam K. Chamberlain Series on Social and Economic Justice

Taxes Are a Woman's Issue: Reframing the Debate
Mimi Abramovitz and Sandra Morgen with the
National Council for Research on Women

TAKING ON THE BIG BOYS

OR WHY FEMINISM IS GOOD FOR FAMILIES, BUSINESS, AND THE NATION

Ellen Bravo

The Feminist Press
at the City University of New York
New York

Published by The Feminist Press at the City University of New York
The Graduate Center
365 Fifth Avenue
New York, NY 10016
www.feministpress.org

First Feminist Press Edition, 2007.

Lyrics from the song "Sister" by Antibalas appear courtesy of Ninja tune.

Library of Congress Cataloging-in-Publication Data

Bravo, Ellen.
  Taking on the big boys: or Why feminism is good for families, business, and the nation /
Ellen Bravo. — 1st Feminist Press ed.
      p. cm.
  Includes bibliographical references.
  ISBN-13: 978-1-55861-545-8 (pbk.)
  ISBN-13: 978-1-55861-546-5 (library cloth)

  1. Feminism. 2. Feminist theory. I. Title. II. Title: Taking on the big boys. III. Title:
Why feminism is good for families, business, and the nation.
  HQ1190.B75 2007
  305.420973—dc22

                              2006024679

The Feminist Press would like to thank Mariam K. Chamberlain for her generosity in
supporting this project.

Text design by Lisa Force
Printed in Canada

10 09 08 07   5 4 3 2 1

To the Miller Boys, Larry, Nat, and Craig—inspiration and proof

People have to be made to understand that they cannot look for salvation anywhere but to themselves.
—Ella J. Baker

Try to imagine a world worth living in, and then ask yourself if that isn't worth fighting for.
—Leslie Feinberg, *Stone Butch Blues*

The wicked brother . . .
He gone be afraid if
   sister sees her strength
   sister feels her strength
   sister knows her strength.
He gone be afraid if
   sister smarter than him
   sister faster than him
   sister stronger than him. . . .
But strong brother no need to fear.
He going to be safe
In sister strength like him brother.
He going to listen to sister wisdom.
He not hate him sister.
He not patronize him sister.
Strong brother,
Call him feminist.
—From the song "Sister" by Antibalas,
album *What Is This America?*

CONTENTS

ACKNOWLEDGMENTS

First a number of big publishers said things to this effect: "Impressive, inspiring, at times shocking, even humorous, but sorry, we already have our woman for this year," or "Not sure there's an audience for a book like this." Then Florence Howe at The Feminist Press called and said, "We love your book." Thanks to everyone at The Feminist Press, especially Florence, Anjoli Roy, Gloria Jacobs, Lisa Force, and Franklin Dennis, for their enthusiastic support and incredible work.

I'm grateful to the many people I interviewed, particularly those who shared how they and their organizations took on the Big Boys: Kathy Augustine, Linda Chavez-Thompson, Christine Hansen, Anita Hill, LaDon James, Nadia Marin-Molina, Congresswoman Gwen Moore, Tyleatha Samuels, Debbie Schneider, former Congresswoman Pat Schroeder, Deeda Seed, Young Shin, Harriette Ternipsede, and Judy Victor.

Huge thanks to those who believed in this book and made it better, especially my twin sister, Lynne Bravo Rosewater, for her wise suggestions; friend and editor extraordinare, Barbara Deinhardt; and chat group members, Ellen Cassedy, Carolyn Daffron, and Natalie Wexler. I appreciate all those who gave me support and assistance, including Ingrid Ankerson, Eileen Appelbaum, Allison Beck, Jeremy Bishop, Linda Burnham, Dara Burwell, Cindia Cameron, Dorothy Cobble, Dennis Dresang, Joel Dresang, Margaret Egan, Pam Fendt, Netsy Firestein, Kim Foltz, Jocelyn Frye, Linda Garcia-Barnard, George Gonos, Arne Kalleberg, Shannah Kurland, Vicki Lovell, Linda Meric, Barbara Miner, Kathleen Mulligan-Hansel, Mildred

Navedo, Karen Nussbaum, Mary Ochs, Candace Owley, Barbara Zack Quindel, Bob Peterson, Michael Rosen, Cathy Ruckelshaus, T Santora, Rinku Sen, Amy Shapiro, Amy Stear, Dan Silverman, Nona Martin Stuck, Chris Tilly, Jeffrey Wenger, and Joan Williams.

A special thanks to Gerda Lerner, for her early support; to my circle of FOAD defiers and confidence boosters, especially Zohreh Emami, Anita Kline, Sandra Priebe, and the late Mileka Aljuwani; Betsy and Donna at the copy shop, who said, "Wow, I'd buy this book" the first time they saw the title; and to everyone at the post office who gave blessings as well as great service.

I couldn't have written this book without the scores of 9to5 leaders and others who shared their stories with me over the years and the untold numbers who've been part of the struggles I describe. Their courage, resolve, and wisdom give me inspiration and hope.

Above all, thanks to my mother, the late Dorothy Bravo, for trusting me to find my own way; to Nat and Craig, who greeted my obsessing with affection and encouragement; and to Larry, who fed me, held me, and made me laugh.

TAKING ON THE BIG BOYS

TABLE OF CONTENTS

1. OVERVIEW

Soon after the publication of my book *The Job/Family Challenge* (1995), I appeared on a popular Sunday night interview show in Milwaukee. The next day my husband went to buy a new bicycle. The guy behind the counter pointed to my name on the check.

"Do you live with *her*?" he asked.

"She's my wife," Larry replied.

The bike shop owner leaned over the counter as if about to divulge a secret: "I saw her on that show last night. And the amazing thing is, she didn't say one thing I disagreed with. She even made me laugh."

"What'd you expect?" Larry started to ask. But he didn't—because he already knew (plus he really wanted to get home and ride that bike). When the shop owner clicked on my interview, he was waiting for me to say, "All men are pigs," "All women are saints," "Women who stay home with kids are wasting their lives." Instead he heard how little this society values families, and how much men as well as women suffer when workplaces function as if everyone had a wife at home full time. He was surprised to learn that the changes feminists want are not favors to women, but a better way to do business, raise families, build society. And yes, most men have a lot of changing to do—but here I was, arguing they have much more to gain than to give up.

And what do you know, I had a sense of humor.

I wanted to tell you this story so you'd see what a nice, reasonable, and amusing person I am. But the more I thought about it, the more I became, you should pardon the expression, PISSED OFF. Think about it—the majority of women in the United States earn less than $25,000 a year. The average woman loses nearly a half million dollars over her lifetime because of pay inequities. Cameroon, Brazil, and India offer better maternity leave than we do. The percentage of female executives is down and the percentage of kids in poverty has gone back up. And feminists like me are the ones with a bad reputation?

It's hard not to be outraged. But I'm not mad at most people, not even most men. Who I'm really mad at are the Big Boys.

Who Are the Big Boys?

The Big Boys are what I call the relatively small number of men who have a real stake in maintaining gender discrimination. They're the ones who control wealth and power in this country. You may think of them as the "powers-that-be" or the ruling class or the owning class or "the Man." They profit from our labor, set the conditions under which we work, and create or greatly influence public policy. They may be executives, elected officials, lobbyists, pundits. I include their spokespeople, whether appointed or self-appointed, since these people help the Big Boys maintain power. Some may wear high heels and lipstick, but regardless of gender, they're part of this group.

It's not enough to run the show—the Big Boys also control its description. By their reckoning, the status quo isn't a particular system that serves their interest. It's inevitable and beneficial to all. Whatever perks they happen to have, they deserve. Because they're in charge, they get to tell the story of what's happening in the world—what's working, what the problems are, what solutions are needed. Anyone can put forward opposing views. But the Big Boys' version is the one we hear most often. The tales they tell, repeated over and over by the media they control, take on the appearance of objective truth. Yet as we'll see, these narratives are often myths designed to misdirect and confuse while they perpetuate the existing distribution of power.

The Big Boys don't function like a club or fraternity. They don't have secret handshakes or smoke-filled meetings where they conspire to keep women down. And they don't all agree on every point. But they do operate from the same general interests and often work together to preserve their authority.

Some men earn the title of "Big Boys" even though they have no wealth and little actual power, based on the role they play at the workplace to keep women out or down. These folks may see themselves as part of "the people," but their behavior toward women in fact helps cement the Big Boys' domination.

By saying the Big Boys are relatively few in number, I certainly don't mean to let men as a whole off the hook. Most men exhibit male supremacy—the notion that males are superior to females—in the way they view and treat women, and the majority don't think that's a problem. Guys who get kicked around in the rest of their lives grow up believing they can at least be "the boss" at home. They're not eager to let that go. But as this book will point out in many different places, most men actually have much to gain from feminism. Only the Big Boys have a lot to lose (and even some of them can be transformed).

To understand how feminists—and women as a whole—got such a bad rap, we have to understand the role of the Big Boys and learn how to take them on.

Back to Basics: How Did This Happen?

The Big Boys didn't always exist, and neither did gender inequality. Some would argue that men have always been masters, or brutes. I don't buy it. Anthropologists have documented a very different story—tribes where gender played a role in how men and women spent their day, but not in how that work was valued.[1]

Picture the earliest humans. The problem wasn't that cavewomen were too emotional to go after a woolly mammoth, or men too macho to tidy up the cave. The men trooped out to hunt because the tribe needed food and they were mobile; women hung out near the cave and gathered edible food and other nearby supplies because they were usually pregnant or lactating. There's every reason to think both forms of work were valuable and valued. When a child was born, the group always knew who the mother was, but the dad connection was much less clear. That reality often added to women's status. In many human societies, mothers were revered and given significant power.[2]

Why did this change in many parts of the world? Here's the most logical explanation I've heard: Most humans at first used up everything they got their hands on. They considered themselves lucky not to freeze or starve. As tribes were able to move beyond day-to-day survival and develop agriculture, land and tools were not scarce, but labor was. Therefore, tribes with greater numbers of women and children were more successful. Tribes could and did steal women, but they needed ways to avoid constant warfare with each other. And at some point early humans learned the lesson that too much intertribal marriage weakened their offspring. Anthropologists have documented how these developments led to an "exchange of women" among tribes.[3] Women—and in particular, women's sexual capacity—became the first private property. In a world without paternity tests, there was only one surefire way to ensure that the woman a man received belonged only to him—preventing her from being sexual with any other man. As some men began to accumulate surplus land and goods, they also had to make certain the property got passed on to rightful heirs (as Samuel Johnson once put it, "The chastity of women is of all importance, as all property depends on it").[4] Controlling women's sexuality went hand in hand with restricting their rights in all spheres. Those who began to accumulate property went on to restrict the rights of the majority of men as well.

Think of these men as the original Big Boys. Once in charge, they found ways to justify their actions. They created an ideology, declaring women to be weaker, inferior, of lesser value (just as it justified that men with wealth were in fact more "worthy" and destined to rule over others).[5] As society developed, these beliefs about women weren't just opinions—they were transformed into laws. Not good enough to own property, women could in fact be treated as the property of their husbands. (I stopped using the expression "rule of thumb" as soon as I learned its origins in British law: The stick with which a husband could beat his wife was to be no thicker than the size of his thumb.) In most cultures, women's "natural" role as mothers didn't translate into any rights to their children. Instead, as societies industrialized, women's ability to bear children became an excuse to keep them out of all kinds of jobs. And the jobs they did perform were considered less valuable.

Flash forward to the twentieth century. Technology brought many changes that helped women, but perhaps none more significant than the development of birth control. Throughout the ages, some women had applied their knowledge of herbs and nature to prevent unwanted pregnancy. But for the majority of women, biology really was destiny. Access to modern contraception (for those not prohibited by pulpit or pocketbook) represented a monumental advance. Having some control over when and whether to have children laid the basis for changes in how women might spend their time—changes many women in this country had begun to demand but hadn't had the power to effect.

Rise of Feminism

Social movements don't spring up out of nowhere. Usually before numbers of people act together in groups, some individuals have begun to make a case for change; isolated acts of rebellion have taken place. This was certainly the case with feminism in the United States.[6] When people use the phrase "first-wave feminism," they generally mean the first time women in this country took action on their own behalf on a significant scale.

The movement started in the mid-nineteenth century when women abolitionists began to question why they were denied so many of the rights they were seeking for slaves. Since women at the time had fewer rights than men who'd been declared insane, it's not surprising that the original list of demands was pretty extensive. The Declaration of Sentiments drafted at Seneca Falls in 1848 called for, among other things, "securing to women an equal participation with men in the various trades, professions and commerce."[7] In the next decades, women in some states scored a few victories, including the right to divorce, to own and inherit property, and to keep their own names. Pioneers like Margaret Sanger fought for women to have access to birth control. But women needed political power to gain reforms. The general list of goals was soon whittled down to the vote—a win white women didn't see until 1920; Puerto Ricans had to wait until 1928, and many African Americans decades more. In addition to massive opposition from the Big Boys, racist views held by many leaders in the women's suffrage movement helped narrow and weaken its outcomes.[8]

The movement appeared to hibernate after the suffrage victory. In fact, groups of women, including African Americans, immigrants, and other low-wage workers, continued to make demands and take action, often boldly, to improve their lot (see Chapter 6). But for the next burst of feminism we had to wait until the 1960s. Young women inspired by the civil rights and antiwar struggles demanded equality in the movement, in the bedroom, and in society at large. At the same time, women privileged to stay home with children began to feel stuck in suburbia and wanted more options. Both groups began to imagine—and then demand—entrance to occupations and status that had been off-limits. Women who'd been told they couldn't, or shouldn't, or wouldn't want to dig underground or fly in outer space or many other things in between found that they certainly could, and more and more of them did.

Today virtually all occupations have at least some females; gender discrimination has been outlawed for more than forty years in the United

States. But whenever a group has legally been declared inferior for centuries, there's bound to be a powerful legacy of inequality and a slew of structural barriers that remain. Imagine if all the best jobs were in buildings designed for short people.[9] One day tall people are told, "Okay, you can work here, too, as long as you walk on your knees or stoop over so you don't bump your head." How many tall people would we expect to find in those jobs? It shouldn't be surprising that women still earn considerably less than men—even in the same professions—are in charge less often, and are treated badly more often. Nor is it surprising that today's Big Boys still try to justify women's lower status. In fact, their arguments have become more sophisticated. Feminism, they say, is not just the wrong solution for women, but the very cause of women's problems.

What Is Feminism Anyway?

According to the dictionary, feminism is the movement for social, political, and economic equality of men and women. The problem isn't that most people disagree with feminism—it's that they don't know what it is. When people are asked directly about this definition, they overwhelmingly support it, even if they avoid the label.

My own definition goes further than the dictionary version. *Feminism is a system of beliefs, laws, and practices that fully values women and work associated with women in order to help all people reach their potential.* It means an end to views of women and "women's work" as being *less valuable.* Doing away with discrimination against women opens the way to full participation and choices both for women and men.

What about the "men are from Mars, women from Venus" theory? Once gender stereotypes—assumptions and generalities about females and males—are eliminated, perhaps we'll still find more women than men in caregiving occupations and more men than women who are good with tools. Who knows? But clearly many in each group go against stereotype right now, and many more would if they weren't punished for doing so. Simply being female or male will one day tell us very little about someone's talents, interests, and dreams.

Like all social movements, the women's movement is not monolithic. The brand of feminism I'm advocating is what's known as "social justice feminism." It takes into account women's different experiences depending on class, race, and sexual orientation. We know there can't be full freedom for women if there's not freedom for *all* women. And we can't end domination by the Big Boys in one area if we allow it to continue in another. That means the fight for gender equality has to be linked with systemic change that opposes all forms of injustice and domination.

In other words, our goal is not equal numbers of females among the Big Boys. What we want isn't just more women in power, but more power to women as a whole and others who have been disenfranchised. To achieve that, we have to do more than smash the glass ceiling—we have to redesign the building.

Why Big Boys Beat Up on Feminism

Ask yourself, Who gains when women get less? The extra money, power, prestige, opportunities do not land in the laps of most men. If I make a dollar an hour less than the guy working next to me, that dollar goes not into his pocket but into the profits of the business owner. Paying women less and treating them as if they *deserved* less has been very profitable for the Big Boys. That's not all. Workers who are divided among themselves because of the color of their skin or the country they were born in or which box they check under "gender" are less likely to band together to challenge the Big Boys' power. That means feminism or any other beliefs that do challenge that power inevitably run into resistance.

The Big Boys' arguments against feminism are often infuriating, sometimes stupefying, and usually predictable. One thing you learn early on is that they don't all take extremist positions. Instead, many exploit the misunderstanding and prejudice spread by those who do.

For example, some opponents of women's suffrage warned that victory would cause women physiological damage—larger, heavier brains and loss of unique feminine mannerisms.[10] Female labor would bring even worse devastation, destroying not just women's nature but the home: "[I]t is the knife of the assassin aimed at the family circle."[11] Most Big Boys were less heavy-handed. They just asserted that little women had more important things to do than worry their pretty heads about sordid world affairs[12]—at the same time ensuring that suffragists who took to the streets were dealt with harshly.

The visible rise of feminist groups in the late 1960s and '70s was seen both as a bad joke and a big danger. While the National Organization for Men dismissed feminists as "brain-damaged man haters," some men also depicted them as causing massive trouble for the family and for society. "Forcing fire departments . . . to lower their standards to accommodate women," one argued, "amounts to nothing less than the offering of human sacrifices."[13] Underlying these attacks was the equation of "women" with "inferior."

The antifeminists' argument went something like this: Women can be many things, but having men in charge is only natural. It's been the norm forever. The norm is fine. Therefore, those who oppose the norm must have something wrong with *them*. Feminists can't make it as women. They're ugly women who can't get a man. They're resentful, they hate men, they envy men, they wish they were men. If you want to be like them, something is wrong with you, too.[14]

Although some pretty high-ranking people took this position,[15] most Big Boys at the time were more subtle. As you'll see throughout this book, they even admitted then (and now) that some areas need tweaking. Nevertheless, they took advantage of the image spread by these more outlandish comments to preserve the status quo (along with their own power and privilege). Feminism was made to seem extreme, ridiculous, outside the mainstream. Like pornography, the word *feminist* became associated with the adjective *hard core*.

What feminists actually stood for—the goals of equity and fairness—along with their documentation of inequity, disappeared in this man-hating/man-envying, unattractive/unhappy woman framework. With considerable help from the media, the framework stuck. The media dubbed feminists "libbers" (what other movement, however maligned, has ever been dismissed with such a name?) and described their objectives as freedom from bras and babies. Feminists were equated with lesbians, and lesbians were equated not with women who happened to love another woman, but with failed women who hated all men. Typically feminists were painted as sourpusses. The photo or quote featured the most strident or offbeat. A disproportionate amount of airtime and print were—and still are—given to the opponents.

The April 25, 2004, March for Women's Lives in Washington, DC is a good example. A million supporters marched past a smattering of antichoice opponents. Yet most news stories featured "the other side" at length to be "fair." As Gloria Steinem has pointed out, "An issue may be supported by a majority of women, 60/40 or even 70/30, but confining its discussion to two women arguing will give the impression that women are divided 50/50, also that two women can't get along."[16] Focusing on these "catfights"[17] between women was used to cast feminism as outside the mainstream. Despite the fact that the majority of women agree with feminism's goals, calling yourself a feminist was tantamount to *isolating* yourself from those around you.

The Backlash

In the 1980s, the Big Boys added another dimension to their rhetoric. Not only had feminism failed to provide solutions for the majority of women, it actually was responsible for most of their problems. As Susan Faludi documented in painstaking detail, a backlash developed that told women they'd never had so much—or been so miserable. Feminism gave women equality, but was said to rob them of love and to cause "nearly every woe besetting women, from mental depression to meager savings accounts, from teenage suicides to eating disorders to bad complexions."[18]

Today the backlash has a new feature. Women, we're told, can be whatever they want. If few are in the best jobs, it's because they don't want to be there. Those unwilling to work like maniacs are less competent and committed. If they leave, they're not driven out—they're "opting out" to be at home. Women with children who hang on to these jobs are selfish, handing over their kids to strangers to raise. They earn less than men, but that's okay, because motherhood is the most important job—except for women who are poor. They'd *better* work at whatever job's available regardless of hours, or they're lazy and bad role models. And if their kids are home alone and don't see much of Mom? Well, at least they have their pride.

As for feminists who would change the status quo, their image hasn't changed much. When I taught women studies in 1970, I asked students what their friends and loved ones thought about feminists. Their response: hairy, raging, humorless, man-hating dykes. Thirty-five years later, I'm teaching women's studies again and asking the same question. Incredibly, I hear the same replies, along with some new variations. "My grandpa said, 'You're going to need a helmet in that class,'" Rob told us. Becky added, "My boyfriend begged me not to sign up."

Adding Fuel to the Fire

Feminists can't put all the blame on the Big Boys. After a talk I gave in Worcester, Massachusetts in March 2004, a young woman came up to thank me "for being so reasonable." I asked her to explain, thinking she'd been affected by the backlash. In fact, she'd been turned off by some other women students who told her, "Be just like us, reject all things feminine, or you're hurting the cause." From Worcester I drove to Boston for a reunion with a college roommate, a strong and strikingly independent woman. When I told her about this book, she expressed her view that the word "feminist" had taken on an aggressive connotation. "If I saw a notice for a meeting of feminists," she said, "I wouldn't go."

What's known as the women's movement has a lot of work to do. Many women of color think of feminists as white women who are at best oblivious about white supremacy or at worst clinging to it. In fact, there are multiple women's movements, including many groups invisible to the mainstream media but doing amazing work. I'll tell you about some of them in this book.

But above all I want to show you that ending sexism—the view that women and work associated with women are of lesser value—means working together to take on the Big Boys, exposing the myths they tell to maintain power, while documenting the real problems women face and the need for feminist solutions.

How I Came to Feminism

I grew up on the wrong side of the rapid transit tracks in an otherwise wealthy community in Cleveland, Ohio. My father didn't make much money, but our family of five (I have an older brother and twin sister) got by on one income. When we kids were teenagers, my mother decided to go back to work to save money for us to go to college. Shortly afterward, my dad slammed into a parked truck. Turned out he'd been driving blind for who knows how long, due to cataracts on his eyes. Between mending from the injuries and then from the cataract surgeries, he was out of work for more than a year. Suddenly my mother's "extra" wages were the family's only means of support—and we had a lot of trouble getting by. I got my first training in how to handle calls from bill collectors and bought my first rummage-sale dress, hoping it hadn't come from a schoolmate's closet. I knew my mom was smart and worked hard at her social work job. But I didn't question why she earned so little money—that was life.

My reaction to growing up with so much less than my classmates was to reject the materialist world and become a scholar. Thanks to financial aid, I went to Cornell to study the classics. It didn't take long to figure out that the ivory tower was as corrupt as the rest of the world. Still, I loved my studies and suddenly found myself in crisis at age nineteen: I knew I wanted to marry and have a family, but I also wanted to have a career. How would I choose? A favorite professor found me distraught outside our ivy-covered building and asked what was wrong. When I told him, he handed me his hankie and said, "I know three women who've done both." I listened to the names of those three professors, names I didn't know and have long forgotten, wiped my eyes, and said, Fine. If there could be exceptions, I'd be one.

Although I wasn't questioning unequal choices for women, I was caught up in the fervor of the civil rights movement and the antiwar movement. Like many Jewish people who grew up after World War II, I was preoccupied with the silence of those who knew about the Holocaust. Being a bystander was never an option for me. I graduated in 1966, spent the summer in Cleveland working against the Vietnam War, then went to Cambridge University in England, where I divided my time between arcane studies and protest. I also traveled to Athens to visit Kosti, a Greek student I'd dated at Cornell—someone I'd viewed as older, learned, and unattainable. To my surprise, he asked me to marry him and I said yes. A few months later, while I was in England and he was back at Cornell, a military dictatorship took control in Greece. We quickly became involved in efforts to restore democracy, writing letters, marching, speaking out. I assumed we'd live in his country when it was possible for him to go back, and that I would take his name. That's the way it was done.

In December of 1967, I took the train from London to Greece to see Kosti's family. The last night his father and I ended up alone in the study. While my future mother-in-law and I could always communicate, even when I knew only thirty words of Greek, my future father-in-law and I had never had a conversation by ourselves. He hadn't sought me out. And I was a little awestruck, having heard many stories of his bravery in fighting the Nazis and going to jail for being part of the resistance. Eager to create a bond that night, I chattered about the wedding plans and mentioned the rabbi from my childhood who would perform the ceremony. This aging partisan stood by his desk, fiddling with a bouquet of newly sharpened pencils until I finished. Then he folded his arms across his substantial belly. Out of the question, he informed me. No one knew I was Jewish. How could he let his son's friends, so jealous of Kosti's scholarship to study in the States, gloat and say, "Yeah, but look what happened, he married a Jew." Of course, my future father-in-law assured me, he himself wasn't anti-Semitic. Several times he ticked off his wartime exploits and the number of Jews the resistance had saved. But surely I didn't expect him to disclose my ancestry to his mother, a peasant woman in her nineties who still believed Jews killed Christian children and drank their blood.

Standing there as the sky darkened, I felt leaden. I didn't have the language skills or know the protocol—were you allowed to take on your father-in-law? Worse, it was as if he'd reached down my throat and yanked out some vital organ that controlled my joints and my voice. I don't remember how I got out of that room. But afterward, I couldn't rationalize my silence. I knew I never again wanted to be in a situation where my value was questioned and I didn't speak up.

My husband-to-be was appalled when he learned of his father's speech. (So was his mother, who said she told everyone I was Jewish.) A few months after we married (with a judge presiding, but only because the rabbi refused to perform an interfaith ceremony), Kosti and I moved to Montreal. There I was the only woman and only non-Greek who participated in meetings of the Greek movement for democracy. The other women sold raffle tickets and supported their men; I was grateful to be allowed into the action. But when a Canadian friend invited me to a women's consciousness-raising group, I attended as Ellen Bravo, my birth name. How heady those discussions were. So that's why my mother got paid so little! That's why there were so few professional women with families! To his credit, Kosti immediately accepted the need to change the way we lived. He took over the cooking and ironed his own clothes. How could we fight for equality in one sphere and deny it in our home?

Unfortunately, this early women's group, like many of the time, was all white and middle class. It didn't speak to the Greek women I was meeting whose lives were taken up with low-wage jobs and staggering interest rates. The women's group marched for abortion rights; my Greek friends searched for ways to feed their children. I kept looking for a women's group where these women would feel at home, but I didn't find one.

In 1970 we moved to southern Maryland, where the administration of the state college "allowed" me to teach a women's studies course so that Kosti would agree to teach economics there. My students, most of them the first in their family to go to college, were thrilled with the discoveries in our classes. They had new understanding, new role models, and new expectations. Many of the ones ready to graduate told me some version of this: "Okay, you've changed our lives, we're ready to change the world. Where should we go?" I didn't have a clue.

Soon I would join them in that search. After moving to Baltimore, Kosti and I split up—we'd grown in different directions, although we remain friends. No one was about to hire me to teach newfangled women's studies. So to support the organizing I was trying to do with women in my neighborhood, I got a clerical job in a hospital (I type 100 words a minute)—and soon realized that this was what I should be organizing about. The women I worked with were smart and hardworking, yet like my mother, we earned meager pay. What before I took for granted, I now saw to be an undervaluation of women that had to change.

I began attending meetings of the Dump Nixon Coalition, where I noticed a bright, passionate (and extremely cute) guy named Larry Miller and asked him out. He worked at a steel mill and wasn't very savvy about feminists. On our first date, he protested when I went to pay for my meal. "People don't do that," he insisted. But he really listened to women, he loved spending time with kids, and he was fighting against pornography in his all-male work unit. He made me laugh. When we moved in together, he assumed we'd share chores. I was hooked.

In 1976 we married and over the next few years had two wonderful sons. We moved to Chicago, where I worked in the office of a small, left-wing publisher and took each baby to work with me for the first several months. When Larry's mother died unexpectedly, we decided to come to Milwaukee to be closer to his dad. One of us had to get a job with health insurance. Thanks to those typing skills, I got hired at the phone company—and ran smack into inflexible workplace rules (see Chapter 3). All those years I continued to search for a women's group that would look like the women I worked with and speak to their lives. And then in 1982, I found 9to5.

9to5: A Different Brand of Feminism

I had heard of the organization because it was then headquartered in Cleveland, where my parents and siblings still lived. That summer, I learned of a weekend leadership conference at Bryn Mawr College in Pennsylvania and drove eighteen hours to attend. I forgot about my exhaustion when I walked into the old brick building where 9to5's "Summer School" was held. Here was a multiracial group of women talking about all the issues that mattered to me—pay equity, family leave, sexual harassment. Their goal was to win raises, rights, and respect for women workers, especially support staff. Panelists included women who seemed to be speaking publicly for the first time, but were doing it well—this was clearly a group that valued leadership development. In breakout sessions under leafy trees, I heard women just like my coworkers describe action they'd taken on their jobs. And they knew how to use humor—I went home with a button that read, "My consciousness is fine. It's my pay that needs raising." Back in Milwaukee, I found a group of women to start a chapter with me. After a few years, I began working part-time for the national organization. And when the founder, Karen Nussbaum, left to become head of the Women's Bureau of the U.S. Department of Labor, I took over as director.

During more than two decades at 9to5, I participated in historic campaigns in which we went up against a lot of Big Boys, including right-wing pundits, legislators and talk-show hosts, the head of the U.S. Chamber of Commerce, representatives of the state and local chambers, and members of the conservative Independent Women's Forum. (Often we lucked out—our opponents had names like Lump and Lawless.) Again and again my sisters and I had to learn how to take these Big Boys on.

How the Big Boys Operate

Four decades in the women's movement has taught me that the Big Boys rely on a series of myths to prop up the reality that benefits them. Women are making great strides, they say, and where that's not the case, women have only themselves to blame. When feminists challenge those myths and propose concrete policy changes, the Big Boys hustle to defend their positions. Following the well-known creed that the best defense is hardball offense, they rely on a variety of tactics to try to discredit us, shifting from one to the other with ease. One minute they dismiss us, the next they warn that the sky will fall if we get what we want. I came up with this shorthand to describe how the Big Boys operate. They:

- *Minimize*—What problem? ("Women have it made.")
- *Trivialize*—That's a problem? ("Feminism means ugly women will sue to get a man.")
- *Patronize*—You don't understand the needs of business. ("You think you can socially engineer behavior.")
- *Demonize*—You're the problem. ("Women shouldn't have kids if they can't afford to raise them.")
- *Catastrophize*—Your solution will cause greater problems for the very ones you want to help. ("These laws you want to pass will lead to discrimination against women. You'll drive business out and cause people to lose their jobs.")
- *Compartmentalize*—If you get what you want, it will hurt some other group. ("Why should non-parents bear the burden of mothers taking time off from work to deal with their kids?")

The ideology of sexism or male supremacy is different from racism or white supremacy, relying more on trivializing women's role and patronizing than on demonizing them. Yet whenever necessary, as you'll see throughout the book, the Big Boys take off the gloves. This is especially true when sexism and racism overlap.

What You'll Learn from This Book

Taking on the Big Boys makes the case for feminism and why and how we—men and women—should advance it. I see the economic arena as the key place to challenge sexism. We've got lots of work to do on personal relationships, but to be on equal footing at home or successfully leave an abusive relationship, women must have economic sufficiency. And if men are to share parenting, we have to end penalties on the job for those with caregiving responsibilities. My book examines the main issues for women in the workplace. Each chapter exposes the myths, clarifies the problem, proposes detailed solutions, and dismantles the propaganda against those solutions by showing how we took on the Big Boys. The examples of collective action all come from real-life experiences, mostly from the 9to5 movement; each chapter also highlights a victory won by some other grassroots organization. Some examples are very recent, others go back to the 1980s and '90s. I wish I could tell you the Big Boys' reactions would be different today, but the narrative, alas, remains the same. This book is also filled with stories told to me by many of the women I've worked with over the years. Except where otherwise noted, quotes refer to informal conversations.

Taking on the Big Boys will give you practical tips on everything from dealing with a sexual harasser to getting family members to share the chores—and convincing your mate that an equal relationship is the most rewarding. Reading this book, you'll find out the real impetus behind welfare reform, the lowdown on why women earn so little money (and what to do about it), and the advice of management consultants for keeping a group like 9to5 out of the office (and our success at exposing management's tactics). You'll see in detail what a feminist future would look like, why it matters to all of us, and how you can be part of making it happen. I'm delighted to share tales of Big Boys made humble—including business leaders on pay equity, former Wisconsin governor Tommy Thompson on family leave, Bryant Gumbel on sexual harassment, U.S. congressmen on overtime pay.

The Issues This Book Will Cover

Why Social Workers Earn Less than Accountants: Pay Equity. Chapter 2 knocks down the myths of women earning less because of personal choices or deficiencies. Instead, it lays out the history of the undervaluation of women's work and public policies to correct that. The chapter recounts our fight for pay equity in Wisconsin, where the Big Boys included politicians, corporate leaders, and women who claimed that they'd pulled themselves up by their high heels—and other women could, too. And it tells how a group of childcare providers in Rhode Island fought to have their work revalued.

Can You Have a Job *and* a Life? Work-Family Issues. The Big Boys claim it's all about balance, but in Chapter 3 you'll learn how the workplace is still designed for men with wives at home full time. You'll also learn what a family friendly workplace should look like and how to create a society that truly values families and time with loved ones, whether or not they're of the same blood or the opposite gender. Find out how we took on the business lobbyists and demolished their arguments in the successful fight for family leave, and how a group of women in Utah brought their kids to the governor's office to preserve childcare funding.

Can a Woman Do a Man's Job? Chapter 4 exposes the myths and practices that limit women's participation in certain occupations. It clarifies what it will take not just to smash the glass ceiling, but to redesign the building, and shows how we took on the Big Boys, specifically opponents of civil rights and affirmative action, some firefighters who said women didn't belong and senior executives who said they did—they just couldn't find them. You'll also meet a Cleveland group who made the hard hat a unisex item.

You Want to See My *What*? Sexual Harassment. Find out what sexual harassment is—and is not—and some sensible policies to prevent it or stop it quickly should it occur. Hear about women who've fought for change and the Big Boys we've taken on, including hosts on CNN and *The Today Show*, as well as some labor leaders. Chapter 5 explains why you can't care about women and hate gays. And it introduces you to an organization of military women fighting to end sexual mistreatment of female soldiers.

Nine to Five: Not Just a Movie—The Right to Organize. The Big Boys don't want women comparing notes or stirring things up. You'll find out why the best way to get what you need for yourself is to work with others on behalf of everyone—and what specific changes would enable workers to make that choice. Chapter 6 describes how we went up against a big "union-free" management firm, and how our sister union took on the administration of a major university.

Working Other than Nine to Five: Part-Time and Temporary Jobs. The growth in part-time and temp jobs has potential for women—but only if laws and practices change so that these jobs become voluntary and equitable. In Chapter 7 you'll see how we took on various Big Boys, from a mayor's chief of staff to the national association for temp agencies. You'll also learn about a dozen Chinese garment workers in Oakland, California, who challenged a giant manufacturer.

What This Nation Really Thinks of Motherhood: Welfare Reform. Nothing exposes the lie of mothers on a pedestal more than the treatment of mothers who happen to be poor. Chapter 8 lays out the myths about those on welfare and points to the real key to ending poverty: reform of *work*. From Wisconsin governor Tommy Thompson to right-wing think tanks and liberal politicians, taking on the Big Boys has involved telling the truth about poverty and race and about the way women are valued. A New York group called Stand with Sisters for Economic Dignity found an unusual and powerful way to do this.

Revaluing Women's Work Outside of Work. Chapter 9 looks at relationships and the home front. Contrary to claims by the Big Boys, greater rights for women does not mean equal rights or an end to violence against women. You'll learn the cost of denial of marriage rights to same-sex partners. You'll see why equal relationships are more loving, what men have to gain from being full participants in caring for kids—and how to make sure that happens. This chapter also looks at who's doing the dirty work, why feminists shouldn't be exploiters of domestic help, and what a group of Long Island immigrant workers are doing about exploitation.

How You Can Help Get There. In the final chapter, readers, even those with limited time and resources, will learn how to get involved. Activists and leaders will gain detailed tips on ways to be effective in taking on the Big Boys and building a movement for lasting and systemic change.

2. WHY SOCIAL WORKERS EARN LESS THAN ACCOUNTANTS: PAY EQUITY

"So, if you have your way and we have comparable worth, you'll be destroying our society and killing our children. . . . Our society needs cheap labor to survive."—Brigadier general speaking to me over lunch at a federal employees Secretary's Day celebration

On a fall evening twenty some years ago, I kissed my husband and young sons and drove across town to see the movie *Nine to Five* (1980)—inspired by the organization I would later join. Although I went by myself, I soon felt as if I knew everyone at the theater. We roared and cheered as Violet, Dora, and Judy tied up Mr. Hart, their lecherous boss,[1] and proceeded to run the office, humanize the culture, launch a childcare center, institute flexible schedules, and raise pay—all the while improving productivity and profits. At the end of the film, the goateed CEO, Mr. Tinsworthy, arrives for a personal tour. At each stop he heaps praise on a clueless Mr. Hart, marveling at how the changes have boosted the bottom line. Then Tinsworthy leans over and whispers in Mr. Hart's ear: "That equal pay thing, though—that has to go."

And that's how we knew the movie was a comedy, not a fantasy. On most issues discussed in this book, the Big Boys will allow some wiggle room. But as a group, they reserve their fiercest opposition to the idea that women are underpaid. Indeed, the undervaluation of women's work remains the key to women's subordinate role in the workplace and in society.

How Bad Is It?

When I speak to students about women's pay in relation to men's, I remind them that there are two categories of jobs—those where women and men do the same work, and those performed primarily by one gender or the other. Most people look for examples of equity in the first category, especially professional jobs, so that's where I start. I ask volunteers to come up and represent the field they hope to join. A long line forms. One at a time, I hold my hand over the heads of a future manager, lawyer, doctor, reporter, financial specialist, and others, while the audience weighs in on which occupations have equal pay for women and men. If they think the pay's the same, they raise their left hand—"L" for likely. If they disagree, they raise their right hand—"R" for "Are you out of your mind?" Often they shout the words at the same time. Opinions vary; we cluster those with the highest likely votes over to one side. Then I reveal the answers—and have volunteers sit in the portion of a chair that represents women's share of men's pay in that job.

I won't keep you guessing. In none of the fields does a volunteer get to sit comfortably on the whole seat. Most have to contort their bodies to squeeze into three-quarters of a chair or less.

Because the truth is that women make less than men at every level, from corporate manager (68 percent) and professional positions such as doctor (77 percent) and financial manager (69 percent) to low-wage jobs like retail sales (64 percent) and poultry workers (71 percent). Even in new industries, like the Internet, female professionals with the same job and equal seniority pull in only 88 percent of men's earnings.[2] That's not all. Women earn less than men even in female-dominated jobs like secretary (90 percent).

Explaining the Wage Gap

Some of women's lower pay is due to blatant discrimination of the old-fashioned kind—like the woman who was told her male colleague got a bigger raise because "he had a family to support." (So does she.) The fact that such behavior is illegal doesn't mean it's disappeared. Still, it accounts for only a small part of the pay gap between men and women.

Myth: Women Make Less Because They Work Less

If you think women's lower wages are related to the fact that they work fewer hours and fewer years than men, you're right. Women do work less overall and this does affect the gap—but not the one you read about in the media. That figure—how many cents women earn for every dollar paid to men (most recently 77 cents for women overall, 72 cents for African American women, 58 cents for Latinas, 87 cents for women of Asian descent)[3]—is based on men and women who work *full time, year round*. When we look at women in general, including those who work part-time and have taken time off, the gap between their pay and men's stretches to a chasm, with women bringing home only 38 percent of men's earnings.[4] Researchers conclude that no more than half this differential can be attributed to actual number of hours worked.

The reality is that those who work part time or who take some time off to care for family members experience a *penalty* for their choice. No law says part-timers have to be paid the same hourly rate as those who do the identical job full time—and they aren't; part-timers on average earn much less per hour and receive few if any benefits (see Chapter 7). And that's only part of the story. Women do take more time off than men to care for family members. We expect them to experience some loss of earnings as a result. But how big a hit should they take and how long should the penalty last? Consider these statistics: Over a period of fifteen years, taking one year off amounts to a penalty of 32 percent in earning power. Two years chops your pay by 46 percent, and three by more than half—56 percent.[5] "I knew there'd be some cost," wrote Laura, a Wisconsin engineer who left the workforce for three years when her children were babies.[6] "But I had no idea that I'd still be paying the price fifteen years later." Few could argue that staying home with a newborn or a dying parent should flatten pay by such a staggering amount.

And what about women who do spend long hours on the job? You'd expect the wage gap to narrow as the number of hours increases, right? In fact, it *widens*. Women working 41 to 44 hours per week earn 84.6 percent of men's pay for the same hours; when they put in 60 hours a week or more, the proportion goes *down* to 78.3 percent. Adding insult to injury, many women have to work longer than men do to receive the promotions that lead to higher pay. For example, according to the National Center for Education Statistics, women school principals spend an average of three additional years as teachers before moving to administration.

It takes more than work hours to explain away the wage gap.

Myth: Women Make Less Because They Don't Ask for More

Recent studies show that women are much less likely than men to initiate salary negotiations and much more likely to accept whatever an employer offers.[7] For a group of graduates with master's degrees, the difference in starting pay between women and men was $4,000—almost exactly the amount gained as a result of negotiations. This gap keeps growing as the years go by, since raises are usually based on percentages of salary and new employers often start by asking how much you made on your last job.

But women don't earn less in the same jobs simply because they're less assertive. You have to factor in other realities of life for women in Corporate America—fewer raises, smaller bonuses, less frequent promotions (see Chapter 4). I remember talking with a television personality, a woman over fifty who knew she was paid considerably less than her male counterparts despite having more experience. "You can argue ratings, talent, objective criteria 'til you're blue in the face," she said. "The bottom line is, [management is] more committed to the men and they're going to pay whatever they have to in order to keep them."

The issue of negotiations, of course, applies only in the higher level or union jobs where you engage in some discussion about pay. In most of the jobs women fill, you're simply told, "This is the pay rate. Take it or leave it." And in many jobs, asking how much others are making can cost you your job.

In fact, the way women are treated when they do the same jobs as men is still only a small part of the story of the wage gap.

Myth: Women Make Less Because They're Less Educated

Some people think men have more education than women and that's why they earn more. But the numbers don't bear this out. Women's educational achievements are almost equivalent to men's. What's more, women at every level of schooling earn less than their male counterparts.

Level of Education	Women's Pay as Percentage of Men's[8]
Less than 9th grade	80 percent
High school	74 percent
Some college	73 percent
Associate's degree	75 percent
Bachelor's	73 percent
Master's	71 percent
Doctorate	77 percent
Professional degrees	66 percent

The Big Boys like to point out that the gap has decreased over the years, and so it has. What they fail to mention are three key facts: The gap is biggest at the highest level of education. Half or more of the narrowing of the overall pay difference comes from *loss* of pay for men, particularly men of color. Gains for women were mostly among nonmothers—the "mommy wage gap" actually increased. This isn't the kind of "progress" we had in mind. [9]

Reality: Why Women Earn So Little Money

Women don't just earn less than men—they often earn very little. Consider, for instance, that 17 percent of women but only 1 percent of men working full time average less than $15,000 per year.[10] More than 90 percent of long-term low earners among prime-age adults are women. They're childcare workers who can't afford childcare, health-care workers with no health insurance, college clericals who can't pay for higher education for their kids. What accounts for this? The best researchers in the country got together to figure it out. They talked, they examined all the research, they ran multiple regression analyses, and here's what they came up with: The reason women earn so little money is—their employers *pay them so little money*. Why do their employers pay them so little? Because they can, and because they think they have to in order to compete.[11]

The heart of the pay gap lies in how society values what women do.

I once heard Robert Reich tell the story of becoming secretary of labor under President Bill Clinton. His very first act, said Reich, was to abolish the executive dining room. All the hot shots would eat in the employee cafeteria along with everyone else. So there he was, standing in line, and he struck up a conversation with the woman in front of him. After telling him all about her job, the woman asked, "And what do you do?" "I'm the Secretary," Reich replied. "Oh," she said, "whose secretary are you?"

Reich always gets a laugh with that story. But for me the message was why the most trusted advisors of the president are called *secretaries*. That's exactly what secretaries were—the most trusted advisor to the person in charge. The jobs were high status, high paid—and virtually all held by men. Then came the Civil War and a shortage of males for many jobs previously closed to women. Along with necessity, what convinced employers to give women a shot was the cost savings involved. Since the government has to pass a statute in order to create a new job category, we have a legislative record of the arguments in favor of creating these positions. Here's what the Librarian of Congress argued, for example: "I know many industrious, practically educated women who would be glad to do for $1,200 a year the job that male librarians do for $1,800."[12] None of the congressmen (that's all there were at the time) disputed the amounts. They presumed that women needed less money because they had parents and then a husband to pay the way—never mind that this was never true for large groups of workers, especially African Americans and immigrants. Congress created the job slots and established the wage rates at one-half to two-thirds that of men doing the same work.

Not surprisingly, the women who filled these jobs in both the public and private sector proved to be quite capable, and the savings were substantial. More and more were hired until certain jobs became female-dominated. And guess what happened—the discriminatory rate became the prevailing wage or "market rate." When the Equal Pay Act was passed in 1963, which required that men and women doing the same job for the same company be paid the same wage, most women and men no longer performed the same jobs—and the ones done by women paid less simply because women did them. That's true of jobs that had typically been women's work—taking care of children, the elderly, the sick—as well as jobs that were once performed mainly by men. In fact, the National Academy of Sciences concluded that "the more an occupation is dominated by women, the less it pays."[13] You could actually plot it out on a graph—for every 1 percent increase in the percentage of women in an occupation, the pay would fall $42 a year (in 1971 dollars).[14]

Today almost every job category, from doctor to drill sergeant, carpenter to CEO, has some women in it. But most women are doing the same jobs women have always done. Nearly three-fifths of women workers are employed in service, sales, and clerical jobs. Fewer than one in seven work in jobs typically held by men. Even within certain occupations, women are clustered in the lower-paying jobs. Walk into a gift or novelty shop and chances are four out of five that the person helping you will be a female. Then stop by a higher-paying car dealership—the probability of a woman handling your purchase drops to one in five. Ask who's cleaning houses, changing bedpans, caring for toddlers, and you're most likely to find not just a woman, but a woman of color.

Sex segregation isn't only about what women do. Fewer than 8 percent of men hold female-dominated positions. Yes, we want more women designing and building houses, fixing cars, and putting out fires—but we also want more men tending to young kids and frail elders. And that won't happen until those jobs pay a decent wage. Whether at the top or bottom of the job ladder, jobs done predominantly by women pay less than jobs performed mainly by men.[15]

The Consequences of that Reality

The issue of the undervaluation of women's work hit home for me in the mid-1970s. My first husband Kosti and I had moved to Baltimore so he could be closer to a Greek community. Although I'd been teaching women's studies for three years, the field was still new and far from accepted in most institutions. So I joined a women's group and looked for ways to get to know women in my neighborhood, many of whom were on welfare or in low-wage jobs. When Kosti and I separated, I had to find a paying job. I decided to look for a position where I could use my clerical skills; that's how I'd supplemented my financial aid during college. I also wanted more insight on issues facing women in "regular"—not university or professional—jobs. My thinking was I'd sock away some money and return to community organizing. Many male activists I knew would pick up jobs painting houses or something similar, then go back to doing movement work full time. But once hired in the electrocardiogram (EKG) department of a local hospital, I was locked in. This wasn't because of health insurance—like many young people, I didn't worry about falling ill. The problem was pay. Here I was, single, no children, and I earned so little money, I couldn't afford to take time off. Looking at my male movement buddies, I appreciated that the jobs they did involved hard work, but so did mine—administering EKGs (this was before the job required special certification) and deciphering and typing the doctor's taped reports. Patients' lives depended on my accuracy. For hours each day my coworkers and I ran our carts up and down the hospital halls, carefully administering the tests, often to patients who were old or frightened and needed to be reassured that the strange-looking circles I was pasting on their chest wouldn't shock them or cause other harm. Then I had to hurry back and begin typing piles of tapes (the cardiologist happened to be Greek and I was the only one who really understood his accent). We were always told how important our work was—but our wages sent a very different message.

A close look at other typically female jobs shows a similar pattern. We pay the people who care for our children less than those who tend to our cars, our pets, our lawns. Consider prekindergarten teachers in state-funded programs—seven out of ten earn salaries in the low-income category and one in six works a second job to make ends meet.[16] I applaud the goal of encouraging more females to move into math and science. But we also have to ask why mathematicians are paid so much more than social workers or prekindergarten teachers.

Women aren't the only ones who suffer from these disparities. When I met Larry in Baltimore he worked in a steel mill, where women were scarce and pay was high. We moved to Chicago to be closer to his family in Wisconsin and he got a job building hot water heaters. The plant had more women, not a lot, and the pay was still good, though not as much as steel. Then we came to Milwaukee and Larry got hired at General Electric manufacturing cables for magnetic resonance imaging (MRI) machines. He earned less but still a decent wage; his department had a pretty good representation of women. After he got laid off, Larry realized he wasn't going to find these factory jobs anymore and decided to go to college to become a teacher. Four years later he had a bachelor's degree and began work in a female-dominated field—where he earned less than he had in any of those other jobs.

Families, not just women, benefit when pay inequities are removed. The American Federation of Labor and Congress of Industrial Organizations (AFL-CIO) determined that if female workers received the same pay as males of the same age who work the same number of hours, have the same education and union status, and live in the same region of the country, these women's annual family income would rise by $4,000. Poverty rates would be cut in half. The gain to working families? A staggering $200 billion in family income every year.[17]

In order to get to that point, we have to ask not just who performs which job, but who decides how much those jobs are worth.

Myth: The Market Decides

The Big Boys like to tell us that the market decides how much each job should pay. I got a helpful lesson in how the market functions when we first started the 9to5 chapter in Milwaukee. A woman who identified herself as an executive secretary at a major corporation called to ask if she could take me to lunch. We met the next day. She looked quite conventional, an older woman with large glasses and permed hair, but her message was subversive. "I want to explain something about how things work around here," she told me over Caesar salad. Her boss, who we'll call George, would go out to lunch with let's call him Sam, a buddy who ran another major company. They'd chat about this and that. At one point, Sam would say, "So, what are you giving your girl this year?" "Fifty cents," George might respond. "Oh, really? I was going to give a quarter." "Okay," George would reply. "That sounds good to me." George and Sam didn't have lunch in order to conspire. They weren't engaging in deliberate price fixing. It was just a chat between two buddies, one conversation among many. My confidante, who had finally gotten her boss to reveal this process, looked me in the eye: "Your group has to change that," she said.

So much for the market.

And what is the market anyway? To a large extent, it's a reflection of the prevailing culture. Social mores, not God, determined that women needed and deserved less than men—or that ex-slaves deserved less than whites. For a long time society viewed women as less able to do what men do (provide, protect, govern), and viewed the caretaking work performed by women (both paid and unpaid) as less valuable than tasks typically performed by men. Those in charge also assumed a woman would—or should—have a man to take care of her. Even as the rationale for these views fell away and society accepted the principle of equality, the *legacy* of discrimination had been built into the pay scale and the way jobs were evaluated.

Myth: "Objective" Job Evaluation Determines Wages

Employers have been relying on various job evaluation surveys for nearly a century. Evaluators use some group of criteria to determine what skill, effort, responsibility, and working conditions characterize every job category and then assign a certain number of points to each; the greater the points, the higher the pay. This sounds objective—but subjectivity can play a big role in determining what questions to ask and how many points to assign to each factor. Those who designed job evaluation systems often based them on an industry model; they either overlooked or underrated skills associated with women. Here are two of my favorite examples. A job evaluator once gave female bindery workers zero points for knowing how to sew the binderies because, he said, that's the kind of sewing all women know how to do. Another evaluation used the following question to ascertain the unpleasantness of a nurse's job: "Do you work with grease?" Nurses had to answer "no," although they obviously do work with unpleasant substances and odors.

Many skills women utilize, including language skills, office machine skills, people skills, don't show up on the evaluation forms. "Planning, scheduling, and coordinating," for example, are all considered important competencies in managerial positions and count toward compensation, but these are seldom recognized in support staff jobs. You might not rate the skills and responsibilities of a dogcatcher higher than those of nursery school teachers, but a job evaluation system did.[18]

Some people will argue that risk does and should play a big factor in determining pay. I agree. Yet the *Washington Post* found that one of the poorest paid occupations, nurses' aides, faces a risk of serious injury higher than that of a coal miner or steel worker.[19] Lifting and moving patients can and often does lead to back injuries. Assaults by patients are not uncommon. In 1997, nurses' aides suffered 27 percent of all serious workplace assaults in private industry, compared with 7 percent for security guards. (As for dirt and danger, which certainly should play a role in determining pay, some of the lowest-wage jobs—often performed by nonwhite immigrant workers of both genders—are those with grueling physical labor, nonexistent rest breaks, and the highest exposure to dangerous substances.)

In each of the examples above, the skill, effort, and risk involved with these female-dominated jobs were simply invisible to those evaluating the jobs and setting pay. The "market rate" usually plays a big role in deciding how to compensate various skills. If the market rates reflect sex, race, or ethnic bias, as we've seen, well, that just gets folded into the "objective" outcome.

What's needed is a form of job evaluation that *removes gender and race bias* from the compensation system.

Moving Toward Solutions: A New Approach to Job Evaluation

Maybe you can't compare a nurse with a plumber. But you can compare what skills, effort, responsibility, and working conditions each job requires as well as other factors, such as the consequence of errors. Given the degree of sex segregation in the workforce, groups of women workers began to search for a remedy that would consider these job components, so that pay for female-dominated jobs could be brought in line with pay for male-dominated positions that were *comparable*. This idea of "comparable worth" is not a new one; the War Labor Board introduced it during the two world wars. In the mid 1970s, city nurses in Denver who worked in intensive care filed a sex discrimination lawsuit when they found they were paid less than sign painters, tire repairmen, meter servicemen, and tree trimmers. School secretaries in Iowa sued because the custodians received a dollar an hour raise and secretaries didn't—the secretaries thought both groups deserved the extra pay. In Madison, Wisconsin, public health nurses (mostly women) sued because they were paid less than health sanitarians (mostly men). In each case, the court ruled against the women, saying more or less that yes, there was a disparity but the market permitted it and that the courts couldn't correct social inequity.

A more promising ruling came in 1981 in an Oregon case.[20] Here prison matrons filed suit because they were paid less than prison guards whose duties were not exactly the same but were comparable in terms of skills, effort, and so forth. The state's attorneys argued that the women had no grounds to sue because the jobs weren't equal. They insisted that a provision in Title VII of the Civil Rights Act[21] restricted pay discrimination suits to cases of equal pay for equal work. The Supreme Court ruled that Title VII could be used to argue for comparable worth, although that wasn't the basis on which they decided the case and they didn't indicate how they would rule if such an argument were presented. Instead, they based their decision in favor of the prison matrons on a narrow sex discrimination issue: The state had done a study showing the women should be paid 95 percent of what the male guards earned, yet continued to pay the prison matrons only 75 percent of the higher rate.

Sex discrimination was also the basis of a decision in a Washington state case in September 1983, when Federal Judge Jack Tanner ruled that the state had engaged in "direct, overt and institutionalized discrimination." As in Oregon, the state had commissioned a study in 1974 that showed pay disparities of about 20 percent for female-dominated jobs, but had taken no action to correct the problem.

Title VII might provide a remedy when women and men do different jobs, but pursuing that route can be long and complicated. Feminists supporting the concept of comparable worth or pay equity have come up with other solutions.

FEMINIST SOLUTIONS

Raising women's pay will take a multipronged approach, including redesigning the way companies recruit and reward (see Chapter 4), ending the caregiver penalty (see Chapters 3 and 7), and expanding women's bargaining power (see Chapter 6). It also means raising the wage floor, the bottom amount anyone can be paid (see Chapter 8). Here I want to address jobs where women and men do either substantially similar work, or different but comparable work, for the same employer.

Same Employer, Same Jobs: Enforce the Laws and Give Them Teeth

Since 1963 the law's been clear that businesses must pay the same wages to women and men in their employ who perform the same jobs. Laws themselves, of course, don't solve all the problems. I remember taking a call in the 1980s from a woman who had known for years that male coworkers earned considerably more than she did and that this was illegal. Still, she'd never done anything about it. Why not? "I was afraid I'd get fired," she told me. When I asked why she was calling us now, the woman laughed bitterly. She'd just been fired. Her situation was not unique. A 1999 study crossing all industries and areas of the country found that one-quarter to one-half of the pay gap is due solely to differences in pay between men and women working in the same establishments and in similar jobs.[22]

If laws aren't the whole answer, they are a start. But they need to be enforced and to impose *consequences* on wrongdoers. A measure to beef up enforcement of the Equal Pay Act has been pending in Congress since 1999. Known as the Paycheck Fairness Act, it would increase resources available to the Equal Employment Opportunity Commission (EEOC), the agency that oversees antidiscrimination laws. The bill would also provide for better training of EEOC staff on wage discrimination and compliance, and clarify that the law applies to all of an employer's "establishments," regardless of location. It would give the law more heft by protecting complainants from retaliation, making it easier to file class-action lawsuits, and allowing people to seek not just back pay, but compensatory and punitive damages. Right now many employers can fire you for talking about salary with coworkers, even though that information could shine a light on disparities in pay. The Paycheck Fairness Act would prohibit such salary secrecy requirements. And it would require greater proof from employers who claim they have some reason other than gender for the pay differential.

The administration of George W. Bush decided equal pay isn't worth bothering about—the Department of Labor simply stopped publishing information about the pay gap. The Paycheck Fairness Act would reverse that by requiring the secretary of labor to conduct studies and promote research on the elimination of sex-based wage disparities.

Same Employers, Different Jobs: Equal Pay for Jobs of Equivalent Value

A second piece of legislation, the Fair Pay Act, addresses jobs at a given employer that are comparable but not the same. It would amend the Equal Pay Act to require equal pay for jobs of *equivalent* value. In addition to gender, the Fair Pay Act prohibits wage discrimination based on race or national origin. Each business would evaluate its own jobs but would have to use a legitimate and nondiscriminatory job evaluation system like the ones described above. Adjustments in pay would have to raise the lower pay rates—no cutting men's pay in the name of pay equity.

Some states have already applied such a remedy to jobs of public employees, and taxes didn't rise, businesses didn't flee, the sky didn't fall. Costs were modest and certain job categories saw significant improvements. In Minnesota, for example, where the legislature passed the State Government Pay Equity Act in 1982, the cost of pay equity adjustments was less than 1 percent of the budget each year for a four-year period. Thousands of Minnesota women in state jobs saw their earnings rise significantly above the poverty level.[23]

The Canadian province of Ontario was the first to institute a pay equity policy that applies to private as well as public sector jobs. Experts have created several models of job evaluation systems that are gender neutral, valuing job content in the range of female work as well as male and removing bias embedded in typical market-driven systems. Five additional provinces followed with some version of a pay equity law, with one other, Quebec, extending to the private sector.

Any pay equity system has to build in continual monitoring and enforcement. Wisconsin provides a useful lesson of what happens when pay adjustments are a one-shot deal. Under sixteen years of an administration opposed to pay equity, support staff saw gains steadily erode as "market adjustments" were made for certain jobs. According to Michael Lowery, a member of the bargaining team at the University of Wisconsin–Milwaukee, "the market only recognizes guys—prison guards, police, custodians, etc."[24] There were never adjustments for female-dominated positions. "We're back where we started," Lowery said.

In Canada, a national task force recommended establishing a separate commission to ensure monitoring and compliance with pay equity laws. This body would also carry out public education on the issue, provide technical assistance, and investigate and attempt to resolve disputes. We should do the same.

Different Jobs, Different Employers: Revalue Women's Work

Even if statutes providing for pay equity were enacted and administered properly, they wouldn't solve the entire problem of women's low pay. Not all jobs have positions to compare. Childcare centers, for example, don't offer a lot of job categories besides caring for kids. Many women work for employers who hire virtually all women, or who pay males and females equally bad wages—think of them as equal opportunity oppressors.

The principles in this chapter, however, are relevant wherever the undervaluation of work associated with women or with men of color has helped suppress the pay for an occupation or job category. When groups like homecare workers, childcare providers, domestics, or others organize for better pay, demands for new wage rates should highlight the social history of the current pay scale and the lessons learned from employers where jobs can be compared. Similarly, employers can conduct their own payroll audits and make adjustments, even if all or most of the jobs are held by women.

Moving into Better Jobs: Increase Educational Opportunities

Many women would benefit from educational and training opportunities to sharpen their skills. Welfare-to-work and other job training efforts should focus on training for jobs that pay a living wage (see Chapter 8). Schools at every level need to do a better job in steering women into higher paying fields like math and science (see Chapter 4). But we also have to challenge a system under which social workers earn so much less than accountants. The main problem isn't that women are unskilled—rather, their skills are undervalued.

Which takes us right back to Mr. Tinsworthy.

TAKING ON THE BIG BOYS

Like the CEO in the movie *Nine to Five*, the Big Boys have been resolute in opposing pay equity. One even called it "the looniest idea since Loony Tunes"[25]—a lovely example of *trivializing* the issue. They *patronized* women, claiming they cheerfully choose to trade income for flexibility and other perks. When advocates organized to win pay equity in the public sector, opponents jumped to *demonize* "fat cat" state workers, *compartmentalize* them from private sector workers (and women from men, union from non-union, white from people of color), and *catastrophize* about the harm to the business climate. Newly appointed Chief Justice John Roberts dismissed the concept as a "pernicious" redistribution of wealth: "Their slogan may as well be, 'From each according to his ability, to each according to her gender.'"[26]

The pay equity fight is where I earned my debating spurs and my favorite newspaper write-up.

Winning Friends and Influencing People

My involvement in fighting for pay equity began in earnest in 1984, when then-governor of Wisconsin Tony Earl appointed me as an "official observer" to the state's Task Force on Comparable Worth.[27] The fancy designation was meant to compensate for not being named as an actual commissioner. The meetings were public; anyone could observe, but observers didn't have the right to speak. We didn't let that get in our way. Right away we petitioned and won a thirty-minute slot for public comment at each Task Force meeting—and grew to be good friends and allies with the Task Force leaders. It didn't take long to see how much we needed each other.

Wisconsin wasn't the first state to put pay equity on the public agenda, but it was the first where the opposition mobilized on a grand scale and with the support of national forces. Led by the Wisconsin Manufacturers and Commerce, opponents bombarded legislators with weekly bulletins. They set out to prove that pay equity would be deadly to the state's business climate. Only a large, well-organized, and unified movement of supporters could win over public opinion and effectively counter this opposition. The activists began by framing pay equity as a justice issue—our slogan was "Justice Is Worth It"—and appealing to the largest grouping possible. Our alliance totaled fifty-six women's groups, and religious, civil rights, labor, professional, and community organizations, each of whom mobilized their own constituency. A coordinating group in Madison known as the "Lunch Bunch" sent out bimonthly fact sheets to all the organizations, as well as to legislators and the media. Each sheet had a different focus—explanations of the pay equity concept, a roundup of activity in other states, an overview of litigation on the issue, a summary of the Task Force's methodology, and so on. I became part of a core of debaters who shared our combat experience and helped prepare materials and alerts. Activists were able to compare notes on legislators' responses and quickly concentrate attention on those who needed it.

In the end, pay equity passed in the Wisconsin budget because of hardball politicking around what had deteriorated into a highly partisan issue.[28] But the grassroots work was the backdrop without which victory would have been impossible.

Losing Innocence

I was already forty years old when we began this campaign. I'd certainly been around the block. But dealing with politicians in the state capitol in the winter of 1985 made me feel like a high school kid who just learned about Watergate. First I went to see my own senator. "Tell the governor to call me if he wants my vote," he said. Just like that! To my face! Then I went off to find my assembly representative, a man by the name of Tom Crawford. He tried to shoo me away as he prepared to leave his office. "I already know what you think," he said. "How can you?" I asked. "We've never met." Crawford hurried down the hall with me at his heels eagerly sharing my views—until he walked into the men's room, leaving me wide-jawed and stranded outside the door.

I didn't follow him into the men's room, but I did make a vow: We would make ourselves heard.

Getting Heard

9to5 worked hard to put faces to the statistics. But our goal was also to counter the efforts to *marginalize* this fight and to use *divide-and-conquer* tactics. Meet some of our most effective speakers.

Carlene Carr ran the office in a warehouse. A single mother with two kids, she'd originally called us in 1983 for information because she was working side-by-side with the boss's son, who had the title "management trainee" and considerably higher pay but the same job assignment she did, except that he refused to do things like filing "because Daddy told me I didn't have to." In the testimony she developed for a public hearing,[29] Carlene described her job responsibilities as including "invoicing, inventory, cost analysis, pricing for more than 1,000 products and 500 customers in various sell categories, accounts receivable, inventory control, in-house programming, direct sales for a cash-and-carry program, typing a weekly sales newsletter, other typing as necessary, and handling customer service calls." Her official title was computer operator. Her wage: $4.75 an hour (at the time, only $1.04 over the minimum wage).

Everyone else in the plant made more than Carlene, including those in the warehouse and dock and in maintenance. "Their jobs required hard work and skill," she noted; "surely mine did, too. If my job were done improperly, not only would millions of dollars of accounts be jeopardized, but none of the other workers could complete their jobs." She went on to list the raft of public assistance programs she was eligible for as a result of her low wage, including food stamps, government-subsidized housing, childcare assistance, the free-milk program at school. Unfortunately, she earned "too much to qualify for the program I needed the most, Title XIX health care."

The pay equity campaign applied only to state workers. But Carlene desperately wanted the state to be a *model* for her employer and others. "I am not the exception," she told legislators, "I am closer to the norm. There are many thousands of us—working women in poverty—and it hurts. It hurts to work full time and not be able to pay your own way. It hurts to be angry when your child needs shoes. It hurts to do your job and be undervalued."

We got to know Deborah after she was featured in an article in the *Milwaukee Journal* about the black family being in a state of crisis. Here was another woman living in poverty even though she worked full time as the secretary in a social-service agency. "My family would not be in crisis if I were paid commensurate with my skills and responsibilities," she said at one of our press events. When opponents demonized women by arguing that pay equity was an excuse for women not to work hard, I pointed to Deborah, who somehow managed a second, minimum-wage job and studied real estate on the side, while caring for her two sons.

In my talks, I also referred to a group of parish secretaries I met with one summer evening in a suburban Milwaukee church. These were women who had raised a family and then taken clerical jobs, skilled women in their forties or fifties earning less than $10,000 a year. They were not suffering financially because they were married to men with decent paying jobs, but along with tea and cookies, they shared how much they resented the fact that their work was unappreciated. That night they were upset for another reason. One of their group was absent because her husband had recently died. Suddenly her less-than-$10,000 wage was her family's only income. Medical insurance had come through her husband's job, not hers. Although he had life insurance, she'd put that away for retirement because she had no pension, and now she was afraid she'd lose her home. Each woman in the group knew this could be her story.

The Debates

Throughout the campaign we organized as many debates as possible, in order to win public opinion and increase pressure on the legislators. I took on a series of business lobbyists—some of whom, I'm proud to say, ended their debating career (at least on this subject) after our encounter.

My first opponent, Wayne Correy from the Allen-Bradley manufacturing corporation, belongs in that category. I'd never met him before the debate, but we got a glimpse of each other a couple hours earlier when a local TV station interviewed us for the five-o'clock news and paired us on the screen. He wasn't a particularly imposing figure and apparently felt he needed an advantage. As soon as I arrived at the debate site, he rushed over to greet me. "You were much better looking on TV," he told me. "Really, and you were much taller," I said. (Okay, I just wish I had said that.) But instead of intimidating me, he brought out my competitive urges.

Before our encounter, a group of us made a list of all the arguments we thought Correy would use and ideas for how to answer them. Happily, he stuck to the playbook, and I blocked every play he made. He began with patronizing—women make less as a result of their own choices, trading income for flexibility, preferring jobs with easy access and easy exit. I pointed out that the lowest-paying jobs are in fact the least flexible. "You want to see an easy exit from a job," I said. "Meet a woman with no maternity leave." Easy access implies that women's jobs don't change at all over the years—a myth easily dispelled by talking to any nurse, secretary, or social worker who's struggled with technological change.

My opponent plodded through various explanations for women's lower pay: Wages reflect supply and demand. Higher paid jobs are more productive. "Oh!" I replied, "there must be a shortage of liquor-store clerks in Maryland and *that's* why they earn more than teachers in that state." I referred to a study in Minnesota to determine the relationship between availability of labor, on the one hand, and wages on the other. Guess what they found? Virtually no relationship except in a few cases of highly technical labor in short supply. Under pay equity, such a legitimate market factor would still be taken into account; the jobs would be overcompensated accordingly. As for productivity, clerical workers' productivity shot up with the computer, yet in some cases their pay declined. Unlike the manual lifting job now performed by the forklift, which was considered more skilled and therefore more valuable with automation, technology was thought to make office work "easier." I quoted a conservative Republican, Robert Isaacs, who instituted pay equity as mayor of Colorado Springs, Colorado. "We did something that was fair and just," he said, "and in return we got higher productivity, lower absenteeism, improved morale. Isn't that what the private sector always wants?"

Unable to prove his economic theories, Mr. Correy turned to demonizing, blaming male-dominated unions for "negotiating" lower wages. I reminded him that this is like saying parents share the blame for child labor because they "allowed" their children to work. Unions operate within a certain environment and can't easily bargain outside of that. Certainly male chauvinism exists within organized labor as everywhere else in society, but unions have also led the way in fighting for pay equity. Besides, the overwhelming majority of women are not represented by unions.

Correy also denounced bureaucrats comparing janitors with clericals and equated that to comparing apples and oranges. (I have never understood why people use this phrase. After all, apples and oranges have a lot in common—they're both fruits, both round, both good sources of vitamin C. Why not say, compare apples and antipasto? I feel the same about the expression "You want to have your cake and eat it, too." Who'd bother making the cake if no one was going to eat it? The real problem is that women have to do most of the baking and often are left with only crumbs.) From my experience on the Task Force, I was able to detail how the job evaluations were actually being done—three job evaluation committees made up of equal numbers of managers and employees utilized a survey instrument to compare not job titles but job components and assign points to those. In order to test the reliability of the process, each group was given about 1,000 of the same survey questions to review. More than nine times out of ten, they came up with the same answers—an extremely high reliability rating.

Anyone who thinks she's underpaid can always quit, Correy muttered. Talk about minimizing. "Quitting—the ultimate American freedom," I replied. "But like moving, it requires a security deposit—you have to know you'll have another job, and that the next position won't be just as bad. That's why America has another tradition: organizing to improve your lot."

The catastrophizing came last—pay equity will be a boondoggle we just can't afford, Correy tried to persuade the audience. I reminded them (to great cheers, I might add) that as a nation, we had long ago decided that discrimination is wrong, period, not just when remedying it could be cheap or easy. But I also delivered the good news: The price tag for this advance had not been great in Washington and Minnesota, and would not prove to be elsewhere. Factoring in the huge gains for working families and for everyone in reducing poverty, how could we afford not to take this step?

Correy kindly (but unwittingly) gave 9to5 the material for our guide for activists, called "Twenty-Five Arguments Against Pay Equity and How to Answer Them."

When the Big Boys Tell It Like It Is

Some of the Big Boys, like the brigadier general I quoted at the beginning of this chapter, were refreshingly candid about their reasons for hanging on to the status quo. I once debated a lawyer on a radio show who summarized his opposition to pay equity with this statement: "Capitalism is about paying people as little as possible in order to make as much profit as possible."[30] Indeed. But most Big Boys were more suave. Several lobbyists acknowledged past discrimination and argued for "alternatives" to pay equity such as childcare and affirmative action. We need those, we pointed out, but since they don't address the undervaluation of women's work, they wouldn't substitute for reform that revalued women's work.

"I Pulled Myself Up by My High Heels"

The pay equity fight in Wisconsin was my first, but certainly not my last, experience going up against a so-called feminist. Attorney Ann Shindell never claimed that women should stay home or leave the larger salaries to their husbands. To the contrary, her argument—an indirect form of demonizing—went something like this: "I pulled myself up by my high heels and so can you. Asking the government to intervene makes women look like weak creatures that can't work hard and earn their own advancement. This is all a matter of power and negotiation."

It wasn't hard to show how few jobs populated by women allow for negotiation of any sort. Calling someone weak puts the blame on them. We call women exploited—placing the blame squarely where it belongs, on their employers and on the legacy of discrimination embedded in wage evaluation systems.

The opposition also ran ads featuring women saying, "I'm a plumber [or some other job] and I'm against comparable worth." These lost their effectiveness when we revealed the fact that the women were actresses.

The so-called feminists who argued against pay equity generally worked for law firms, consultants, or public-relations outfits that represented management. When they spoke to business audiences, their emphasis was not only on why to avoid pay equity but *how*—with their firms ready to pick up the new clients. If labor organizers could hand out union cards the way these folks hand out business cards, the AFL-CIO would be bursting at the seams. Fortunately, many business and professional women don't see their own careers tied to defeat of pay equity; the Wisconsin chapter of Business and Professional Women/USA was an active member of our coalition.

Tripping Through the Technicalities

All our debate opponents also tried to discredit the pay equity study by taking points out of context and making hay out of seemingly ridiculous examples. One of their favorites was that a "simple clerical" got more points for "effect of action" than a pilot—never mind that "effect of action" refers to how many people the job impacts; the pilot received many more points than the clerical on "consequence of error." The sheer weight of numbers of examples can hurt here, giving a veneer of credibility to the view that the study was subjective. Our side compared notes after each debate so we were well aware of the examples the other side would use and were able to counter with specifics. You don't always have the opportunity to get back to each point the opponent makes. I would be sure to answer two or three examples of such criticism in my remarks, but above all I lambasted the opposition for continuing to raise these distortions when every one of the examples had already been refuted by Task Force leaders.

Another favorite tactic of the opponents was to argue that if women's jobs were underpaid, some men's jobs must be overpaid. The way to avoid a pay-adjustment scheme that would cost money and thereby raise taxes, create skyrocketing inflation, business flight, you name it, was to adjust both ends of the scales. Obviously this was part of a compartmentalizing effort to turn men against us, along with women who didn't want their men to get less pay. It conveniently ignored the essence of the problem: The discriminatory wage originally set for women when it was legally and morally acceptable to pay women less than men, even for doing exactly the same job for the same employer, determined the prevailing wage for female-dominated jobs a century later. It's illegal to remedy discrimination against one group by lowering the pay of others. Doing so, we pointed out, wouldn't end discrimination but perpetuate it by incorporating it into paychecks of people who had previously been better off.

Sometimes Bawdy

After we'd won the pay equity item in the state budget in July of 1985, a mainline Milwaukee law firm held a seminar on the subject for corporate leaders and invited me to be one of the speakers. At first this puzzled me. Why would a firm that had opposed the bill give 9to5 a platform? It didn't take long to figure it out—they wanted to know what we were up to and especially whether we would try to impose pay equity on private sector employers.

The seminar was held at a fancy hotel, attended by hundreds of well-dressed, well-connected people. I wore my best (and only) summer suit. "I know you asked me here to find out our plans," I told them, "and I'm happy to share them. But first I have to give you some background, so you'll understand where we came up with the idea for the next stage of our campaign." I explained how I'd been influenced by a state legislator from Eau Claire named Joe Looby, a union activist with an easygoing manner, an imposing set of eyebrows, and a booming voice. One day in the spring of 1985 while I was in Madison fighting for pay equity, I sat in on a caucus meeting of Democrats in the assembly. Looby rose to explain why he'd switched from opposing the bill to supporting it after a recent medical experience. "When you have surgery," I remember Looby telling his colleagues, "first the area has to get 'prepped.' You know how they're always comparing nurses and electricians, nurses and plumbers? Well, there I was waiting to get prepped, and in walks the electrician with his giant tool belt, and the nurse with a nice, neat little kit. 'Please, God,' I said, 'please let the nurse be the one that does the prep and the electrician be here to fix something in the wall, and if this guy is making fifteen dollars an hour, please let her be making that much, too.'" The nurse efficiently completed the prep and Looby moved along to surgery. Later a doctor came in to see how he was doing. "Is everything working?" the doctor asked. "Not exactly," Looby replied. "Well," the doctor informed him, "you can't go home until everything is working." In walked a plumber with his roto-rooter, followed by the nurse with a nice, neat little kit. Again Looby prayed that the nurse would be the one to do the procedure, and that she'd be earning the same salary as the plumber. He got the nurse—and Looby's vote was sealed. He took his seat amid howls of laughter.

Immediately another state representative, Marlin Schneider, bounced up. "Let me tell you what really happened," he said. "Looby's lying on the bed waiting to be prepped and in walks the nurse with a straight-edge razor. She holds the razor over the affected area. 'Hey, Looby,' she shouts, 'are you for comparable worth?'"

I could see the corporate audience wondering where I was going. "Here's our plan," I told them. "We're finding out the surgery schedule for top executives. Our organizing will focus on operating-room nurses. We'll be handing out straight-edge razors and conducting training sessions. The name of our campaign? 'Use it or lose it.'"

The next day a business editor for the *Milwaukee Journal* published a long article on the seminar. He described my remarks as "moving, witty and sometimes bawdy."[31]

Continuing the Fight

Unfortunately, Carlene Carr's dream of the state being a model for private sector employees hasn't materialized. 9to5 and other groups work with the National Committee on Pay Equity (NCPE) to spread awareness of the problem and policy solutions. Every year the NCPE selects a Tuesday in April as Equal Pay Day; Tuesday was chosen because that's the day when women's wages catch up to men's wages from the previous week. Supporters of equal pay wear red to symbolize how women are "in the red" because of pay inequity. 9to5 also created an array of workshops with titles like "What Could You Do with an Extra Quarter, Thirty-Five, or Forty-Five Cents?" referring to the shortfall in earnings for white, black, and Latina women compared to every dollar earned by men. These trainings helped women learn specific tips for evaluating their own job skills and asking for higher pay, and also prepared them for broader policy campaigns.

9to5 chapters and others have been delightfully creative in designing activities for Equal Pay Day. Colorado 9to5, for example, presented legislators with candy bars with a chunk missing, representing women's lower pay. A group of early childhood teachers associated with the American Federation of Teachers (AFT) delivered a petition and bag of peanuts to all 535 members of Congress on behalf of thousands of activists across the nation, protesting that those doing such vital work for our children earn only peanuts.

RAISING THE PAY OF FAMILY CHILDCARE PROVIDERS

Childcare is a prime example of the undervaluation of jobs that are seen as "women's work." A group of family childcare providers in Rhode Island set out to change that reality by making visible the cost and the value of the care they administer every day.

The Home Daycare Justice Campaign began in Providence, Rhode Island in 1990 as part of an organization known as DARE—Direct Action for Rights and Equality. Pearlie Mae Thomas, a DARE member, was one of many women hired by the state's Department of Human Services (DHS) to provide care in their homes for children of women eligible for assistance. The pay wasn't only low, often it arrived as much as three months late. Pearlie Mae Thomas decided to do something about that. She and DARE staff began to survey providers in the community and soon found fifteen others who joined the campaign to demand timely payment from DHS. After getting the brush-off, a group that had grown to twenty-five providers brought the press with them to the associate director's office. The next daycare payroll came on time.

After this victory, the women turned their attention to compensation and eventually spun off into a co-op of providers. Judy Victor became one of the co-op leaders during the nine years she spent as a family childcare provider. "I sort of fell into this," Victor told me, describing the long hours and constantly changing shifts she worked earlier at a nursing home. "I was a single mom who hardly saw my kids—sometimes I had to leave them alone. I wanted to be there."[32]

Victor calls the co-op not just a good idea but a "necessity to make sure providers weren't exploited and were treated as a valuable asset not only to the state agency, but to the families they served." The group launched a campaign they called the Cost of Care. With the help of a professor from nearby Wheelock College, they designed a survey and interviewed a random sample of providers to find out exactly what providers were spending on food, equipment, space, and other expenses; how many children they watched; and how much money they received in compensation. Even Judy Victor was startled by the results, which the co-op published in a booklet in 2002. Many providers were making as little at $2.76 an hour (the highest pay was $11 an hour) for fifty to sixty hours of work every week.

"The way providers are valued basically reflects what society thinks about women," Victor said. "That's women's work. They're supposed to be home watching children anyway." The providers worked to expose this problem and to show that, like Head Start teachers, they educate children. "They may not have degrees, but they do the work," says Victor. "They're expected to teach the children things, take them on field trips, have activities and curriculum. If I give you nine hours of this kind of service, I should be entitled to some kind of decent pay and benefits."

The parents of kids Victor cared for were often immigrants who "looked to me for things beyond what they'd look to a teacher in a center or Head Start. They wanted social support. Family childcare goes beyond caring for kids—in many cases, it means caring for the whole family."

The co-op presented lawmakers with the Cost of Care and other research. They utilized a 2003 study done by the Rhode Island Institute for Labor Studies that showed every dollar the state spends on childcare brings $1.72 in return from sources such as payroll taxes and people spending more money. The women also looked at what other occupations earned— janitors, sanitation workers, and others, were all paid more than they were. They knew those jobs were important, "but so were ours," Victor said. "They look at us as babysitters. Family childcare providers are so much more than that—we're teachers, we're counselors, we give the kids guidance. We're a valuable workforce."

Winning Respect

Because of the work of the co-op, that value is beginning to be recognized. Rates of payment from the Rhode Island DSS have gone up by 40 percent. Providers taking care of at least two children, earning at least $1,800 every six months, became entitled to participate in the state's Medicaid program, known as Right Care. Much more money is now available for training, and partnerships have sprung up with colleges offering two- or four-year degrees in early childhood education. United Way of America and the Rhode Island Childcare Facilities Fund awarded mini grants to providers who want to beautify their property, buy equipment, and do professional development. For two years the co-op ran a successful pilot project to provide substitutes when a provider was ill or wanted a vacation. Unfortunately, the state refused to provide funds to continue that initiative.

The Service Employees International Union is now working with providers to win recognition as a union, so that they can negotiate not only wages and benefits, but funds for training, substitutes, and professional days for continuing education. "The State expects providers to care for each kid at least nine hours a day," Victor explained. "They regulate the money we get, the things we could do. If you have a workforce you have that much control over, they're basically your employees. Providers don't really want to be employees of the state, but they want to be recognized as a valuable asset, as a profession that needs to be rewarded as such."

Victor, who's no longer with the co-op, is proud "that I had even a little bit to do with it. Even though we didn't get all the things we wanted to—and I think they eventually will, the governor is trying to put off the inevitable, they will become a union and bargain for what they need—after all the work in the last nine or ten years, family childcare providers as women have gotten a lot of respect in this state and nationally. People at the capitol realize this is not something women are doing to make some pocket money. This is a career for the majority of us. It's being recognized as a profession."

FINAL THOUGHTS: DOING THE RIGHT THING

One year on Valentine's day, the Milwaukee 9to5 chapter gave a "Full-of-Heart" award to Ralph Sherman, who was then director of Jewish Family Services. The support staff at the agency, led by a 9to5 board member, had barraged Sherman with materials about how their jobs were undervalued and the consequences for them and their families. "You'll have to convince me," Sherman told the women. They did. He went on to persuade the agency's board of directors to revalue those jobs and significantly raise the pay. At the 9to5 ceremony, Sherman was reluctant to accept his award. "Why honor me for doing what we should have done all along?" he said. (When I attended his funeral a couple years ago, I learned that this recognition meant more to him than all the accolades he'd accumulated during his lengthy career.)

Ralph Sherman was right. Valuing women's work is what we should have been doing all along. Thanks to women like the clericals on his staff and the Rhode Island childcare providers—ordinary women taking on the Big Boys from the bottom up—someday all workers will experience fair pay as a matter of course.

3. CAN YOU HAVE A JOB *AND* A LIFE?

"You need to decide whether you want to work here or whether you want to be a mom."—Milwaukee office manager to 9to5 member Tina Orth after she took an unpaid day off to care for her sick five-year-old daughter[1]

You've come a long way, mama.

Consider yourself lucky this slogan doesn't grace some brand of cigarette or diaper or feminine hygiene product. Ad executives surely know that the most dramatic changes for women in the workplace have occurred among mothers. For better or worse, most moms are employed outside the home, even the majority of mothers of infants—a number the Bureau of Labor Statistics didn't even track until the mid-1970s.[2] Employers no longer have the right to fire women for being pregnant. Mothers—and fathers—are allowed to spend time with new or seriously ill children, thanks to the Family and Medical Leave Act (FMLA).[3]

Myth: All Women Have Maternity Leave

That's the good news. The bad news is this hard-won legal protection has loopholes large enough for a pregnant woman to walk through sideways. Take the 1978 Pregnancy Discrimination Act. This law states that if you're expecting a baby, you can't be fired or refused a job or treated differently from other employees. So far, so good. But it doesn't require your employer to keep your job open during maternity leave. I've never understood how giving away your job fails to qualify as firing you—but remember, we live in a world where the highest court once ruled that pregnancy has nothing to do with sex.[4] If your employer offers temporary disability insurance, the policy must treat pregnancy the same as other short-term disabilities. In other words, if a coworker gets paid time off when his gall bladder is removed, you're entitled to the same benefits when you deliver a baby. That's a step forward from the days when pregnancy was excluded as a disability along with injuries that were "willfully self-inflicted or incurred during the perpetration of a high misdemeanor."[5] But it doesn't help the majority of women who work for firms with no short-term disability policies to begin with. And not all employers gave it willingly. In the mid-1980s, when Sheila Ashley was a captain in the army, her superior officer tried to limit her maternity leave to four weeks instead of six. "He said women are getting pregnant for those six weeks of leave," she told me. "Like six weeks off makes up for a lifetime of parenthood."

Some of the problem was addressed in 1993 with passage of the Family and Medical Leave Act. Thanks to this law, not only does your employer have to allow you to take time off to have a baby, you also have the right to return from leave to the same or equivalent job. But here's the fine print: In order to qualify under the law, you must work for a firm of more than 50 employees, have been on the job for at least a year, and work there more than 25 hours a week. As a result, more than two in five private sector workers aren't covered. And many of those who are covered can't afford to take the leave because it's unpaid.[6] Others work for employers who simply break the law—like the woman whose boss looked at her in her eighth month of pregnancy and said, "I was going to put you in charge of the office, but look at you now."[7] Or the pregnant employee whose manager was ordered to fire her for wearing flat shoes and needing to sit down occasionally—even though she worked in a maternity clothing store. When the manager failed to carry out the order, she was fired along with the subordinate.[8]

Myth: Most Workers Can Take Time to Care for Sick Family Members

The FMLA has other limitations. Family is narrowly defined. When I served on the bipartisan Commission on Leave, appointed by Congress in 1994 to evaluate the impact of this law on employers and employees, a woman testifying at one of our hearings thanked us for allowing her to spend time with her brother when he was dying of AIDS. "Thank your employer," I told her during the break. The law doesn't include siblings—or domestic partners, grandparents, in-laws, or any other relative besides children, spouse, and parents.

Think of Rosemary, for example. Her desk has no picture of her long-time partner, Louise, because Rosemary works for an employer who could and would fire her if he knew she were a lesbian (see Chapter 4). What's worse in Rosemary's view is that she couldn't take off when Louise had breast cancer surgery. "I'd have used vacation days," she said, "but we have to give advance notice and the cancer just wasn't considerate enough to warn us." Rosemary did use vacation days to accompany Louise to most of her chemotherapy sessions—"a helluva vacation," she added.

That's another shortcoming of the FMLA—it applies only to "serious illness." Fortunately, not all children get leukemia—but they do all get the flu and ear infections, which are not covered. From time to time, children need their parents to be at school for a conference or play or sporting event; they have routine doctor appointments; they must be immunized or school won't admit them. Yet the law provides time off for none of these events. For low-wage workers, three-fourths of whom lack paid sick days, taking a day to be with a sick child can mean not only losing your wages but facing disciplinary action as well. The results? Teachers we interviewed say they've never seen so many kids coming to school sick because their parents can't take time off from work.[9] As for their parents, many are like Judy, a factory worker in northern Wisconsin, who told me, "I go to work when I'm sick or in pain."[10] As for doctor or dental appointments for herself or her kids? "We don't go, or I use my vacation."

Myth: The Workplace Is Family Friendly

Even when workers have the right and the means to take time off, corporate culture pressures them not to. We're deluged with commercials for cold and flu treatments that tell you how to make it to work when you're sick. Men who take more than the occasional day or week of vacation when a new baby is born are badgered about whether they're really writing a novel. "What are doing, breastfeeding that baby yourself?" demanded a friend's supervisor after this new father had been off (using vacation time) for one week.

The problem has even made its way into popular culture. If you have young children or take many long flights, you may have seen the movie *Home Alone 3*. In this one, the boy comes down with chickenpox. His mother is caring for him when the boss calls to demand she come in for a meeting. "Thanks for making me choose between making the house payment and taking care of my child," she says. Regretfully she informs her son he'll have to stay home alone for a while. "But, Mom," he pleads, "what about the Family Leave Act?" The law's on his side—but the boss isn't.

Adding to the culture problem is the lack of training and accountability for many supervisors. A few years ago, the vice president of a large retail corporation came to see me. She was drafting a memo from the CEO to managers about how they sabotaged the company's leave policies. Here's the gist of the memo: "When our people ask you about leave policies, you tell them what's available—but then you add, 'Boy, will you be sorry if you use them.' They hear only the second message." Alas, this enlightened CEO (not to mention his female VP), whose memo went on to require an end to these tactics, stands among the exceptions. More common are examples cited by work-life consultants, such as the CEO at a dot-com company who, when asked about instituting concierge services to handle dry cleaning and take-out food, replied: "Anything that will glue these people to their desk for an extra hour is worth its weight in gold." Responding to a survey about flexible schedules, a financial company CEO summed up his enthusiastic support: "My chief in-house counsel has lots of flexibility. She can work her 80 hours any way she wants."

Indeed, most of Corporate America continues to function as if all employees were still men with wives at home full time. Faith Wohl, formerly work-family manager at DuPont, described a senior finance executive who balked when she met with him to explain the company's new work-life policies.[11] "I don't believe your statistics," he said, referring to numbers that showed the majority of DuPont's employees are in dual-earner couples. Wohl pointed out that he made his living working with numbers. "Yes," he said, "but no one in my neighborhood, my church, or my circle of friends has a wife who works outside the home. How could it be true of the majority of our employees?" If you think your world is *the* world and you're a top decision-maker, your front-line workers are in for a heap of trouble.

Reality: A Lot of Lip Service

Even the so-called best places to work are often not what they're cracked up to be. In 1992, Sprint won a place on *Working Mother* magazine's list of the top 100 places for women to work. Sprint operators were amazed as they read the descriptions of flextime, job-sharing, and adoption aid, which none of them enjoyed. It turned out the company did have such policies—but only for managers. If you were a customer agent, the sole flexible option open to you was to be 15 minutes late once within a three-month period, provided you made up the 15 minutes at the end of that shift. (The operators signed a petition to the magazine expressing their objection—the company failed to make the list the following year.) A friend's husband works at a company frequently on "best lists" for its work-life policies. Yet when he applied for a promotion, his manager told him his "family obligations were a factor against him." Only after an expensive nationwide search failed to find someone did they offer him the job.

Many employers say they have flexible policies—but a closer look reveals that the policies are up to manager discretion.[12] Consider the printing company on Long Island, which had won awards for its on-site childcare center but also had a policy of mandatory overtime. In the late 1990s, one worker told me what happened when her mother was dying and she wanted to leave work at 5 P.M. every day. "What's the problem?" her manager told her. "Your child is in the center and they're open until 6." She explained about her mother's condition. "Well," he demanded, "how long is this thing with your mother going to last?"

Jack Welch, former CEO of General Electric who's reinvented himself as a corporate guru, let the cat out of the bag in his 2005 book, *Winning*. "I have a sense of how bosses think about the issue," he alerts the reader. In reality, the family friendly lingo you hear is mostly "lip service."[13] And that's not a problem, according to Welch, because if the boss is "doing his job right, he is making your job so exciting that your personal life becomes a less compelling draw." Welch fondly recalls what a "blast" he had all those Saturdays at the office. His advice: Figure out that work-family stuff on your own and keep your mouth shut about it. "People who publicly struggle with work-life balance problems and continually turn to the company for help," he warns, "get pigeonholed as ambivalent, entitled, uncommitted, incompetent—or all of the above."

When I asked a group of my graduate students, all HR staff, to respond, they blasted Welch for wasting the opportunity to give leadership on the topic. The most poignant response came from a woman who signed her paper as "the child of a twenty-plus-year GE employee who never saw her mom at sporting events, had to make her own meals since she was eight years old, and who grew up in second place to a job."

Reality: To Advance, You Need a Wife

The policies we need already exist in many companies, and studies consistently show these to be good for the bottom line. In particular, research confirms that the cost of leave is much less than the cost of replacing the employee permanently.[14]

But most policies exist on the fringes of a company's operation. They don't touch a fundamental problem about Corporate America, namely, in order to get ahead, you have to be available for long hours of "face time," and be able to meet, move, or travel at a moment's notice. It's very hard to do that unless you have a wife at home full-time, or no life. As high-profile executive divorces remind us, few CEO's move up without a wife to entertain, volunteer in the community, and take care of the home front (see Chapter 9).

I remember hearing Barbara Jones, then-editor at *Harper's*, tell of interviewing managers concerning work-family issues. One had confronted a male senior executive who called a meeting at 7 P.M. "I know you have kids, too," the lower-level manager said. "How can you be at this meeting?" The answer: "I have a wife." No wonder that 80 percent of top executives are men with wives at home full time—and more than half of female senior executives have no children.

FEMINIST SOLUTIONS

Can you have a job *and* a life without having a wife at home full time? Sure—but only with significant change in how business does business, how society values families and how families divide up the work. We'll come back to that last part in Chapter 9.

What's needed is not that complicated—time to care for loved ones or yourself, access to reliable, quality caregivers when you're unable to provide care, and enough income to afford both the time off and the outside help.

Time to Care

Time means flexibility at work so you can take your mother for her mammogram or attend your child's school play, as well as flexible start and end times so you don't have to leave your kindergartner alone at the bus stop. It also means time off for routine illness in addition to more demanding events like a new child or a seriously ill family member. I'll always remember the testimony at a Commission on Leave hearing from Kenneth Weaver, an oil technician who was able to take time to be with his eleven-year-old daughter in the last weeks of her life. He told his supervisors, "I'm going to use the Family [and] Medical Leave Act, and I'm out of here."[15] In the break he told me, "We already had so much stress to deal with. Just knowing I had the time off and didn't have to haggle over it was a huge relief."

The only way to secure this flexibility for everyone is to create a reasonable minimum standard. That would mean expanding the FMLA to cover all workers, with the leave prorated for part-timers (see Chapter 7). It would also mean a definition of family that includes same-sex and domestic partners, siblings, in-laws, and grandparents. Workers would be able to use the time off for routine school and medical appointments as well as serious illness.

Finally, time to care means control over schedule, a reasonable workweek, and no mandatory overtime.

Affordable Leave

Employees and their employers would be able to afford extended leaves if needed if the time were funded through an insurance pool paid for by employees, employers, and some public monies. Five states and Puerto Rico already have Temporary Disability Insurance funds (TDI) that have been operating in some cases for seventy years. These are funded either by modest contributions from employers or employees or both. I did a study on these funds in the early 1990s and the administrators all said they were solvent, easy to administer, and a boon to employers as well as workers because they enabled people to return to work. New Jersey's governor at the time, Thomas H. Kean, described the partial wage replacement provided by TDI as fostering "the economic survival of low- and middle-income women who wish to bear children." Governor Kean concluded that TDI "has not caused a significant economic strain on employers," calling the employer contribution "an important investment in an employee's future well-being."[16] The only thing lacking has been the political will to expand such funds to all the states and allow them to cover the spectrum of reasons workers occasionally need leave, as California did in 2004 (see p. 64).

Even the members of the Commission on Leave who opposed the original law acknowledged that we needed to make it affordable. All of our economic competitors manage to provide paid leave. And we don't just mean Sweden and Norway, which allow parents to share a year's leave at 80 percent of pay. Germany, Japan, Canada—even Third World countries like Cameroon and Bangladesh—all do better than the United States.[17]

Use It or Lose It

One interesting note about Sweden and Norway is that they *require* men to take at least a month of that leave or the family loses the time. Sweden is now debating whether to lengthen the portion of time men are required to take; Iceland already requires three months. This "use it or lose it" feature ensures that men will expand their caregiving role, and should be part of the leave we design here.

Time for Routine Illness

In addition to FMLA, all workers need a guaranteed minimum number of paid sick days for routine illness. A new bill called the Healthy Families Act, introduced by Sen. Edward Kennedy and Rep. Rosa deLauro, would ensure that workers receive at least seven paid sick days to care for themselves or a sick family member. I've known for a long time that people go to work sick or send their kids to school sick when they don't have this protection. But Carissa Peppard, the twenty-one-year-old daughter of 9to5-leader Kiki Peppard in Pennsylvania (see Chapter 4), reminded me that kids also make these decisions. "Kids know everything," Carissa told me at a 2004 9to5 leadership conference in DC where groups were preparing for meetings the next day with their senators. "Whenever I was sick, I'd ask myself, 'Should I tell Mom? Will we have groceries this week if she stays home with me?' Whenever I could, I just dragged myself to school."

Help with Dependent Care

Anyone who's ever been responsible for dependent children or ailing parents while trying to earn a living knows you need some help from experienced caregivers. For me and millions of other parents, having access to skilled childcare providers—and for my mother, skilled nursing home workers—has meant more than someone to fill in when I couldn't be there. It meant my children learned creative and social skills greater than what my husband or I could teach them. For my mother, it meant receiving patient and knowledgeable care to keep body and mind agile.

Such care exists in the United States right now, but for most people it's expensive, and for many, hard to find. Childcare is like a tug of war between two sides who can never win—parents who for the most part can't afford what they're already paying, and childcare workers who leave to take jobs in retail because they can't pay their bills. There's got to be a better way.

Fortunately, there is.

When I was pregnant with my first child in 1977, I received a letter from a good friend in France. "I'm so sorry for you that you have to have this baby in the United States," she wrote. She went on to describe the lengthy paid leave mothers in France received. But that wasn't all. Infant care was available to all on a sliding scale fee. The childcare providers received excellent training and good wages, along with assorted government assistance such as equipment and health-care screeners for the kids. Once children reached the age of two and a half, they were eligible for free preschools, the quality of which was so high that 99 percent of the population sent their children there even if the mother was not employed outside the home. At the time, I was dumbfounded and embarrassed for having thought my country was the most advanced in the world.

We could have a system like France's (and many other countries) simply by making real a value most of us already hold—the importance of early childhood development. Public school, after all, wasn't always free or open to all of the public. That concept evolved over time because employers couldn't function with illiterate workers. The culture and laws changed enough to include African Americans and other groups that at first were willfully excluded or relegated to inferior facilities. Gradually lawmakers lengthened the number of years students were required to attend; many have now added optional kindergarten for four-year-olds and even three-year-olds.

We could make quality early childhood education available in public schools for all children ages three and up. We could expand existing models of after-school care, where instead of being parked alone in front of a TV or video game, kids are offered sports, music, other cultural and language arts, help with homework. We could also transform the tug-of-war of childcare into a sturdy three-legged stool by adding public support and sliding scale payments.

"Why should my taxes go to pay for other people's kids?" a caller to a radio show once asked me. "I'm glad you're concerned about where your taxes go," I replied. "So am I. But we pay for kids one way or another. Let's pay for it upfront in support for good childcare and early education, rather than paying for it later in remedial care, prisons, and public assistance. To start, let's take the money from the billions being spent on corporate welfare, subsidies from the government to large corporations."[18] The money exists—we just need the people, rather than the Big Boys, to determine how it gets spent.

As for the argument that we don't want to turn our children over to "strangers," my children's caregivers quickly became beloved people in their lives. Studies show that what matters most is the quality of care—whether at home or at a center or private provider's house.

A New Model of Families that Work

Even if we could find ways to provide fabulous care for our children at all hours of the day or night, we also want time—quantity as well as quality—to spend with them ourselves. For that, we need a new model. Two sociologists, Janet Gornick and Marcia Meyers, have come up with a much more reasonable, and not terribly expensive, approach.[19] They call it a "dual-earner/dual-carer" model, assuming a two-parent couple where both parents are employed outside the home and both care for the children. This can be adapted for single-parent households and for those caring for elderly parents rather than kids. The model depends on the kinds of changes we describe above—ample job-protected leave policies with pay, quality childcare and early education programs, and changes in the workplace to allow for reduced schedules for both parents. In the first two years of a child's life, after an extensive leave, each parent might work 20 to 25 hours a week so that someone is home with the infant all or most of the time. Parents of kids three to five years old might each work 30 to 35 hours a week. And as children progress in school, their parents might work a full week, redefined as 37.5 hours (35 would be even better).

How much would it cost? Gornick and Meyers estimate that a full package of programs to allow for leave and early childhood education and care would cost 1.5 percent of the Gross Domestic Product. That's a mere fifth of what the government is now spending on corporate subsidies.[20]

Changing the Way We Work

Along with changes in public policy, allowing all workers to have a job *and* a life requires a fundamental restructuring of the workplace. In Chapter 6 we'll talk about a greater voice for workers on the job, Chapter 7 will look at how to achieve equity for part-time workers, and Chapter 9 will look at ways for men to share in caregiving. Clearly, money is a work-family issue. But we also need change in how work is *done*.

The workplace I'm describing has more people working for more reasonable periods of time. To allow that to happen, we need greater collaboration and better planning. I remember speaking to a group of women physicians who thought it was impossible to reconcile a successful practice with a successful home life. One described missing her daughter's graduation because she was called to deliver a baby. "If I were your physician," she said, "you'd want me to be there when you had your baby." It's true—I'd want the doctor I knew and trusted to be there. But I'd also want her to be at that graduation. The solution? Have patients get to know two or three doctors. A more team approach in medicine, law, business, and government, means that the best jobs don't have to go to those who are willing to work ridiculously long hours, whatever the consequences to their lives and the lives of their family members.

Here, too, we aren't talking about pie in the sky. Some employers have already piloted changes in work organization because they wanted a better way to run a workplace. Engineers at Xerox, for example, hired researchers to help them figure out how to meet deadlines without spending manic sessions away from their families. By moving flexibility from a nice concept at the margins of the department's operations to a core value, the engineers were able to redesign how they got the job done. Researchers helped them work more collaboratively, schedule uninterrupted blocks of time, and plan more efficiently. As a result, they were finished in fewer hours, but produced what they considered higher quality work.[21]

At SAS system, a software company, the gates close at 6 P.M. No one, including the CEO, stays later than that. Yet the company has never had a down year, even when the rest of the tech economy tanked.

In order for these changes to be meaningful, those who take advantage of flexible schedules or leave—including several years off—have to know they won't be penalized in pay or advancement (see Chapters 2 and 4). That means allowing exits and reentry points for those who want to take time out to care for a new child or ailing parent, to connect with busy teenagers, or to pursue a passion of some kind.

Some farsighted corporate leaders will make these changes on their own. But to guarantee them for everyone, we need a vision that transcends what's politically winnable at the moment. And we need to take on the Big Boys.

TAKING ON THE BIG BOYS

My first experience speaking up about work-family policies came in 1981, when I was working at Wisconsin Bell in Milwaukee. My husband and I decided to come here after his mother died, in order to be closer to Larry's father in Janesville. I knew with my typing skills I could get hired at the phone company, and I did receive family health benefits there. But I also experienced the most rigid work environment I'd ever known. For starters, I was told I could not get sick for the first five years. The benefits manager, a petite Japanese woman in a regulation navy-blue suit, apologized as she informed me of this rule. "You're probably wondering how the hell you're going to do that," she said. "Well, you just have to." People were constantly coming to work sick, infecting others, and staying sick much longer than they would have if they'd just been able to take a day or two off. In my department, we also had to arrive at work by 7:30 A.M., no excused lateness—even if your five-year-old's school bus was late and you weren't about to leave him on the corner alone. And my favorite rule: If you knew you had to schedule a doctor's appointment during work hours, you could make up the time as long as you gave advance notice. But if your unruly children woke up sick and you had to take them to the doctor, you couldn't make up the time because you hadn't told your supervisor in advance. (I tried to train my children to warn me at least 24 hours before a stomach bug or ear infection, really, but I failed.)

After a few months (I lasted only nine), I attended a listening session conducted by the head of corporate services, Mr. Z. I remember him as having a flushed face and a comb-over, but I believe he was actually trim and well groomed. I'd heard that he and his secretary would leave the room and allow the workers to write any question anonymously on a large pad of paper. The whole process sounded appealing—until the guy began to speak. Twenty female support staff filled three sides of a giant rectangular table while Mr. Z presided at the other end, where he lectured us on the appalling habits of American workers. A number of the women nodded as he spoke; I worried that I'd been assigned to a meek group. But as soon as he left us alone, all the women surged to the front to scribble furious questions on the newsprint. Mr. Z returned five minutes later and proceeded through the questions one by one. I was astonished by his arrogance. In response to why we had to make coffee and managers didn't, for instance, he said, "I don't know—it wouldn't bother me." Among other things, someone had asked why workers, unlike managers, had no flexibility. Mr. Z rambled on about his tough requirements for managers. "They have to be on call 24 hours a day and be willing to change their vacation schedule at a moment's notice," he said. "That's why I give them more flexibility on scheduling."

It was not my intention to make trouble on this job. But a hand shot up and a voice spoke out and I realized they belonged to me. "Does this mean mothers of young children can't be managers at the phone company?" I asked. Mr. Z cut his eyes at me and flashed a scowl that seemed to ask, "Who let you in here?" He muttered something about the company's non-discrimination policy and the number of women in management—never mind that the actual number in high positions was minuscule, and that few of them had kids.

Thus began the first of many encounters with the most common Big Boy tactic on family friendly policies: *minimizing* the problem. Over and over we were told the solution we were proposing was unnecessary because the problem didn't really exist.

Campaign for Family Leave

Our experience fighting for family leave in Wisconsin is a prime example. Unlike pay equity, the concept of family leave was hard for the Big Boys to discredit. Instead, they acted as if all employers already provided it and the real problem was government mandating unreasonable requirements. This, they *catastrophized*, would lead to untold harm to business and—of course—to women.

"No business that's worth its salt is not going to bend over backwards to take care of its employees," said Timothy Sheehy, chief lobbyist for the Metropolitan Milwaukee Association of Commerce.[22] He claimed that 95 percent of the nation's 1,500 largest companies already offered some form of family leave.

In fact, as that bipartisan Commission on Leave later discovered, two-thirds of all employers covered by the federal FMLA had to change at least one or more of their policies in order to comply with the law. Many of these had to do with allowing time off for men as well as women, leave for adoption as well as biological births, and time for the care of seriously ill children. The so-called family leave already offered by large employers usually meant firms with short-term disability policies allowing six weeks disability for mothers giving birth—as required by the Pregnancy Discrimination Act.

Catastrophizing

On the catastrophizing front, the Big Boys argued that mandating family leave would destroy small business and end up hurting women. I helped organize forums on family leave in several cities in Wisconsin, where we heard many variations of this argument, including the following:

- A small business owner argued that he couldn't afford to do without his female office manager. My response: "That's why a reasonable family leave policy makes good business sense. If you don't offer some time off, you'll lose that person entirely."

- A business lobbyist insisted we were taking away employer flexibility and freedom: "Employers will accommodate good employees, but they shouldn't have to give extensive time off to bad ones." I agreed that employers had the right to correct the behavior of a problem employee or let the person go. "But don't wait until that worker's husband has cancer to tell her she has a problem," I advised.

- A representative of a large manufacturing firm complained that passage of family leave legislation would mean his company could no longer give the more generous benefits they now offered. Women workers would suffer because of us. "The *minimum required* is hardly the same as the maximum allowed," I pointed out. Firms have enormous flexibility in offering more generous leave. The bill would provide a floor, not a ceiling.

We used a report from the General Accounting Office (GAO), showing only modest costs for such legislation, to silence the Chicken Little cries of the Big Boys.[23] And we talked about the price tag for *not* providing leave—the costs of reduced earning power and public assistance programs, not to mention the human costs to workers and their families.[24] As for those who insisted that family-leave legislation would lead to discrimination against women, we countered with the fact that the bill applied to men as well as women, and to non-parents caring for a parent. "Let's face it," I argued, "it's inconvenient when workers get pregnant or sick. But we've learned to deal with vacations and heart attacks—it's high time we learned to deal with pregnancy and sick children as well." This also helped head off efforts to *compartmentalize* the issue—set mothers against those without kids by claiming they would be getting "special privileges."

Business Support

To bolster our position that the problem was greater and the solutions less dire than posited by the Big Boys, we found some employers to testify in support of the bill. Robert Weisenberg, general manager and co-owner of Effective Management Systems, had himself taken some time off when his four-year-old son had severe asthma and had to be on breathing machines. "Legislation is the only way to ensure a fair treatment of employees across all companies," Weisenberg told legislators.

But above all, we left the minimizers in the dust by bringing forward the many workers we knew whose employers did *not* offer meaningful leave. First we focused on women. Brenda Liddell was a hotel worker who returned from maternity leave to discover she'd been placed in a lower-paying job on second shift; she had no car and there were no buses to her neighborhood at 11 P.M. when that shift let out. Brenda lost her job and wound up on welfare. Sandra Seymour had asked her school district supervisor for a one-week unpaid leave when her eighty-five-year-old father had two heart attacks in another state. The supervisor denied her request, but promised she could have three days bereavement instead of two if her father died because he was more than 100 miles away. Brenda and Sandra were among the many women we worked with who told their stories to legislators and the media.

In the years of working for state and national family leave laws, we also included stories of men who were denied leave. Among them was Kevin Knussman, a paramedic with the Maryland State Police. Knussman wanted time off when he was caring for his newborn daughter and his wife, who had developed dangerous complications during her pregnancy. Only women qualified for leave, Knussman was told by a personnel manager. "Until I could breastfeed a baby," he said, "there was no way I could be the primary care provider." Later he was informed he might indeed qualify "if his wife were in a coma or dead."[25]

Our Secret Weapon: Kids

Before passage of the federal Family and Medical Leave Act, a number of states enacted their own versions of the bill. Our fight for such a law in Wisconsin ran smack into one of the most powerful Big Boys, Governor Tommy Thompson. A scrappy guy from the town of Elroy in Wisconsin, he'd made his position clear: He'd support a leave of only thirty days and only for maternity. Employers were in the best position to determine these things, he said. Anything more from government was simply unnecessary.

We decided the most effective way to show why we needed leave for family illness was to involve another group of those affected—the children. In February 1988, our statewide coalition escorted a dozen kids, ages seven to seventeen, to the capitol in Madison. Their personal experiences covered the range of reasons why we needed a broader bill.

Our goal was to meet with the governor himself, but he delegated the task to his then-secretary of employment relations, John Tries. The secretary met with us in a formal conference room, where the children took their seats around a large, polished table. Later the kids told an AP reporter they'd speculated on the way to Madison what Tries would be like. They had expected a fat, gruff, bald man who smoked a pipe. "He was skinny, he was nice, and he had hair," one of them said.

Just as we did with members at 9to5, we'd spent time with each of the children beforehand and had them tell us their experience while we took notes. Then we typed up the statements and gave it to them to read or just to hold while they talked. Now one by one they told Secretary Tries their stories.

Noah Michaelson was big for a nine-year-old. I had trouble picturing him hairless and skinny from cancer four years earlier. The boy from Racine, Wisconsin, recounted how both his parents would accompany him when he had to get treated, one to hold him and one to tell him a story while they put the needle in. His voice was steady as his hands demonstrated the size of the needle. "Operations and tests hurt more when your parents aren't there," he said. Noah remembered noticing other children at the hospital who were all alone—what he didn't know then, but understood now was that their parents had to be at work or they'd lose their jobs and their insurance.

Chris Chrisler from DeForest, Wisconsin, was adopted for the first time at the age of twelve. A friend, Francie Phelps, read his story. "I was so happy to finally have a home," he'd written, after spending twelve years being moved from foster home to foster home in Texas. "Now I have the stability and security of my family. At least we are trying to be stable. My brothers and sisters and I must go to bed by 8:00 at night so that mom can tuck us in and be at her job all night." The adoption agency required her to be home during the day, but her employer wouldn't give her leave—the only solution was working the night shift.

Then Francie, an earnest preteen from Madison, talked about the recent loss of her grandma. "It was hard enough for my mother to lose her mother," Francie said. "I don't know what she'd have done if she also lost her job."

Michael McGrew's sister is developmentally disabled. In a quiet voice from a mouth surrounded by faint new facial hair, the Milwaukee teenager described the many problems the family had when she was little. "But the main problem," he said, "was my mom having to put her job in jeopardy. She would either have to worry about being replaced or losing money when my sister would need her at home."

The youngest and smallest of the children who told their stories was Craig Miller, age seven—my younger son. Two years earlier he'd been hit by a car. Luckily, the driver had been going slowly and slammed on her brakes as soon as he darted out into the street. Still, he had to be hospitalized for twenty-four hours for a concussion—an experience he found quite traumatic, considering the brace on his neck and the bruises all over his body and being awakened by a flashlight every hour. (At midnight, he begged me to take the neck brace off. When I explained why we couldn't, he wailed, "Nobody loves me!") Craig sat extra straight and held his testimony in front of his freckled face as he described the experience and how he couldn't imagine having to go through that without his parents at his side. He ended with this challenge: "I'd like to say to the governor, how would you like it if your son was sick and you couldn't take the time off from work to be with your sick kid?"

Getting a Commitment

When the children finished, John Tries had a grin on his face and a tear in his eye. "You know," he told them, "we're so used to dealing with lobbyists, we forget about those who are affected by our legislation." Just so, he'd forgotten that some of us were busy writing down every word he said. He thanked the kids and asked if any of them had a question. Craig immediately raised his hand.

"Yeah," he said. "I want to know why wouldn't the governor sign this bill?"

Tries laughed and looked straight at Craig. "I promise you that the governor will sign some version of this."

The kids then held a press conference for legislators and told their stories again—this time adding the secretary's promise. Newspaper headlines the next day read, "Young 'Lobbyists' Win Lawmakers' Hearts," and the stories included John Tries' agreement to work toward a bill "everyone could support."[26]

A few weeks later, the governor did sign the Wisconsin Family and Medical Leave Act, which called for six weeks leave for a new parent, fathers as well as mothers, and two weeks leave to care for a seriously ill family member. It was only the second state law to include time for family care, and the first to allow the right for workers to substitute any paid time off they might have for the unpaid leave. I took Craig with me to the bill signing. Much to our surprise, the governor acknowledged that the children's testimony was the reason he agreed to accept the family leave provision—and he offered Craig the pen he used to sign the bill. My son turned to me with a look that said, "I know this is a bad guy, but I *really* want that pen." We still have it.

That Was Just Round One

Once the legislation passed in Wisconsin, the Big Boys tried to undermine it, challenging the provision allowing workers to substitute paid time off for their unpaid leave. In addition to the other tactics, the Big Boys turned to *trivializing*. Julie Buchanan, a Milwaukee management attorney, claimed male workers were taking the time off to go fishing and alligator hunting.[27] We responded with stories of men finally being able to afford to spend some time with their new babies by using their own sick time—and of the women who were desperate for their involvement.

In 1995 I attended the Fourth World Conference on Women in Beijing. There I met men from Norway and Sweden eager to talk about the new provisions in their countries' family leave laws. Remember, these are the countries where fathers not only receive paid paternity leave, but *have* to use at least a month or the families lost the time. The men I met were convinced that this early bonding with infants would lead to much greater involvement by men throughout their children's lives.

Both in Beijing and upon my return, reporters from the States peppered me with questions about the experience. "Weren't you proud to be from America?" they asked. Well, I certainly was grateful that women here don't experience the genital mutilation, stoning for adultery, and abandonment of female infants we heard about from women in other countries. But most of my time at the conference was spent in workshops about work-family issues. I was profoundly aware of how *backward* the United States was compared to most of the world, including many Third World countries. Representatives from newly liberated South Africa talked about how they were working to lengthen their three months paid leave to six. Whatever region of the world they were from, the delegates I met enjoyed a floor much higher than we had ever asked for here.

Today the Big Boys continue to minimize the need to expand FMLA to cover more workers, for more reasons, with some form of wage replacement. In 1999 I testified at a Senate hearing where lobbyists who had fought fiercely to stop the FMLA from passing now claimed it was a fine bill, no problem; they'd used it when they adopted a baby or their husband had a heart attack—but, they said, the bill needed a little "tweaking" (like taking away the right to use it for chronic illnesses such as asthma) and certainly did not need expanding.[28] "Even the most modest sick leave policies," they argued, cover conditions in which treatment and recovery are brief.[29] I responded by sharing the stories of those who don't have any flexibility, much less access to any sick leave policy, and highlighting the consequences to children's health and well-being, to job retention, to family stability.

Even when a proposed policy has no costs to business, the Big Boys put up the catastrophizing fight. In 2004 California passed the first paid leave law in this country. It builds upon an existing Temporary Disability Insurance Fund program and is entirely paid for by employees (at an expected cost of $27 per worker per year). A study by economists at the University of California showed the measure would mean a *savings* to business of $89 million and to taxpayers of $25 million in public assistance costs. Nevertheless, business lobbyists unleashed a massive campaign to stop the bill or prevent then-governor Gray Davis from signing it. Thanks to the work of a large and diverse coalition, they were unsuccessful.

Patronizing

Much of the time the Big Boys are trying to halt some effort initiated by feminists and their allies. But sometimes the opposition introduces a measure of their own. It's hard to make the case that workers should spend more time away from their family. So the Big Boys turn to *patronizing* in order to move such legislation.

A case in point is the Family Time Flexibility Act, which would have allowed workers to "choose" to substitute time off (comp time) for overtime pay—time-and-a-half for hours worked in excess of the forty-hour week. The very title of the bill and the use of the word "choice" were part of a significant effort to convince Congress that giving up overtime pay was just what working women wanted in order to spend more time with their families.

Spearheaded by the AFL-CIO, the coalition working to defeat the bill was permitted to have one person testify against it at a congressional hearing in March 2003.[30] Given the way the legislation was promoted, the coalition decided this should be a representative of a working women's group and asked 9to5; our members had been speaking out on the issue. I was delighted to have the opportunity to share their stories and point out the chief contradiction of the proposal: You'd get to spend more time with your family only after you were forced to work overtime and spend more time *away* from your family. This legislation would do nothing to stop the problem of mandatory overtime. Also, employers, not employees, had the power to choose when workers took the comp time. I gave the example of a California paralegal who already worked in this fashion; whenever she needed time off, the lawyers said they were too busy—then offered her a week in November, when her kids were in school. Flexible employers who wanted to help workers could already do so by providing unpaid time off; workers could then bank their overtime pay and pay themselves on those unpaid days. I recommended renaming the bill the "Employer Overtime Protection Act," since its real purpose was to make overtime cheaper. That would make it more plentiful, at great harm to families.

If you've ever seen a congressional hearing on the news, you can picture the scene. The Committee members were perched in ascending rows of seats, looking down at a long table of those testifying and at the spectators behind them. At first the Committee chair, Rep. Charles Norwood, and the other legislators in support of the bill directed questions only to those testifying in favor. They emphasized how the legislation creates choice, provides flexibility, helps families. Whenever I was allowed to speak, I continued to debunk those notions. Finally Rep. Johnny Isakson (R-GA) looked down directly at me and said, "I acknowledge that there are bad actors, . . . but I just wanted it to be said that all businesses are not bad."[31]

"I certainly know there are good employers," I replied. "The problem is the good employers do not need a law to be flexible. They can do it right now. This law will not transform bad employers into good employers. We need laws that set a floor and that protect against abuses."

Despite the support of the administration and an enormous lobbying campaign, the Family Time Flexibility Act never came to the floor for a vote in the 2003 session. At least fourteen Republicans indicated they would vote against it.

When All Else Fails, Demonize
Demonizing, though not the main weapon of the Big Boys on family leave, pops up over and over. On a public interest television show, for example,

I appeared with a member of the Eagle Forum who blamed all problems in the family, from teen suicide to alcoholism, on mothers who work outside the home. With great indignation, she described volunteering in her children's school and calling mothers of sick kids, only to be told they couldn't come in because they couldn't get off work. "I'd be angry, too," I said—"but at their employers, not the mothers, who had no choice." To those who argued that you shouldn't have children if you can't afford to stay home with them, we pointed out the economic reality: Ward and June Cleaver may be recycled on cable television, but they're disappearing from the neighborhood.[32] Parents work because they need to—and as a society, we need to find a way to make it possible for them to be both good parents and good employees.

SHAKING THINGS UP IN UTAH

In addition to leave, support for quality dependent care is a major front in the battle to have a job *and* a life. Many groups have been active in efforts to increase access and quality of care. One of my favorites had the unexpected name of JEDI and operated in, of all places, Salt Lake City, Utah. JEDI stands for Justice, Economic Dignity, and Independence for Women. In 1994, this group of low-income women waged a frenetic and creative campaign to save full funding for the childcare subsidy program.

Deeda Seed, then director of the group, told me she was astonished to learn that the state intended to cut funding and create a waiting list at the very time it was pushing women from welfare into the workforce.[33] "Probably 90 percent of our members were mothers, many with young children," said Seed. "If they were going to move from welfare to work, they needed a reliable, affordable source of childcare. Many more women would have been on welfare without this program. If someone's making minimum wage or even $10 an hour, it's practically impossible to cover childcare costs in the state for one child, much less two."

The group decided to try every available method to have the half million dollar cuts restored, not an outrageous request considering the state had a budget surplus. First they demanded and got a hearing on the issue. "They made the mistake of holding what was supposed to be a statewide hearing in a very tiny room," said Seed. "We had fifty to sixty women with us. Those who spoke described from very personal perspectives what happens if you don't have childcare assistance and you're a low-income worker.

It was really clear to everybody that this was a problem."

JEDI members launched a letter-writing campaign, with lots of support from women at all income levels. When the issue moved to the legislature, so did they. They made a giant key out of poster board and wrote on it "the key to getting off welfare is childcare." As always, they'd alerted the news media and got lots of coverage. In the coming weeks they testified and lobbied, sent hearts on Valentine's day, held picket lines. The legislators claimed to agree with them and passed the buck to the governor. JEDI sent numerous letters requesting a meeting with the governor, but got no response.

"We were at the end of our rope," said Seed. "The legislative session was drawing to a close. We decided we had to take our message to the governor in person and if it came to it, we wouldn't leave. That was a pretty big decision to make." About twenty-five women and "a bunch of our kids" arrived at the capitol to hold a news conference. As luck had it, a group of schoolchildren were touring the capitol and wanted to know what these women and kids were doing with all those TV cameras. Seed described the result: "To the horror of their teachers, these kids spontaneously joined us. Probably one hundred kids were yelling, 'Childcare, childcare, we need childcare.'" The students stayed with the group as they marched right into the governor's boardroom. Frantic security forces joined the nervous teachers. Eventually the JEDI group were on their own. They politely explained to the receptionist how many letters they sent and how some of them could wind up on welfare because of these cuts. When Governor Mike Leavitt (now head of the federal Health and Human Services division) failed to come out, the women settled in with their kids.

Tidy Protesters

"We came prepared with diapers and toys," said Seed. "Our news media had not seen anything like this." Their protest became the top story on four TV stations as it turned into a sleep-in, complete with sandwiches from legislators and a small TV to watch the Olympics figure skating competition in Lillyhammer. "The governor looked like a fool," said Seed. "Our cause was very just and everyone got it." The *Salt Lake Tribune* joined the Morman paper in endorsing reversing the cuts.

All night the women waited for police to come, but it never happened. "I think they knew arresting women with small children was probably not a good idea," Seed said. The next morning the governor's chief of staff picked his way across sleeping bags to schedule a meeting for the following Friday. The governor restored the funds.

"It was very empowering for those involved," said Seed. She attributes their effectiveness to having a very good issue, being right, and demonstrating that they'd tried everything. Seed, who now serves as the communications director for Salt Lake's Mayor Rocky Anderson, noted that the group were "very tidy protesters. They made a big point of telling us we were sleeping on a $30,000 Persian rug. We brought in a vacuum and vacuumed it. Only women protesters would do that."

FINAL THOUGHTS: LEARNING TO THINK BIG

Some people may wish to spend several years at home caring for young children or other family members. Right now we have only the illusion of choice in this country. To make real options available, we need the full array of changes outlined in this book, available to men as well as women.

And that means challenging ourselves to think big. This can be hard—we have so little practice. We have to learn to become our own eye doctor, shifting the lens until we can see the whole picture.

4. CAN A WOMAN DO A MAN'S JOB?

"The wonderful thing about America is our freedom of choice. I chose to be a bank president. My secretary chose to be a secretary."
—Philadelphia bank president speaking to 9to5 founder
Karen Nussbaum before her luncheon speech

Whenever I speak on the status of women, most people in the audience—women's groups, students, academics, managers—are stunned to learn how few women there are in the highest paid and most powerful jobs. Sixteen percent of Congress? Six percent of top corporate earners? Just two percent of Fortune 500 CEOs? But wait, someone will say, look at all those women graduating from law schools and PhD programs. True enough, I reply, and then I have to fill in the rest of the story about those graduates: Women account for 12 percent of law firm partners—make that 1 percent for women of color—and fewer than one in four tenured professors. Most women never make it to the glass ceiling because they're trapped on the sticky floor or bouncing off maternal walls (see Chapter 3). In response I hear everything from disgust to despair, but from college students in particular, I hear betrayal. Most of these women have been told they could be anything they want and they expected the numbers to confirm that promise. What's behind this dismal record, they demand to know, and what's being done about it?

Myth: Women Don't Want those Jobs

Some commentators claim women are "opting out" of those jobs. They don't rule the world because "they don't want to"—they'd rather be home with their kids.[1] Others think women just don't have what it takes. This view got new life in 2005 when Lawrence Summers, the president of no less prestigious an institution than Harvard, suggested that "issues of intrinsic aptitude" may be the chief reason women are underrepresented in top science and technology jobs, along with their "unwillingness to put in the long hours required." Oh, he added, discrimination may also play a role.

Focusing on women's "choices" and DNA is like the magician's patter—the abracadabra and other chit chat you hear while he (why are there so few women magicians anyway?) makes those scarves disappear and reappear. The greater the diversion, the less aware we are of what's really going on—in this case, the institutional attitudes and practices that keep women out or drive them out of positions of status and power.

In the old days, the fear about letting women take on certain occupations was focused on the damage to women themselves. Dr. Edward Clarke of Harvard Medical School told the audience gathered at the New England Women's Club in Boston one December night in 1872 that education for women was actually dangerous.[2] Physical consequences could include "monstrous brains and puny bodies; abnormally active cerebration and abnormally weak digestion; flowing thought and constipated bowels." Most at risk was the womb—the very center of womanliness. Dr. Clarke's prescription? "Rest cures" for ambitious women. Given that the audience included movers and shakers such as poet Julia Ward Howe, author Louisa May Alcott, and abolitionists Lucretia Mott and Lucy Stone (one of the first married women to keep her name), the doctor may have been lucky to escape with his own, uh, organs intact.

Nowadays, we've apparently accepted that women's brains and wombs can handle the strain of accomplishment. Instead, some fret that admitting females to previously male preserves will imperil the safety or well-being of the organization or the public. I count at least four kinds of myths about women's ability to do the job: assuming they can't, assuming they shouldn't because of their maternal role, failing to see that they already do, and my personal favorite, abracadabra arithmetic—believing one or a few equals plenty.

Myth: Women Can't Handle these Jobs

Melissa Fojtek in Racine, Wisconsin, had been lifting weights and doing heavy labor for some time when she decided in the early 1990s that she'd like to be a firefighter. The males in her training class insisted she couldn't handle the job, even though she was stronger than many of them and passed all the tests. In case the rigor of the program didn't drive her out, some of the guys decided to add to the challenge. She told me about a typical day at the training school. The class was performing an exercise that simulated being trapped in a smoky place, unable to see. You had to slide face first out of a structure that had been set up in the room. Fojtek found herself landing between the open legs of another trainee, her face against his crotch. Not only did the teacher laugh—he was the one who set this up.

"I expected problems from some of the other students," Fojtek said. "But when the person in charge is the ringleader, you know you're in trouble."

Linda, a police captain in a Midwest city, has had to put up with everything from small indignities to sexual harassment and other challenges from colleagues and superiors.[3] When she was promoted to sergeant, subordinates called her by her first name rather than by her rank. "They wouldn't have called a man by his first name," she said. "I hear people talking about other women in leadership, saying they don't know what they're doing and they're not leaders." For a time Linda was desk sergeant, in charge of scheduling for her district. Her supervisor knew that every sergeant in the district had access to her and other schedulers' lists and made their own changes in the line-up. "I wanted to move to beat patrol but was actually told I couldn't leave my position until I was 100 percent efficient with that line-up," she told me. "I'm thinking, 'How can I ever be when it's more than just me generating information?'"

Recently a group of white men sued the department for "reverse discrimination" in promotions. "Sometimes it's hard to figure out if the issue is sex or race," noted Linda, who is African American. One man, who served as lieutenant when she was a sergeant, brought up the old line-up complaint. They also said she wasn't qualified "because the papers on my desk weren't stacked neatly." Unlike the majority of those plaintiffs, Linda has a bachelor's degree along with attendance at numerous seminars, extensive community involvement, and almost twenty-five years seniority. "It doesn't matter what you do," she lamented, "you're never qualified enough."

Myth: Mothers Shouldn't Be Doing these Jobs

Most modern managers are too sophisticated to say women aren't up to snuff. Yet a surprising number feel free to make all sorts of derogatory comments about women who happen to have kids.[4] Underlying their declarations are strong views about what mothers *should* and *shouldn't* do.

A case in point is Joann Trezza, an attorney and mother of two young children, who filed a suit against The Hartford, an investment and insurance company.[5] Despite a sterling record and outstanding performance evaluations, she kept being passed over for advancement. Managing attorneys first promoted two less qualified men (both fathers) and then a less senior and less experienced—and childless—woman. Why? They hadn't even considered her, the higher-ups told Ms. Trezza, because the new position required extensive traveling and they assumed she wouldn't want to be away from her family. You may think lawyers are good at double talk, but a senior vice president put it right out there, complaining to Trezza about the "incompetence and laziness of women who are also working mothers." They're not good planners, he told her (leave that guy for a day with an infant, a toddler, and a school-aged child and see how he manages without a plan). Above all, in the view of this executive, women can't be good mothers *and* good workers. "I don't see how you can do either job well," he concluded.

The assistant general counsel went even further. If Trezza's husband, also an attorney, won "another big verdict," he assumed she'd be "sitting at home eating bon bons." Ruling in her favor, a U.S. District Court noted that only seven of the company's forty-six managing attorneys were females and that none of them were mothers.

Studies show mothers are 44 percent less likely to be hired than nonmothers with the same resume, and are offered significantly less money when they are hired. You'd think we'd have advanced more since the days when Pat Schroeder, lead author of the Family and Medical Leave Act and the first woman elected to Congress from Colorado, was asked at every campaign event, "'How can you be a congresswoman and a mother?" She had two children; her opponent had six—no one ever asked him a similar question. (Schroeder told me she finally "lost it" one day and came up with her famous response—"I have a brain and a uterus, and they both work.")[6]

Myth: If You Don't Have the Title, You're Not Doing the Job

The third type of myth can be especially painful—without a particular title, you must not be doing the job. A woman I'll call Phyllis once confided a striking example of this. It was the year after Wisconsin passed pay equity legislation (see Chapter 2). I'd been invited to participate in a debate on the subject at a daylong forum sponsored by Journal Communications, Inc., the publisher of the main Milwaukee newspaper. Phyllis served as secretary to a high-ranking executive at the *Journal* and single-handedly organized all the details of this event. One day we met to go over details. A tall, sturdy woman who wore a flowery dress and practical shoes, Phyllis expressed interest in my topic and rolled her eyes as I shared various statistics and examples. It didn't take much prodding for her to tell me her own story.

Among her many tasks, Phyllis was responsible for typing managers' performance evaluations. Over the years she'd noticed one guy who never seemed to go anywhere. He was a nice guy and Phyllis always rooted for him to get a promotion. Then one day her boss called her in to report a new job was being created and would go to this very man. Phyllis was delighted—until she wrote down the job description the boss was dictating. Fifteen of the seventeen job duties were ones she already performed; the new position paid more than twice her salary.

The executive could see she was upset. "What's the matter?" he asked.

"These are things I do," she told him. "Why didn't you consider me for this job?" Dumbfounded, her boss pointed out two tasks that would be new for her. They would also be new for the guy being promoted, she replied, as she well knew from having typed his job description all those years. "He didn't say it," Phyllis told me, "but we both knew the answer—he didn't even think of me for the job, because I was just a secretary."

Did her candor in speaking up change anything? I asked. Phyllis rubbed her hands along the sides of her skirt. "The next day I had flowers on my desk."

Myth: One or a Few Equals Plenty

And then there's the peculiar habit of many Big Boys who point to one or two women on their board or among their top earners and say, "There! We've got diversity!" Abracadabra arithmetic isn't just bad math (and President Summers thinks *women* have problems running the numbers), it's also bad management. Resting on the laurels of one or a few means there's no need to look further; many talented people will be underutilized or effectively driven out.

Hiring or promoting a token woman (or any other underrepresented group) virtually assures that the individual will be an outsider who'll have difficulty speaking up without being seen as a troublemaker. And it lends itself to that all-too-common excuse for failing to address inequity: "Well, I hired a [fill-in-the-blank-group] once and she/he just didn't work out."

Reality: Bad Practices

The fact that women are so underrepresented in top jobs isn't just about bad attitudes. Above all, it has to do with *institutional practices*—how corporations organize work. The "Good Old Boys' Network," so hard to make visible yet so powerful, too often determines who gets the best assignments, opportunities, leads, resources, training, and mentoring. Sometimes this boils down to where and when deals are made, how many hours people are expected to work—and how people are treated when they call attention to the problems.

Milwaukee architect Ursula Twombly says it's almost "a knee-jerk reaction" that female architects are placed in interiors or health care or other planning areas rather than getting opportunities to learn how to put buildings together or do construction administration.[7] "That's where the power is," she says. "It is this technical knowledge that makes you a good architect and then gives you the opportunity to move on and expand your career."

A series of class-action suits against major players on Wall Street—Smith Barney, Merrill Lynch, Morgan Stanley—revealed a lot about the workings of sex discrimination. Sometimes the environment rivaled a frat house—you may have read about the boom-boom room in the Garden City, New York, office of Smith Barney/Shearson, where the manager allegedly sent condoms to female employees through pneumatic tubes, and some brokers spent more time seeking lap dances from coworkers than stock sales from customers (so much for doing business "the old-fashioned way").[8]

Even more buttoned-down offices proved to be hostile to women. Consider the testimony of Allison Schieffelin, lead plaintiff in the Morgan Stanley case in 2001. Schieffelin and the others claimed the firm denied them pay and promotion commensurate with those of male counterparts, even when they performed better.[9] She described a workplace where men commonly made sexist comments and organized trips to topless bars and strip clubs. I'm not just talking about how men and women spent their spare time—women were excluded from the outings, clients weren't. Schieffelin also said women who took maternity leave lost out on raises and desirable assignments.

Like the other big firms who were sued, Morgan Stanley eventually ponied up (in 2004, the company wound up paying $54 million to as many as 340 plaintiffs). But the firm's initial reaction to the suit was denial and, according to Schieffelin, retaliation. After she filed her charge with the Equal Employment Opportunity Commission, Schieffelin said, "senior managers at the firm sought to denigrate my work, ostracize me. . . . They took away projects that I had worked on for years. They diminished my daily responsibilities. I believe that they thought that if they made my day-to-day life miserable enough that I would just pack up and leave." When she didn't leave, she was fired, after fourteen years of service.

Some would argue that Wall Street firms have come a long way since the 1970s, when Merrill Lynch gave all applicants a test that included this question: "Which quality in women do you consider most important?"[10] The choices included beauty, intelligence, dependency, independence, and something labeled "affectionateness." Here's how the points were assigned—two each for dependency and affectionateness, one for beauty. If you answered intelligence or independence, you got a big zero.

But the women who filed charges against Merrill thirty years later don't see much progress. Taking the lead were Valery Craane and her daughter Janine, known as star brokers at the firm, who echo the view that male managers systematically belittled women and limited their opportunities. According to Janine Craane, each Wall Street firm is like a fraternity. "They feel that women don't belong in that club," she told a *New York Times* reporter. "You have your boys, your soldiers, the guys that you trust. Whether they're not so talented is maybe not so important as their loyalty to that group."[11] These attitudes translate into practices that disadvantage women.

Reality: Women Are Less Likely to Get the Goods

A friend I'll call Patricia, a stockbroker at a branch of one of the big national firms, elaborated on the problem.[12] A theme in the various lawsuits is how branch managers distribute the accounts of someone who leaves. The manager is supposed to get on the phone and try to keep each client, assigning the person to somebody else. "There will be an onslaught of people going into the branch manager's office, saying, 'Assign me—I know this client from my brother-in-law or my wife,'" Patricia said. "It's supposed to be equitable, but it's very subjective. Even when women get their share, what's the quality of the accounts they get? It's easy to see that it's not equitable, but hard to prove."

The other big problem, Patricia told me, is the disparity in treatment between men and women who aren't pulling their weight. Say a call comes in from a client who's just moved to the area and wants a local broker. "A lot of times the branch manager will bail out guys who are not working hard at marketing themselves and give them these accounts," Patricia said. "He's part of the fraternity. But if a woman fails, she'd be fired."

When Patricia was hired, after a class-action suit against her firm, women accounted for 10 percent of all the brokers. Eleven years later, they're still only 16 percent. And Patricia has no illusions about the cost of participating in such a suit. "It means you're choosing to hang out your own shingle," she said.

The financial sector is hardly alone in its unfriendly treatment of women. A Chicago-based association for lawyers, the Defense Research Institute, reported on a 2005 internal survey of female attorneys.[13] More than three in five respondents said they had considered leaving the legal practice due to gender-related issues. Two-thirds agreed that a glass ceiling exists for women in the field.

And the 2004 class-action suit at Wal-Mart revealed how common sex discrimination is in retail. Although more than two-thirds of the company's hourly employees are female, they hold fewer than 15 percent of store manager positions. According to Wal-Mart's own workforce data, women in every major job category have been paid less than men with the same seniority in every year since 1997, even though the female employees on average have higher performance ratings. Internal Wal-Mart documents acknowledge that the company is "behind the rest of the world" in the promotion of women to management ranks.[14]

Female academics at MIT, University of Michigan, and elsewhere have taken the lead in pointing out the gender bias that affects hiring and other opportunities for women. Mel Hochster, a senior mathematics professor at Michigan, told a reporter how a presentation on sex bias in his department opened his eyes. Numerous studies have documented an array of problems, such as men being given longer and more specific letters of recommendation than women; women being held to higher standards; women being left out of information loops; men and women being more likely to vote for a male applicant than a female even when they have identical records.[15] Orchestras that hold auditions where they can't see the applicants hire women 30 to 55 percent more often than when the musicians are visible.

"I vastly underestimated the problem," Professor Hochster said. "People tend to think that if there's a problem, it's with a few old-fashioned people with old-fashioned ideas. That's not true. Everybody has unconscious gender bias. It shows up in every study."

Reality: Getting Ahead Requires Long Hours

Another significant barrier for women is work hours. "In architecture school, you're trained to work overnight," Ursula Twombly says. "Normal hours are fifty a week or more. Women who ended up starting families have a huge conflict. One of the big reasons I achieved what I did is that my husband and I decided not to have any kids." Twombly now owns her own firm with another woman and mentors women architects.

C.J. Richards is one of Twombly's mentees and current staff. Richards has had her shares of sexist attitudes from men in the field. "It came with the territory," she said. But at a top firm eight years ago, she ran into something unexpected when she was fired without warning for not "progressing" fast enough—a code word for not working enough extra hours. While employed at the firm, she had two children close in age. "I've been told [that firm] now has part-time schedules," Richards says, "but I was also told it's make believe, to make them look good. Later I heard unless you were childless and preferably husbandless, you wouldn't make it."

Richards didn't realize until recently that she wasn't the only one this had happened to. "I was blaming myself," she says, "saying I can't be a mother and be in architecture, that's the way it is. I found out I'm not the only one who got fired for something that's just natural." At the time she had talked to a lawyer but never sued for fear it would be career suicide.

Other women do put in the hours, to the detriment of family time. Dawn Drake, a school administrator in Platteville, Wisconsin, wants to be a positive role model for other women, but says, "that means work is all encompassing. Expectations are higher for women than men in the profession. If you can't produce at that level, opportunities melt away. You're hired because they know you're a workhorse. My seven-year-old said, 'I'm not going to be an educator. You have to work too much. I never get to see you.'"[16]

Reality: Slamming into the Glass Ceiling

One factor that both reflects the bias against women and allows it to flourish is the lack of women at the top. A 2001 report by Dennis Vacco, then attorney general of New York, showed at least seven of the top ten Wall Street firms had no women at all at the highest levels. For Fortune 500 companies, the overall picture today is a little better, but not much. One in seven of these firms has no women among corporate officers (senior vice president or above), and a third have only one—including many who are heralded on lists of the best places for women to work[17] (back to abraca-dabra arithmetic). Altogether, women account for only 16 percent of the top jobs in the top firms.

It's hard for women who experience barriers at these companies to ask the board of directors to intervene, given how few women sit on them. Only 14 percent of the board seats at Fortune 500 companies are filled by women. In many states, the numbers are even worse—9 percent for the top fifty firms in Wisconsin, for instance, and only 1 percent for women of color.

Someone asked me recently to describe the shape of women's position in the workplace. "A vicious circle," I replied.

What the Law Says

No law prohibits corporations from filling all top positions with white males. But many of the practices I've described that keep women out of these jobs or treat them as second-class employees are, in fact, illegal. Most are prohibited by Title VII of the Civil Rights Act of 1964, which includes sex along with race, religion, color, and national origin among the protect-ed categories that may not be treated *differently* (it's generally legal to treat everyone badly). Sex was added at the last minute by a segregationist named Howard W. Smith (D-VA). The congressman boasted, "I have certainly tried to do everything that I could to hinder, delay and dilapidate this bill,"[18] but he was running out of time. Throwing sex in the mix, he figured, would dilapidate it for sure. Smith and his colleagues had a merry time imagining ugly women who would use the law to sue because they couldn't find a husband—until they were confronted by Martha Wright Griffiths (D-MI), one of only fourteen women in the Congress at the time. "We've sat here for four days discussing the rights of blacks and other minorities," she told them, "and there has been no laughter, not even a smile. But when you suggest you shouldn't discriminate against your own wives, your own mothers, your own daughters, your own granddaughters, or your own sis-ters, then you laugh." Her remarks were followed by absolute silence.[19]

The bill passed.

Patterns of discrimination often can be documented, as the highly public lawsuits in the securities industry, Wal-Mart, and elsewhere have shown. Sometimes the discrimination is astonishingly blatant (as in the case of the Wal-Mart executive in Arizona who told a female manager she was paid less than a less qualified male because she "didn't have the right equipment").[20] But many times the discrimination is subtle and harder to fight. My stockbroker friend Patricia says the branch manager who bails out failing male brokers "doesn't realize he's doing anything wrong. He just thinks he's helping people." Networking with people you know and feel comfortable with isn't always deliberate discrimination—males easily miss the fact that the people they know and feel comfortable with happen also to be male. The same is true for whites, both male and female.

Unfortunately, even when discrimination is blatant, the Equal Employment Opportunity Commission cannot act unless someone makes a complaint. If only staff could call up top execs and say, "Hey, we've noticed nearly all your officers and high-paid staff are white males. Smells fishy to us. We're coming in to do an audit."

Blatant AND Legal

Carolyn would have complained to the EEOC the time she was fired and the times she wasn't hired simply because she is a lesbian, but neither Title VII nor any other federal law prohibits such treatment. Carolyn happens to live in Ohio, one of thirty-three states where it's perfectly legal to discriminate based on a person's actual or perceived sexual orientation. That's right—the fact that someone *appears* to be gay is reason enough to toss them, unless state or local government or company policy says otherwise. Carolyn now works for a national employer where she can be out and even receive benefits for her partner—but she has no recourse when the IRS taxes the benefit as individual income.[21] Nor do the domestic-partner benefits cover their kids, since Carolyn is not the birth mother.

While sexual orientation isn't a protected category, some lawyers have successfully argued that sexual stereotyping is unlawful discrimination. In other words, under Title VII someone can be harassed for being gay, but not for being a guy who's perceived as too feminine or a woman who's perceived as too masculine.[22] Courts differ widely about whether this protection extends to transgendered individuals. Only six states[23] ban discrimination on the basis of gender identity or transgendered status.

Sexual orientation isn't the only grounds for legal discrimination. Ask Kiki Peppard, a 9to5 activist in Effort, Pennsylvania, about the twenty times she was denied a job after answering "No" and "Yes" to "Are you married?" and "Do you have children?" Pennsylvania isn't alone—only nineteen states prohibit discrimination based on marital status, and only Alaska and the District of Colombia prohibit it based on family responsibility.[24] Kiki began waging what has become a ten-year campaign to change state law. She told a reporter about the opposition she's faced from some legislators, including one who argued that "obtaining information about marital status was important in determining who to hire. He said that employers needed the freedom to determine their own [hiring] rules."[25]

Not Even on the Radar Screen

Imagine you're a woman vying for a position—and then put yourself in a wheelchair or add a palsy to your limbs. All people living with disabilities face an added challenge in the workplace, but women have an even greater burden—they fail the widely applied beauty test reserved to females, and they're most likely to be seen as passive, dependent, non-leaders.[26] Only a third of women with disabilities are employed. Their median earnings are substantially less than men with physical disabilities—and less than women without disabilities.[27] In addition to bias on the job, women in this category face a terrible double bind: If they do get hired, they earn too much to be eligible for federal disability benefits—but if they lose their job, it's much harder to regain eligibility.[28] Yet for most of us, this form of discrimination barely registers. Our nation may not hide people with disabilities like some countries do, but they remain largely off the radar screen of decision makers—and of many activists.

What's at Stake

Why should we care about excluding people based on gender or any other category? I like to ask audiences if anyone knows about Josephine Elizabeth Thomas White or Lucinda Foote. Not surprisingly, no one ever does. Of Josephine Elizabeth Thomas White, we know only that as a slave child, she learned to read by doing her sewing in the room where the white children received instruction and later by slipping into the linen closet with any book she could put her hands on. She married the man who started what is now Morehouse College, which admitted women as well as men. Josephine White, then a young mother, attended her husband's school for just one night—when she returned home, she saw the housework awaiting her, "and decided she'd have to choose between the children's getting an education and her getting one."[29] As for Lucinda Foote, in 1783 at the age of twelve, she took the entrance examination for Yale University. She was found "fully qualified except in her sex." Ms. Foote went on to marry and have ten children, a life that might have been rewarding in its own right.

But one can only imagine what Josephine Thomas White, Lucinda Foote, and other women even less extraordinary might have accomplished had they been able to attend those colleges. Uncovering and developing underutilized talent is a key reason to change how society treats women—and men of color, and all others who have been discriminated against.

Employers have several other reasons to shape up. Topping the list is job retention. Not long ago I interviewed a table of women at a professional women's event about their experiences in the corporate world. Three of the six had left big corporations to start their own businesses out of frustration and rage at how they were treated. Julie had spent thirteen years at a large corporation before giving notice. "You have to be willing to give it all to the company," she told me. "There are no role models of women with young kids in upper management. They wanted me to fly somewhere on July Fourth. When I told them I had family plans, they were aghast."

Another incentive is successful outreach to customers and clients. A woman I'll call Donna who worked for a large appliance manufacturer described the meeting where she saved the company from a disastrous mistake. Thirty people were in attendance; Donna was the only female. The team was about to roll out a marketing campaign for a new washing machine. "In the ad, they had a blond woman in an apron standing beside the machine with her two blond, blue-eyed children," Donna told me. She gazed around the room in disbelief. "If you think this is how our customers see themselves," she informed her colleagues, "you haven't got a clue. This campaign will be a miserable failure." The men got rid of the apron and made several versions of women from different ethnic backgrounds—a rescue that wouldn't have happened had Donna not been at the table.

Lawsuits, of course, are always a good reminder of the reason to do the right thing. Executives do not want to wake up and see headlines about groups of women coming forward to point the finger at their company's discriminatory practices. Forget lawyers' fees and settlement payments— it's hard to put a price on the loss of reputation, not to mention all the lost hours, morale, and productivity while employees sit for depositions or just gossip among themselves about the case.

Typical Solutions

What's being done to deal with the problem in Corporate America? Here are the three most typical approaches:

Watch Your Head: In this group I lump all the companies who do nothing but encourage women to lower their expectations so they won't be in too much pain when they hit the glass ceiling.

Watch Our Butts: This category includes those whose only concern is escaping litigation or bad press. Often consultants will appeal to firms on exactly this ground. Some consultants specialize in getting companies on the "best-place-for-women-to-work-lists"—whether or not they deserve to be there.

Design Some Programs: Most organizations that say they're addressing the problem in fact fall under this category, adding some programs or policies at the fringe of their operation without challenging the essential work practices or corporate culture.

None of these approaches, of course, will get us where we need to go. To deal with the problem of sticky floors and glass ceilings, what we have to do is *redesign the building*.

FEMINIST SOLUTIONS

Feminist solutions start with an honest examination of how business does business. If the top jobs in an organization are held mostly by white males, it's a safe bet that talent alone hasn't driven the process. The goal isn't merely to add a few more women at the top, but to *change the way work is performed and evaluated in ways that benefit everyone*. Solutions take the form of both private initiatives and public policy.

When Employers Want to Change: Conducting an Internal Audit

For employers who sincerely want to root out any form of discriminatory treatment, step one is to conduct an organization-wide audit. The audit should look at gender but also at race and other categories, with the goal of documenting who holds every position and how each person got there. That means asking questions like these:

- How was each current manager and board member selected? How wide was the search? Who was involved in making the selection?
- What kind of developmental, skill-enhancing measures are in place? How are decisions made about who will take advantage of them?
- How are compensation, raises, and other rewards determined? How much depends on managers' discretion and individual negotiating skills? Have jobs been reevaluated from a pay equity perspective?

(See Chapter 2.) Are department salary ranges and job openings at all levels regularly posted?

- What are the sexual harassment and other antidiscrimination policies? Do they cover sexual orientation and gender stereotyping? How do they work in practice? What kind of follow-up takes place? Of those who have utilized complaint procedures, how many have been promoted? How many have left?

- What are the policies to help staff manage work and family responsibilities? What are the usage rates among each level of employees, men as well as women? How many people have been promoted after taking a leave? How many have left?

- Are managers held accountable for enforcing nondiscrimination and work-life policies? How?

- What is the corporate culture? What messages are sent out about who the company values? What are the underlying assumptions about competence and commitment?

- How is work organized? How much attention is given to "face time" (presence at the worksite) rather than output? How much control do employees have over schedules and work processes?

- How many levels of advancement are there?

- How much do we know about the people who leave, especially members of underrepresented groups?

- What rules if any are in place for personal conduct by top managers, including membership in males-only or whites-only clubs?

- What rules if any are in place for selection of vendors?

To answer these questions requires more than detailed numerical data, although that's a start. If firm size allows, distributing an anonymous survey is the best way to get honest answers and help reveal what happens in practice, not just on paper. Questions should cover all the basics, including these:

- How did you hear about your job? What were the requirements for hiring? Are they clear to everyone? How much do they correspond to the actual requirements of the work?

- What opportunities have you had for training? Are you regularly informed about training or other growth opportunities? How do you think these opportunities are made available?

- How are work assignments made? Are they given out fairly?

- What work-life policies are you aware of here? Which if any have you needed? Which if any have you used? Do you feel comfortable and supported asking for or using them? In your opinion, do other employees feel comfortable and supported?

• What messages are given out about how many hours you should put in? How are these messages delivered?

• Do you know employees who have left this organization? If so, do you know why they left?

Top managers should create a record listing every employee's starting pay and annual increases. Whoever determined the pay or raise amount should indicate the process used in each case.

Following up those surveys with interviews of a certain number of staff from every level will help fill in the picture. Employers should consider using outside independent experts to oversee this process, to help ensure both the reality and the perception of objectivity.

Eliminating the Good Old Boys' Network

Step one, in short, involves *making visible* any traces of the Good Old Boys' network—institutionalized sexism and racism—and pledging to eliminate them. Once you find problems, you have to fix them. That means detailed remedies for making all hiring, training, promotion, and pay-setting as objective as possible—a step that benefits most men as well as women and other underrepresented groups. The organization will need a process for rectifying inequities in pay and revaluing the work performed mainly by women and by people of color—of course, women of color may experience both gender and race discrimination (see Chapter 2). The process of change will also increase the availability, accessibility, and affordability of policies and programs that help women—and men—integrate work and family responsibilities, and *encourage* employees to utilize them (see Chapter 3). That will probably require changes in the way work is performed, with more control in the hands of employees and managers playing more of a coaching, mentoring, coordinating role—again, a change that benefits the majority of employees. And reasonable guidelines are needed for top managers as well as suppliers—you can't be a "diversity leader" and belong to an all-male golf club or have vendors who happen to be all white and male or pay their employees a substandard wage.

Taking Affirmative Action

For many organizations, finding talented women means looking more carefully in their own ranks. But often it means looking outside as well.

And here's where affirmative action comes in—having a concrete plan to go *out of your way* to find qualified applicants from groups that have been excluded or underrepresented. Affirmative action is simply the opposite of negative action, which means doing nothing to address the legacy of discrimination, continuing to give preference to those already in the circle or who already know the way in.

Genuine affirmative action has nothing to do with tokenism. That's a quick fix, throwing anybody into the position just because they fit the demographic. Instead, employers need to put effort into where to look and how to interpret qualifications. A senior architect told me about the scholarship program his firm instituted at a local university to locate prospective employees of color who were currently students. They met an African American student who seemed outstanding, except that he had a C average. With a little investigation, managers discovered that this student was working several jobs to pay his way through school, including one that required him to get up at 4 A.M. They gave him the scholarship and told him to quit that job. After graduation he came on payroll and has been a successful employee for more than seven years. A rigid rule about grade point average would have disqualified this future architect—and cost the firm a real asset.

Acting affirmatively also means developing concrete ways to help all employees advance, including mentoring, tuition reimbursement, and career development paths. Management must see these programs as part of an overall plan for transforming the organization, and regularly evaluate their effectiveness. Take women and golfing, for example. If women want to learn golf, fine, but organizations should avoid setting up a women's golfing group as a substitute for changing the way deals are made. Likewise, women's networks can be a good thing—but not if they're designed to help women "gain leadership skills," as if they didn't have any, and groom them to compete for a token slot or two.

Will there be resistance to real transformation? Count on it. Employers need to reinforce the changes with training and role models who emphasize the broad benefits of greater transparency, objectivity, and diversity. They'll back this up with clear monitoring and accountability. All the programs in the world won't mean a thing if the fundamental culture hasn't changed. And even the best of intentions won't suffice without benchmarks, regular assessment, and meaningful consequences for managers who fail to meet reasonable hiring, retention, and promotion goals.

Public Policies to Guarantee Opportunity for All

This chapter makes a clear business case for why to make the changes detailed here. But relying on the Big Boys to audit themselves is like asking toddlers to decide when they need a time-out. To make sure all employees benefit from a discrimination-free workplace, we need public policies as well as voluntary initiatives. I detail many of these in other chapters, particularly regarding pay and flexibility. But the following measures will also help:

- Leverage change through allocation of government contracts and tax dollars. The government can and should ask firms for clear gender and race breakdowns in hiring, promotions, and compensations. Officials can also take into account the outcome of lawsuits and other civil actions and refuse contracts to firms shown to have discriminated.[30]

- Enforce Title IX. This provision of the 1972 Education Amendments prohibits sex discrimination in education institutions that receive federal funds. While women make up 46 percent of the overall work force, they represent just 10 percent of engineers and 29 percent of computer scientists and mathematicians. Colleges and universities need to do a better job steering women into these fields and keeping them there.

- Enact the Employment Nondiscrimination Act. This bill would add sexual orientation to the categories protected by Title VII of the Civil Rights Act. The language should be broad enough to cover sexual identity and expression, to protect the rights of transgendered or transsexual individuals.

- Require that firms make salaries public internally. Women can't challenge lower pay if they don't know about it. Disclosing pay by gender and job category within the organization helps make the process of setting pay fairer for everyone.

- Ensure greater voting power to stockholders: Only when stockholders have access to democratic processes and a meaningful say in decisions will we see an end to the cycle of CEO-puts-best-friends-on-the-board-who-then-decide-pay-for-CEO.

- Enact a maximum wage for top executives. A number of compensation consultants and other experts have recommended tying executive pay to company performance and limiting outlandish pay packages and perks.

- Add parental and family status to categories protected under federal antidiscrimination law. No employer should have the "freedom" to tell single mothers they don't belong in the workplace.
- Expand the Work Incentives Improvement Act so that all persons with disabilities can continue to receive health insurance while employed.

TAKING ON THE BIG BOYS

Despite the appalling numbers on women's status in the workplace, the Big Boys dig in their heels to protect the status quo. Some will be crass enough to say outright, "We want our own club; no women allowed." But they're much more likely to rely on these three tactics: They *minimize* the problem of exclusion, claiming that women have it made and that any lagging behind is because of women's own life choices. They *catastrophize* efforts to increase the number of women employed in male-dominated occupations, dismissing affirmative action programs as mandatory quotas that drag unworthy women into work they can't handle. And they do their best to *compartmentalize* people who should be allies, particularly trying to set white women against women and men of color.

Taking them on requires bringing together the broadest coalition possible in order to expand civil rights protections and strengthen enforcement. At 9to5, we undercut the minimizing by shining a light on the problems, and we exposed the catastrophizing by highlighting positive results of these policies. We also used worker training to confront both bad attitudes and institutional barriers in a number of traditionally male fields.

Civil Rights Act of 1991

Those of us who marched for civil rights in the early 1960s remember how vicious the opposition was. In 1990, when a new Civil Rights Act was introduced, the opponents were more sophisticated but just as determined to throw up roadblocks. Happily, once again they failed.

The new Civil Rights Act was introduced two years after a number of Supreme Court decisions weakened protections for victims of race and sex discrimination, including shifting the burden of proof from employers to employees and narrowing what would count as on-the-job racial discrimination. The legislation was meant to undo those rulings and to allow those who experienced sex discrimination to collect damages for pain and

TAKING ON THE BIG BOYS

suffering (see Chapter 5.) In Milwaukee, 9to5 helped form the "No Retreat on Civil Rights Network" to build support for this bill. Members included the AFL-CIO and a number of individual unions, the ACLU, groups from the African American, Latino, and Native American communities, faith-based groups, gay rights organizations, other women's groups, and progressive attorneys. Nationally 9to5 worked with a similar coalition called the Leadership Conference on Civil Rights.

As I sift through the No Retreat file, with its glossy pages of uncut faxes, here's what I find: flyers for meetings, rallies, public hearings, and protests in front of then-senator Bob Kasten's office; meeting notes in faded blue ink; lists dividing up who will contact which groups and officials; educational materials in various stages of development; press releases; testimonies; op-eds; pleas for financial support; piles of signed forms agreeing to "get two to five friends to write letters or come to a rally" or "to be trained to give speeches on this subject and give at least two."

I find a copy of a statement by Caroline Carter, one of the 9to5 leaders, at a rally when President George H.W. Bush came to town in June 1991 after vetoing this bill. I can still hear her voice over a bullhorn:

> Mr. Bush, we've read your lips. This is what we've heard. . . .
> You tell the employers, "Don't discriminate, but if you do, don't
> worry—you won't have to pay a dime." Well, Mr. President, read
> *our* lips. We will no longer cooperate with racism. We will not
> cooperate with sexual harassment. We refuse to be polite in the
> face of discrimination. You say you're against quotas. . . . The Civil
> Rights Act was never about quotas—and you know it. Here's what
> the Civil Rights Act is about: Somebody has to pay for discrimina-
> tion, and that somebody has to stop being us, the average worker,
> and start being the employers responsible for discrimination.

In reaching out to the public, we focused on the fact that discrimination is *an injury* and should be compensated. By bringing together such a diverse coalition, we demonstrated the breadth of those impacted by unfair treatment and our allegiance to each other.

This same network worked against the nomination of Clarence Thomas to the Supreme Court months before we'd ever heard of charges of sexual harassment (see Chapter 5), because of his opposition to affirmative action and to class-action lawsuits. We didn't win on that one. But we were able to tap into spontaneous outrage when Thomas was narrowly confirmed in October 1991 to demand reconsideration of the civil rights legislation. The bill passed again and President Bush didn't dare veto it a second time. That wasn't the only victory. When the elections came the following November, Sen. Bob Kasten, who'd consistently refused to meet with our coalition, was among the opponents of civil rights who were turned out of office.

Preserving Affirmative Action

In 1965 President Lyndon Johnson first issued Executive Order 11246 requiring federal contractors to take "affirmative action" to ensure equality of employment opportunity without regard to race, religion, and national origin. Three years later, gender was added to the list. The measure was a clear response to centuries of exclusion—college-educated African Americans working in factories because they were kept out of most professional jobs, women with law degrees working as legal secretaries because no firm would hire them otherwise, Asian Americans prohibited by law from owning the land on which they toiled, all-white-male police and fire departments staying that way by hiring sons and nephews of current employees. By affirmative action, Johnson meant those who benefited from federal dollars should *do something*—set goals and timetables for increasing the numbers of groups previously shut out.

Despite the need, the program has been a lightning rod for conservatives, and our side has had to play defense time and time again. California and some other states overturned affirmative action programs. Still, civil rights coalitions have been successful in a number of other states in stopping such a repeal. 9to5 was part of that effort, helping to demonstrate patterns of exclusion that existed before affirmative action and ways the program helped qualified people.

In Georgia, for instance, we worked with a broad coalition in 1998 to defeat legislation that would have ended all affirmative action programs in education, employment, and state contracting. Sheryl Woods was a 9to5 leader who organized women to speak at committee hearings, press conferences, and media interviews and attend meetings with legislators and the governor. She shared her own story of having been held back from advancement despite her skills and years of experience until affirmative action was instituted. "We worked to counter the myths about quotas and preference that supporters of this bill spread," she said, vowing to keep on fighting "as if our lives depended on it—because they do."[31]

When opponents of affirmative action trotted out their tirades about unfair preferences, Sheryl and others were ready. They countered the myths with facts, documenting the gaps in status and pay between whites and people of color, between men and women. And they challenged the hypocrisy. If the other side cared about fairness, why had they never opposed blatant forms of partiality such as children of wealthy alumni leapfrogging into college over much more qualified applicants?[32]

Making the Laws Have Teeth

Putting government protections on paper is only half the battle—violators have to face consequences. The agency responsible for enforcing most anti-discrimination laws is the Equal Employment Opportunity Commission (EEOC). Funds for the EEOC had been slashed under Ronald Reagan and never restored, even as its workload climbed. In 1993, 9to5 surveyed callers to our toll-free hotline and asked about their treatment at the agency. We heard from callers in thirty-five states; one in four were women of color. Nearly all of them scribbled in the margins and attached extra sheets to their surveys. We published the results in a report in August 1994.[33] Respondents were dissatisfied with the information they were given (*"The list of rights was loaded with legalese that I couldn't decipher"*); the way they were treated (*"I felt rushed and confused, thought my complaint was invalid. . . . The statue of limitations has now expired"*); and with the investigative process (*"The investigator . . . was not available when I called. He did not interview my witnesses and did not include the written materials I submitted . . . advised me to 'give up—that's just the way it is'"*). Above all, they said the process took too long (*"It's been fifteen months and still nowhere"*). At the time, the EEOC backlog amounted to 93,000 complaints. Some of our respondents had to wait more than a year and a half just to receive a letter giving them the right to sue in federal court. We tried numerous ways to bring the problem to the attention of those running the commission, with no success.

Then President Bill Clinton appointed Gilbert Casellas to head the EEOC. I happened to be in Washington, DC, the day of his confirmation hearing in September 1994 and decided to attend, in the hope that I could put a copy of the report in his hand and ask for a meeting. I positioned myself in the aisle as the hearing came to a close and sure enough, Mr. Casellas stopped and took the report. "I've already read this," he told me. And then he said something I'd never heard before from a government official:

"Thank you so much for this. We need you to stay on our case." *He* asked *me* to arrange a time to meet. My encounters with this man reminded me that electing a president isn't just about the person in the White House, but about who heads government agencies (not to mention who gets appointed to the federal courts). Under Casellas, the EEOC made a number of important reforms and greatly reduced the backlog. Still, when he asked my advice about the new "triage" system, in which cases get priority if they stand to impact a large number of people, I told him it wasn't enough. We were glad to see them move quickly on class-action cases. But ultimately, we wanted the agency to guarantee that every complaint would be handled in a timely and thorough way. We continued to fight for greater funding, more staff training, and more outreach to the community. Along the way we worked with district directors on specific cases and celebrated some progress in cutting backlogs.

Downsizing Means Backsliding

With the election of George W. Bush in 2000, things took a very different turn. Here was someone who'd made clear his plans to downsize and privatize government services. Yet the moves on the EEOC began as a stealth operation—it's hard to brag about scaling back antidiscrimination enforcement. We learned from an insider at one of the regional agencies that Cari Dominguez, Bush's appointee as chair of the commission, had come up with a plan that would close offices—as many as 41 of the 51 current EEOC branches—and outsource questions and complaints to lower-paid contract employees in a toll-free call center. In March of 2003, with no public discussion, Dominguez tried to slip into the Iraq war funding bill a $5 million appropriation to cover the cost of office closings. After the EEOC staff union and 9to5 notified others in the civil rights community, people rallied all over the country. The district office in Milwaukee was one of those targeted for closing. A strong local coalition developed, many of them old allies from the No Retreat on Civil Rights network. We got support from both senators and from Governor Jim Doyle. 9to5 members testified on how much harder it would have been to bring forward a complaint had they not been able to talk with someone personally. Faced with such opposition, an EEOC spokesperson tried to minimize the impact proposed changes would have and "swore on a stack of Bibles" that the Milwaukee office would stay open.[34] It has—but without its district director, downgraded to an area office, and with greatly reduced staff.

In op-eds and media interviews, I was among those challenging the premise, content, and process of these changes. Why decrease the budget at a time when complaints have gone up, we asked. If cuts have to be made, why hasn't the chair looked at ways to cut costs at the top-heavy headquarters in Washington, DC? We labeled downsizing through attrition as "death by a thousand cuts." And we pointed out that cutting staff meant cuts in service. Any information given to the public requires significant training, yet call-center employees would operate from a script and be trained for only one week. An EEOC spokesperson told Sen. Ted Kennedy's staff that work that would be done in the call center was "too boring" for federal employees. Fighting discrimination isn't boring, we said. We also decried the lack of public input, despite repeated and detailed recommendations in a report by the National Academy of Public Administration to involve stakeholders in the field in any potential change. Finally, we linked the changes to the efforts to recast the EEOC as a friend of employers (a "kinder, gentler EEOC" read one business headline) rather than an enforcer of antidiscrimination law.

I wish I could tell you we stopped them. We did get Congress to intervene. The House Committee on Appropriations gave the chair clear directions to start any cuts with EEOC headquarters and not make any other changes without reporting back to Congress. Nevertheless, Dominguez put out bids for the national call center and began operations in Lawrence, Kansas, in March of 2005. On April 19, Equal Pay Day (see Chapter 4), 9to5 mobilized its members and a network of women's groups to contact their elected officials and demand an end to the fleecing of the agency. The press release quoted Gabrielle Martin, president of the National Council of EEOC Locals: "The people who dreamed of the passage of a Civil Rights Act did not dream of this. Can you imagine hundreds of thousands of people marching on the National Mall, hoping one day there might be a telemarketer staring at a script who they could call if they were discriminated against?" Martin pointed out that the call center's price tag for two years came to an extra $4.9 million—at the same time the EEOC projected a $6 million shortfall and had lost 500 employees to a hiring freeze.

Changing Attitudes

In addition to changing government policies, 9to5 uses training of managers and employees to change attitudes and create support for internal change. We worked with firefighters who thought women didn't belong in their workplace and architects who thought they did—they just didn't know why so few were working at their firm.

In 1997, we were brought in to work with firefighters in Kansas City, Missouri, in the aftermath of a sexual discrimination lawsuit (see Chapter 5). I learned a lot about what makes these jobs so unusual. Here are people who spend huge chunks of time together in a very close space. They alternate hours of free time with intense contact with human suffering. Not only do others depend on them, but they literally depend on each other for survival. They develop bonds similar to those among soldiers—and a culture similar in that it relies on hazing, is harsh on those who violate its codes, and takes time to overcome a history of exclusion or second-class status.

Remember that "telephone" game kids play, where one person whispers something into the next person's ear on and on down the line until the last person says the message out loud? By then, it's been completely garbled. Everyone laughs. In Kansas City, I saw firsthand what happens when adults do this, except the people involved had no idea this was going on and the results were no laughing matter.

From the minute we arrived at the training center, a number of firefighters regaled us with stories of how standards had been lowered in the department since the hiring of women—classic catastrophizing. Yet the only specific example anyone could give us was the removal of chin-ups from the mandatory physical exam. During the sessions, when we asked participants to imagine that their own daughter worked for the department, about one in seven said women shouldn't be there at all—they didn't have the upper body strength. How did they know this? Well, they'd been told. From "no more chin-ups" to "lowering the standards to let women in" hadn't taken very many telephone passes.

We went to Louie Wright, the amiable union president. Come to find out it was the union that had insisted on removing the chin-ups—a task, Wright pointed out, which women actually performed better than men. The leadership knew many of its veteran members couldn't pass that part of the exam. We made sure the union got out the real story.

Several firefighters continued to express concern that they'd have to cover for some female who couldn't handle a heavy piece of equipment. "My wife doesn't want me to die because some gal can't haul my ass out of a fire," is how one guy put it. Female firefighters would be what were known as a "load." We found this allegation stunning, given that nearly every group we trained included men who were shockingly out of shape—heavy smokers, people with bellies hanging over their pants, some we suspected or were told were alcoholics. How did those guys keep up, we wondered. The answer was, they didn't. Their crew covered for them out of loyalty. None of the female-resistant firefighters had a problem with this—but the idea of helping a woman (and the ones we met certainly needed no help) remained a major barrier.

In every training session, we took the lid off this hypocrisy. That helped do three important things: It drew out a number of men willing to challenge their coworkers, it helped the women feel supported, and it isolated the most sexist men by removing group sanction for their behavior.

Changing Practices

Unlike the fire department, the architects we worked with weren't reeling from a lawsuit and hadn't been mandated to conduct training. The owners were being proactive, hoping to enlighten their managers—almost all of whom were white males—about various kinds of diversity issues. (Whenever I write the word *issue*, I think of Keisha, the young daughter of a 9to5 colleague in Atlanta. She was playing in the office while a strategic planning session was going on to determine what issues to work on. As she and her mother were driving home, Keisha asked, "Momma, what's an issue?")

Even though this company wanted more women architects, the owners had no outreach plan and no analysis of how their internal processes might hold women back. As in most architectural firms, the majority of women were in interior design or in lower management positions. Some I interviewed lamented a lack of career paths. The financial coordinator in one studio had tried to get an executive to help develop and promote women in administrative positions. "He brushed me off as if I were just being emotional," she told me. "At best, they say they'll think about it but they don't know what to do about it." On more than one occasion, she'd asked for more authority; nothing came of her requests. She also shared how demoralizing it was to overhear men say things like, "Women are more focused on having kids than on work, so maybe we shouldn't give them larger projects." Another woman gave this example: Her studio's annual team-building activity was a football game. "If I don't participate, I'm a bitch," she explained. "If I choose to bring food and be a cheerleader, I'm 'just a woman.' If I play, I get pummeled by the big guys. And if I say anything, I'm making a big thing out of nothing."

I used these and other examples in the training to raise awareness. One guy took me aside during a break. He knew of an important client who requested a male architect—and that's what he got. When I asked the managers about this, a senior executive trivialized the problem. "What's wrong with that?" he asked. "Lots of men request a male physician, just as women request a female." I helped them understand the difference between personal preference and legal obligation and underscored the impact on limiting opportunities for female architects. We brainstormed ways to break down resistance by bringing a woman into the client meeting and letting her shine.

The firm didn't undergo a revolution, but the owners did see that vague yearnings for more gender diversity had to be replaced with concrete steps and culture changes.

HARD HATTED WOMEN

Imagine being the sole woman among 150 people in some trade where, for the most part, no one speaks to you and some actively try to sabotage your work. That pretty much summed up the former work climate of Kathy Augustine, who for fifteen years was the only female electronics technician at her Cleveland, Ohio, worksite. Aside from three African Americans in the group, she had no allies. One day in the mid-1980s, she attended a support group for women in the trades led by an organization called Hard Hatted Women. "I heard other women talking about what it's like to be the only woman, not go to lunch or coffee break with anyone, how you cope all day long," Augustine told me. "I immediately clicked."[35] She became involved as a volunteer and in 1990 was hired as the group's director.

In the early years, Hard Hatted Women would hold public rallies and picket lines when big construction projects started with no females among the workers. In 1986, for example, they watched a huge new building going up story by story in the downtown area with all-male crews. "We tried the route we were told," Augustine said, "meet with Human Resources and the people in charge of hiring, but we just kept getting the runaround. We decided to hold a rally on Public Square and invited women from the community. We had some media. The next week a woman was hired."

At first unions and employers alike "didn't want to see us coming," she said. "They wouldn't return our phone calls." But careful relationship building led to partnerships with a few key union leaders. "I can think of one guy in particular who wouldn't even look at me when I'd come in the room. Then he got to know me one-on-one." Augustine and her colleagues received invitations to union meetings on recruitment and retention of women in the trades. "Some of the leaders began to see the writing on the wall. With aging baby boomers and all the retirees, the skilled trade workplaces need women and minorities. Once they realized the women we're referring were qualified and skilled, they started admitting them."

Behind Augustine's soft curls and wire-rim glasses lay tremendous confidence. She knew the union got a great deal when they stopped excluding females. "Women pay more attention to safety issues, foster more communication among coworkers," Augustine explained. "Women are good union members, though they often feel they don't have a voice in their union. They're very interested in community action."

Turning Opportunities into Progress

Once they had some allies, Hard Hatted Women used a federal courthouse project to set up monthly oversight meetings. Under President Clinton's administration, government contracts paid more attention to hiring women and minority men. The group was determined to see that this provision was implemented. Augustine recalled an employer she called "Denny" who justified his failure to hire women by saying the union claimed there weren't any qualified women available: "The union leaders would say, 'That's not true, we have the list right here.' Denny held out for six months. He kept giving us excuses—'We don't need anybody; I tried a woman on the last project and she didn't work out.' I told him, 'You hire a man who doesn't work out and you don't hold it against all men. If you were hiring a larger pool of women, you wouldn't notice the one who doesn't work out.' And she pointed out what it means to work alone in a hostile setting.

"Denny kept kicking and screaming," Augustine said, "but eventually he hired a couple women just to shut us up."

Referrals come from the organization's pre-apprenticeship twice-a-year training program. "We're always filling the pipeline," Augustine said. They recruit women throughout the year with community presentations, utilizing graduates to speak and serve as role models. In addition to careful screening and thorough training, one secret to their success is never sending a woman in alone. "We always advocate for at least two women—per trade if possible," Augustine says.

Augustine is especially proud of the group's impact on worksites. "When Hard Hatted Women has a physical presence on a construction project," Augustine said, "the atmosphere is different. Women and minority males feel free to tell us about problems—sexual harassment, toilet problems, unfair treatment, white guys getting more overtime, women and minorities being given sweeping rather than actual work. We take those complaints to the proper authority to get them resolved. People who work there realize it's not business as usual. They have a voice."

The group uses a variety of tactics, such as advocating with government officials to give bids only to contractors who have demonstrated that their hiring reflects gender and racial diversity, and giving recognition to those who do. They've formed alliances with groups in communities of color as well as with leaders of skilled trades unions. "Contractors who don't do due diligence" don't get the contracts, she said.

As a result of advocacy by Hard Hatted Women and other groups, Cleveland passed a "sin" tax on cigarettes and alcohol in 1992 to raise funds for a new stadium. Politicians promised if the tax passed, community residents would be hired to work on huge construction projects like the Gateway stadium. The aim was to hire 6.9 percent females; they reached 6.2 percent. For people of color, the federal standard was 16.1 percent—Gateway achieved 23.3 percent.

"When we're all working together to achieve the goals," says Augustine, "it happens. I know we're making a difference. I just didn't know it would take this long."

FINAL THOUGHTS: MAKING CHOICES MEANINGFUL

Not all women want to be firefighters or architects or construction workers—or bank presidents. But many more can or would be if existing barriers were removed. The only way to guarantee real occupational choices is systemic changes in corporate and public policies.

5. YOU WANT TO SEE MY *WHAT?*
SEXUAL HARASSMENT

"Women can be as promiscuous as men . . . what men used to call tramps—then they demand that [they] not be treated like that."
—Pat Buchanan, then host of CNN's *Crossfire*, blaming sexual harassment on the sexual revolution[1]

When 9to5 was founded in 1973, the term *sexual harassment* didn't exist.[2] Most women who were groped or flashed or subjected to sexual threats or lewd remarks or pornographic images didn't tell anyone—they considered it a bitter part of life on the job. That invisibility changed in October of 1991, when the Supreme Court confirmation hearings for Clarence Thomas turned into a forum on whether or not he'd repeatedly made lurid sexual comments and displayed pornography to a former subordinate by the name of Anita Hill. Suddenly everyone knew the term *sexual harassment* and everyone had an opinion on it. Not surprisingly, most of these opinions were wrong. If the Thomas hearings functioned as a national teach-in on sexual harassment, the "teachers," members of the Senate Judiciary Committee, were woefully ignorant on the subject and spread a lot of confusion and misinformation—dismissing the charges as "fantasies," insisting the truth in such cases is "always elusive," maintaining that pornography would be "a poor choice of seduction techniques."[3]

Still, reporters published some useful information, including 9to5's toll-free number. In the two weeks surrounding the confirmation, more than 2,000 women called our hotline. In voices barely above a whisper or hoarse with rage, they told their stories. Most just wanted someone to know what they'd experienced; some of the incidents went back four decades. I pictured those women glued to their TV sets as I was—only while I sat hunched over a yellow legal pad scribbling notes, they were more likely curled up in pained recognition. I was haunted by one caller's story and imagined variations of it playing out in living rooms around the country: This woman had walked off a good job several years earlier because her boss wouldn't keep his hands off her. She never told her husband the reason she left. Every time they had economic problems, he'd carry on about how much better off they'd be if she'd stayed in that job. During the hearings, she pointed at the TV. "That's why I quit," she said. Her husband grabbed her hand. "I'm so sorry," he kept repeating. "I'll never mention that job again."

Fast forward to 1999. A teenager whose boss kept hitting on her in an after-school job sought help from "Dear Abby." "You have my permission to quit the job, " Abby said, "but you have to tell your parents." In a follow-up letter to Abby, 9to5 clarified that the behavior wasn't just out of line, as Abby indicated, but against the law and gave our 800 number. This time nearly 1,000 people contacted us. In many ways their experiences differed from those earlier callers. The silence had been broken, as Anita Hill once told a *60 Minutes* reporter. More women were speaking out. Most callers knew about the law, although they weren't sure what that meant for their individual situations. Unlike eight years earlier, the vast majority had reported the harassment to higher-ups.

So why were they calling? Because they couldn't get the behavior to stop. It wasn't that the harassers didn't "get" it—they were simply getting away with it.

Myth: Sexual Harassment's a Thing of the Past

Now, six years later, I still hear stories that make my jaw drop. Bernice told me about the Midwestern doctor she met in her native Mexico who arranged for her to move to his hospital for a training program in advanced lab technology.[4] At first when he fondled her and made comments about her body in front of patients, she complained only to him. "I didn't know my rights," she confided. Eventually she learned that this behavior was illegal and reported it on several occasions to Human Resources. "They said he apologized," Bernice recalled in rapid English, "so it wasn't a problem." The harassment went on for several years and was so stressful, Bernice wound up as a patient in that hospital and eventually left the program.

During that time she'd married and had a baby. Now negative references from the doctor are preventing her from finding another placement and are causing stress in her marriage. "All I wanted was a good job to help support my family," Bernice told me over the phone, her toddler babbling in the background. "Instead I wake up at night and can't catch my breath."

Women engineers at a large, well-respected company described to me the crude talk they'd experienced on a regular basis for eight years.[5] In the quiet of a lawyer's book-lined library, two of them talked about what it was like to be the only females in a group of fifty men. Mostly they put up with nude posters and comments about women's body parts from other engineers. But when "Charlotte's" boss came on to female interns and began making inappropriate comments to her, she went to Human Resources. Among other things, the manager had arranged for Charlotte to accompany him on a trip to evaluate subordinates—something outside her job description that involved a long car ride to another state. "As soon as we were off company property," she said, "it was like diarrhea of the mouth." Among other things, the manager kept suggested stopping for wine and a dip in a hot tub. The response to Charlotte's complaint from the head of HR? "What happens off company property is outside our purview."

The media feasts on stories of a first grader kicked out of school for giving his classmate a peck on the cheek. But few people hear about the middle school boys who push a sixth-grader to her knees and shove her face against a boy's crotch, or the high school girl who told my husband, her teacher, she probably wouldn't report harassment "because you never know, you could wind up dead." And girls aren't the only targets. The public seldom reads about boys who are ridiculed for being scrawny or hairless or sexually inexperienced or insufficiently macho. In school hallways, sexual harassment is as common as overloaded backpacks.

In fact, it's disturbingly common everywhere. Studies estimate that 35 to 50 percent of women are sexually harassed at some point in their career.[6] A 1999 study by Society for Human Resource Management found that sexual harassment complaints in the workplace were on the rise; two-thirds of the complaints were substantiated after investigation. Female troops fighting to bring safety to others often find themselves in harm's way from their fellow soldiers—35 to 50 percent of women veterans report at least one incident of harassment in their careers, and many say they experienced rape or attempted rape while on active duty.[7] Did they report the incidents to a ranking officer? Three in four said no—some because they didn't know how to do that, and some because they believed rape was "to be expected" in the military.[8]

Several of these women appeared in a 2005 *60 Minutes* segment entitled "Rape in the Military."[9] There they were in their uniforms, stiff upper lips and all, politely answering Ed Bradley's questions and calling him "Sir." Some, like Lt. Jennifer Dyer, had reported the incident right away. When she refused to go back to the same unit, a superior officer informed her that military police would come to arrest her. "I was fearful for my health and safety and sanity," she told Bradley. Others kept quiet. The six fellow soldiers who gang raped Sgt. Sharon Nixon in Saudi Arabia told her they would kill her if she told anybody. "We will always know where to find you," they warned. "If you open your mouth, you know what will happen."

From the military to media moguls to mainline financial institutions, sexual harassment is the pesky little problem that won't go away. No one would argue that women *should* be harassed. Instead, various Big Boy spokesmen maintain that the definition is too vague, the issue designed to pit women against men, the problem blown out of proportion, and the remedies causing more harm than good.

Myth: What Constitutes Harassment Is Totally Subjective

Sexual harassment really isn't that complicated. Here's the best definition I've come up with: Sexual harassment is behavior of a sexual nature at work or school that is unwanted, offensive, usually repeated, and makes it harder to have your job or do your work. That means flirting and even off-color jokes may be fine, as long as they make someone feel good and not uncomfortable. Most people I've trained, from students to firefighters to top executives, have no trouble identifying the difference.

Some things, of course, don't have to be repeated in order to be over the line. You can't tell someone even once to "sleep with me or you're fired." You can never touch someone in a private part of the body (it's hard to say, "Sorry, I didn't know that would offend you"). Some comments are so vulgar, even one occasion may be too much. And if you're the boss, asking someone out on a date may cross a line because of the power imbalance—the subordinate may not feel free to say no.

Managers always ask me if they can pay someone a compliment. No one has ever called 9to5's toll-free hotline to complain that someone said, "You look great." They call because they're being subjected to coarse and abusive behavior and they can't make it stop. Compliments make people feel appreciated; sexual harassment makes them feel degraded. A compliment deteriorates into something else when it's *sexualized* by words or gestures or tone of voice. So, sure, I tell the managers, give compliments—but don't limit them to appearance (or to women). Be sure to let staff know how much you appreciate their work.

Most people, including most men, aren't harassers. Some harassers behave badly without realizing it—like the guy who stayed in his seat during a break in our training and kept repeating, "Wow, I'm the person you're talking about. I must have offended a lot of people here and I had no idea." Overhearing this man, other participants came up to me and whispered, "Yes! Yes!" But most harassers know exactly what they're doing. When we say that harassment isn't about sex but about power, we mean that some people gain a sense of control by making others feel out of control. They've figured out what will make someone feel humiliated or embarrassed—or they simply don't care if what they feel like saying or viewing has that effect on others.

Typically harassers go after someone they perceive as vulnerable. Women of color tend to be harassed in higher numbers than white women both because they're more likely to lack various measures of security on the job, and because harassers are more likely to hold racist as well as sexist views, building on crude stereotypes of African American women in particular as wanton and animalistic.[10]

Another targeted group is women with disabilities. "You're already devalued because of your disability," explained Harilyn Rousso, the director of Disabilities Unlimited Consulting Services.[11] "That gives license to other forms of harassment." Rousso added that women facing employment barriers are also more reluctant to report the abuse. "[P]eople are less likely to believe you. Particularly if you're perceived as sexually undesirable—who would want to harass you?"

Reality: There Has Been Some Progress in the Workplace . . .

Fortunately, we know what to do about sexual harassment, and more employers are taking those steps. They start with a clear policy, make it familiar to all employees and reinforce it with a strong message from the top. Margaret Crawford, then director of Human Resources at Harley Davidson, told me how then-CEO Richard Teerlink called an impromptu meeting of 150 top Harley managers right after the Thomas hearings. "It's not just an issue

YOU WANT TO SEE MY *WHAT?*

of what's legal or illegal," he informed them, "but what's right and wrong and how do you treat people in the workplace." Teerlink made clear that managers would be held accountable for "the environment your workers have to live in." Said Crawford, "That ten-minute off-the-cuff presentation did more than anything else could have done. Word was out in the hallways."

An effective policy offers multiple channels for reporting complaints. Imagine the company handbook telling you to report any problem to the branch manager—but the branch manager happens to be the one literally breathing down your neck. The policy also has to provide for candid, down-to-earth conversation and a safe environment to ask questions and clarify what is and isn't okay. Here's what doesn't count as training: a mention of the sexual harassment policy during employee orientation; a brief lecture; a list of do's and don'ts. A worker at the plant where my husband used to work told Larry about the trainer who came there and handed out such a list, which included in the don't category a practice known as "elevator eyes" (stopping at certain levels). As soon as they left the twenty-minute session, the participants competed in an elevator eyes contest.

Combating sexual harassment doesn't mean discarding due process for the accused. False accusations are rare but they do happen; so do misunderstandings. Everyone has the right to a fair hearing. As for the investigation, it needs to be prompt and effective, and that requires specially trained staff. Every year I teach a master's level class on sexual harassment to people working in human resources. Some have been responsible for investigating complaints for years—despite the fact that they know very little about the subject or about how to ask sensitive questions.

Then there's the question of discipline if the complaint is found to have merit. Discipline should be appropriate to the offense and to the offender's rank. Don't fire a low-level worker for telling an off-color joke—and don't let a big shot get away with sexual humiliation. The process also shouldn't end with punishment. Follow-up and monitoring are needed to make sure the harassment is over, the target of that behavior is healing, and no retaliation is taking place.

How about workplace romance? This can be dicey, since many people meet their mates at work. But again, common sense provides a solution. Companies should have guidelines requiring professional conduct, whether your honey works in the next cubicle or in another state. If a supervisor wants to date a subordinate, he or she should disclose the relationship to a superior and be removed from any supervisory functions over the love interest. We recommend the same on campus—discourage relationships between faculty and their own students, but should one occur, require disclosure and have someone else grade the student. (I've always wanted to know if the student is allowed to see whether the professor who reports her as a romantic interest lists others as well—"In American Lit, I'm sleeping with Sue. Denise is my bedmate in European Postmoderns.")

And in Congress and the Courts . . .

Many employers who developed sexual harassment policies did so because of action on the part of Congress and the courts. Many women's groups and others expressed outrage at the treatment of Anita Hill, then a law professor at the University of Oklahoma, by the Senate Judiciary Committee. (Sen. Alan Simpson, for instance, had warned she would be "injured and destroyed and belittled and hounded and harassed—real harassment, different from the sexual kind, just plain old Washington-variety harassment"—Yikes!) We flooded our senators' offices with demands for action. As a result, the first President Bush signed a new Civil Rights Act—the same one he'd vetoed a few months earlier (see Chapter 4). Until that time, if you were sexually harassed or discriminated against in any way because of gender and you lost your job, you could win back pay and reinstatement. But if you lost your sense of security or mental health, you couldn't get a dime, not even repayment of doctor bills or hospitalization costs. I remember hours spent talking to a woman named Carol Zabkowicz whose coworkers at a warehouse in Racine, Wisconsin, had enjoyed tormenting her by calling out her name and then exposing their genitals or buttocks when she looked up.[12] Even when she brought witnesses and evidence in the form of obscene cartoons, management's position was, "If we didn't see it, it didn't happen." The court case was excruciating for Carol, who in a pretrial deposition was asked everything from her bra size to whether she'd had extramarital affairs. She did win—the judge found the company guilty of "malicious, blatant discrimination." But because she still had her job, she got no monetary award of any kind. Despite a strong marriage and the support of her husband and two sons, Carol told me her heart pounded with fear whenever she passed a group of men.

The new law changed at least the monetary part, allowing for compensatory and punitive damages up to a modest limit. Several states passed laws requiring employers to have a posted policy, and a couple even required training for employees.

The Supreme Court issued several good rulings as well. In 1993, it concluded you don't have to have a nervous breakdown before someone says, "This has gone too far" (see page 115). Five years later, the Court finally recognized that people could harass someone of the same gender. In this case, as is usually true in same-sex harassment, the perpetrators were heterosexual men. Their supervisor thought sodomizing a coworker with soap and threatening him with rape amounted to "male horseplay" that didn't require any intervention.[13] The Court disagreed. What mattered, they said, wasn't the sex of the harasser or target, but whether the sexually offensive behavior was based on the individual's gender.

Two other rulings that same year clarified employer liability. The Court recognized what 9to5's hotline callers knew—only the employer has the power to impose consequences for bad behavior, and thereby put an end to it. In cases where the harasser is a supervisor and the harassment costs you something tangible, like your job or a promotion, the employer will be automatically liable. If the supervisor's harassment doesn't result in such an outcome, top management can present what's known as an affirmative defense. They have to show they took reasonable measures to prevent harassment or stop it once it occurred, and that the complainant unreasonably failed to take advantage of those measures.

. . . But Not Nearly Enough Progress

We may know what employers should do, but too few are doing it. Instead they simply ignore the problem or opt for a quick fix. Their sloppiness is aided by a flaw in the law: It says employers who discriminate will be punished if they get caught, but it doesn't require them to take any steps *not* to discriminate, not even developing and posting a policy. Most people don't realize that the statute outlawing sexual harassment dates back to 1964—the Civil Rights Act that prohibits discrimination on the basis of race, color, religion, national origin, or gender (see Chapter 4). It took a long time before people considered sexual harassment a form of gender discrimination. When women first sued, judges dismissed their cases on the grounds that the Civil Rights Act was not intended to prevent "a physical attack motivated by sexual desire,"[14] or a "personal peculiarity" on the part of a supervisor—the Court couldn't hold an employer responsible for *that*.[15]

Even with greater guidance from the court, employers continue to make a number of errors:

- They may address individual cases of harassment, but not deal with the underlying organizational culture. Rick Brisbin, then Fire Chief in Kansas City, Missouri, told a group of colleagues that the greatest mistake he made was thinking that all he had to do was hire a few women and plunk them in the stations without changing anything else.

- They fail to curb the harasser because he happens to be a big shot in the organization (I call these the UGLIs: Untouchable Godlike Individuals). Check out the story of Dan Wassong of Del Labs, a cosmetics and pharmaceutical company in Farmingdale, New York, on page 111. The company wound up paying a hefty settlement as a result of Wassong's gross behavior, but kept him on as CEO.

- They fail to make it safe to complain. The military is a great example of this, instituting zero tolerance but neglecting the all-powerful role of drill instructors and superior officers. And let's not forget Congress, state and local government units, and most of Corporate America, who leave the investigation of complaints against high-powered officials to people whose own jobs may be affected if that official is forced out.

- They take a criminal defense approach to complaints, seeking to discredit the people coming forward rather than the harassers.

- They fail to prohibit harassment based on sexual orientation or to include language about treating everyone with dignity and respect. People can create a pretty hostile environment by constantly calling someone "faggot" or "sissy" or "dyke," and get away with it, since the behavior isn't overtly sexual.

Consequences for those Harassed

Employers don't do nearly enough, the law doesn't go far enough—what that amounts to is that many people, most of them women, continue to experience harassment and the range of problems it drags with it, from economic loss to depression, anxiety, and stress-related physical health problems. Nearly half of women who complain of sexual harassment say they experience some form of retaliation.[16]

Over the years I've spoken with scores of women and a number of men who've been harassed. I've served as an expert witness in more than a dozen sexual harassment cases. And I've read everything I could get my hands on. The stories differ enormously, but certain similarities emerge: The unwelcome behavior is usually unexpected and takes people off guard.

The person being harassed says, "Stop" in many ways and keeps hoping that this episode will be the last, only to run into a new variation. Above all, sexual harassment is an *injury* with effects that last long afterward. As an Employee Assistance Program director put it, "Crime victims get empathy—and sexual harassment victims get accusations and scrutiny. Crime victims may have broken locks or a broken arm—but sexual harassment victims have a broken spirit for many years."

FEMINIST SOLUTIONS

Sexual harassment doesn't occur in a vacuum. It's a particular way to devalue women, and it functions to keep them in an inferior status. The fact that most harassers are male has nothing to do with biology, but rather with socialization that celebrates sexual conquest, perpetuates a sexual double standard, and confuses toughness with aggression. Unfortunately, some women who've made it into powerful positions have adopted ruthless behaviors they associate with power—including sexual humiliation. Creating equality at work and eradicating behavior based on degradation and fear will be a huge gain for men as well as women. Ending sexual harassment can happen only in a workplace that relies on trust, dignity, and respect for everyone.

Employers need to follow the best practices outlined above. This includes arranging a wholly independent, outside source to investigate complaints lodged against high-level personnel. Workers must be familiar with this option and able to contact the investigator(s) directly, bypassing cronies and others who have a stake in the outcome.

To create the necessary climate, we need these public policy changes:

- Require employers to have a policy and to make it known to employees. This is one way to level the playing field—those who have a policy should welcome the requirement.
- Require employers to provide sexual harassment awareness training to all employees. As Massachusetts and Connecticut have found, this is a reasonable and effective requirement for all states to follow.
- Expand funding for enforcement agencies to increase the speed and effectiveness of follow-through on complaints. The EEOC continues to have a tremendous backlog. Many states are so overburdened, they routinely fail to meet deadlines spelled out in their own regulations. Both federal and state agencies should be able to investigate every complaint within three months of filing.

- Curtail the use of mandatory arbitration. Right now employers can require applicants to sign an agreement to use mandatory arbitration in case of a discrimination complaint. Employees should not be required to surrender their rights as a condition of hiring.
- Extend the statute of limitations. Someone who breaks a leg in your driveway has much more time to take legal action than you do if you're harassed. Yet often it takes harassment victims a long time to decide on a course of action. The statute of limitations (the time allowed for bringing a legal action) should be extended from 300 days to the two years allowed for battery, slander, and breach of contract.
- Extend protection to those not covered by federal laws. The law doesn't apply to people who work for a firm with fewer than fifteen employees, independent contractors, and to doctor/patient, lawyer/client, and other professional relationships. It should.
- Remove the cap on damages. By imposing a limit on the amount of awards, the law sends a message that sex discrimination is not as serious as other kinds of violations. In states where unlimited damages are permitted, large awards are rare. But the threat of serious financial punishment can motivate employers to take proactive measures.
- Repeal the tax on discrimination settlements. The Small Business Job Protection Act of 1996 has a provision taxing all awards "not based on physical injuries or physical sickness." This includes the majority of discrimination awards. (Until 2005, not only did you have to pay taxes on any money you won, but also on the portion of the award paid to your attorney—who was taxed as well.)
- Improve unemployment-compensation statutes. If you quit your job to escape harassment, you'd be turned down for unemployment insurance in many states on the grounds that you left "voluntarily." States should define such a move as a "constructive discharge," the equivalent of involuntary dismissal without cause, and allow for compensation.
- Train judges, lawyers, and agency staff. Personnel at all levels of law enforcement need to be educated about harassment to avoid statements like those of Judge Patrick McNulty in Minnesota, who ruled that women in a class-action suit against Eveleth Mines were "overreactive," "paranoid," or "puritanical." So a coworker masturbated a few times on one woman's clothes in her locker, said McNulty—big deal, no reason for her to confuse "suspicions with reality."[17]

- Pass the Employment Nondiscrimination Act (see Chapter 4). This will help prohibit harassment based on sexual orientation or sexual identity, regardless of whether or not the offensive behavior fits a definition of "sexual" conduct.

TAKING ON THE BIG BOYS

The Big Boys manage to deploy their entire arsenal when it comes to sexual harassment. The radio waves and Internet sites are filled with stories that *minimize* and *trivialize* the issue. I was once on a TV show where another panelist pulled a news clipping out of his shirt pocket that claimed a professor was fired for kissing someone under the mistletoe. Mistletoe—we all get dewy eyed just thinking of it. I don't know the facts in that case, but I do know there are kisses and then there are kisses. Engaging tongue and loins against an unsuspecting student might be pretty intimidating.

Others *patronize.* I was home sick one day when Phyllis Schlafly, leader of the conservative Eagle Forum, appeared on the *Donohue Show* with her own prescription for avoiding sexual harassment: Wear a button that says "lady." If you just act like a lady, Schlafly declared, no one will bother you. I cheered up enormously when someone in the audience asked if she'd notice that you have to stare at a person's chest in order to read what the little button said.

Catastrophizing comes in handy when employer lobbyists want to argue against any required action. Executives are terrified to tell a woman she looks nice, they claim. "Cupid cops" are peering into employees' private lives. Workers are spending day after day in sensitivity training. And women are walking off with huge settlements for behavior that is merely boorish. Says Timothy Lynch of the Cato Institute: "Any fair-minded observer has to come away thinking that it's ridiculous—the government has gone too far."[18] Commentators like this one maintain that employers already take steps to prevent harassment because they know how costly it is ($6.7 million a year just in turnover and lost productivity—and that was in 1988).[19] Requiring training or more serious penalties would cripple employers, run business out of town—and what do you know, hurt the very people we most want to help.

The Big Boys rail against frivolous charges, false accusations, extreme overreactions. Just think, they say, about the school officials who suspended that six-year-old boy in Lexington, North Carolina, in 1996 for a giving a girl a quick kiss on the cheek. Or they recount the cautionary tale of the female employee at Miller Brewing Company in Milwaukee who filed a formal complaint after a coworker, Jerold MacKenzie, told a joke about a *Seinfeld* episode. After being fired for sexual harassment, MacKenzie sued and won $25 million—or so the story goes. In fact, the North Carolina case was atypical (see page 100 for what's really going on in our schools). The woman in the Miller case never made a formal complaint, and MacKenzie—a $95,000-a-year manager, not a coworker—lost his job for poor management, not sexual harassment, sued over a contract dispute, and had his big award overturned.[20] As for frivolous lawsuits, when Bloomberg News journalist Susan Antilla asked the ten largest brokerage firms on Wall Street to supply examples, not one did so.

And let's not forget the *demonizing* that goes on. It was respected senators, after all, who denounced the deeply religious and proper Anita Hill as demented, paving the way for author David Brock to label her "a little nutty and a little slutty." (He later apologized.) A reporter who wanted to write a book on sexual harassment told me she'd title it, "You'd Better Be a Saint," since anything in a person's past was fair game if she tried to fight back.

Defending Your Own

Typically even Big Boys who acknowledge sexual harassment as a problem jump to their own company's defense when an incident is uncovered there. Mitsubishi, for example, spent $2 million to remake itself into a model company after sexual harassment complaints rocked the corporation— tales of cars rolling down the assembly line decorated with pornographic cartoons featuring the faces of female employees, or photos circulating in the lunchroom of supervisors engaged in sex acts with prostitutes. Yet at the very moment consultant Lyn Martin rolled out her thirty-four-point plan to prevent sexual harassment—which, by the way, made no analysis of what had happened and assigned no responsibility—Mitsubishi attorneys had issued 500 subpoenas to former employers, doctors, gynecologists, and psychologists of the twenty-eight women who'd filed a private lawsuit against the company.[21] Questioning during depositions was so aggressive, many of the women felt as if they were the ones accused. Talk about mixed messages—here's what such employers communicate: "We don't want any harassment, but should it happen, don't make a fuss about it. If you do come forward, you'll be very sorry."

Others agree to settle sexual harassment suits but only with sealed documents and strict gag rules. Once again, those who experience harassment find themselves silenced and the perpetrators off the hook.

Shifting the Focus

To undercut the impact of the Big Boys, activists had to bring home the seriousness of the problem and the real costs of letting it fester. We wanted to remind the public that women who are harassed are someone's daughter, mother, sister, wife. We also wanted to lessen the influence of the minimizers and demonizers on male workers—not the minority who are harassers, but the larger number of bystanders: people who know what's going on but do nothing to make it stop. In the process, we wanted to help those experiencing harassment know what to do about it and gain support to stand up. By reclaiming a sense of power, they could help change the conditions that allowed harassment to flourish.

Over the years, people who staff 9to5's Job Survival Hotline have done an extraordinary job providing resources, information, and emotional support to callers. They teach women how to document the harassment, look for others who've experienced it, research and use company channels, and go as high as they need to in order to get a response. They provide sample responses to coworkers: "That's a great example of sexual harassment for our study. Let me make sure I have the exact spelling of your name"; "You want to touch my what? Why don't I call the supervisor and you can say that again." Sometimes the women on the other end of the line take individual action—like the office cleaner whose boss would stick his arm out and make her rub up against him to get to her assigned area. After calling 9to5, she told the supervisor that everything he'd done to her was now documented with a working women's group; he never bothered her again. Others took the information back to a group. At Del Laboratories, for example, forty-five women who at some point had worked for CEO Dan Wassong and been subject to his outrageous behavior (conducting business with his pants's zipper open, urinating with the bathroom door open and in full view of the secretary, calling women by crude sexual terms, asking for oral sex) came forward after the current secretary, Jonneigh Adrion, learned there was a government agency they could go to. When she tried internal company channels, she'd been told, "Why all of a sudden is this bothering you? You know what he's like."

What was most moving was how often the callers said, "I don't ever want this to happen to me again—and I don't want it to happen to anyone else." They talked to reporters, testified at hearings, started support groups, organized with coworkers, and demanded policy change.

Whenever we could, we encouraged women who'd been harassed to speak along with us. I remember going on a local African American radio program with Sonia, a 9to5 member who'd been driven out of her job after she objected to her boss's unwanted advances. The host invited us on because of all the debate in the black community over Clarence Thomas. ("Sure he did it," my friend Sheila told me over a bid whist card game, "but she shouldn't have told. He's still a brother. Once he's on the Court, he'll do good things." After his first vote, Sheila sent me and a lot of other people a note of apology.) Sonia and I draped our heads in those boxy earphones and adjusted our mikes. She was using a pseudonym on the show, but a caller recognized her voice. "I know this woman," the caller said, "She's my best friend. I never knew she'd been sexually harassed—and until this moment she didn't know that I have been as well." The radio host listened in amazement as Sonia, tears streaming down her face, thanked her friend and arranged to get together that evening. Afterward he told me how powerful that moment had been—it turned him from someone looking for a lively topic to a committed advocate for change.

"If She Looks Like Dolly Parton . . ."

When you speak on certain topics related to women in the workplace, like managing work and family or shattering the glass ceiling, people introducing you tend to stick to a straightforward approach. Not so with sexual harassment. I can't count the number of bad jokes I've heard over the years—"Finally, a training on sexual harassment. I've always wanted to know how to do that!" "How come no one ever sexually harasses *me*!" Still, I have fond memories of one tasteless introduction, back in the mid-1980s. I was about to address 100 United Auto Workers members at a Region 10 conference in a cavernous union hall in Oak Creek, Wisconsin. The audience was 99 percent male. I was the only female on the panel of six and the only speaker on sexual harassment. The union officer (we'll call him Hal) began by saying in three or four different ways that he hoped I could take a joke and wasn't easily offended. Audience members began shifting in their metal folding chairs. Hal then shared his conversation with the regional director, Bob Vickers, who had invited me and had delegated this introduction. Their chat went something like this:

Hal: "Introduce Ellen Bravo? How will I know who she is?"

Bob: "Well, Hal, she should be easy to pick out in this crowd."

Hal: "Okay, but 9to5—what's 9to5? I've never heard of it."

Bob: "Didn't you see the movie?"

Hal: "The one with Dolly Parton? She looks like Dolly Parton? Oh my gosh, if she looks like Dolly Parton, these guys are going to have a hard time keeping their eyes in the right place."

By that point almost every person in the audience had slipped down in his chair, many had their hands over their mouths, and few could look me in the eye. I cheerfully took the mike and asked, "How many think the way Hal just introduced me was sexual harassment?" Every hand shot up in the air.

"Actually, it wasn't," I assured them. "First of all, Hal went out of his way to say he didn't want to offend me. Sexual comments of a relatively minor nature need to be repeated in order to rise to the level of sexual harassment, and I'm quite sure Hal will never introduce someone like this again. Now, was it stupid? Juvenile? In bad taste?" I went on listing various adjectives while the audience roared and Hal signaled his acknowledgment by turning scarlet and nodding his head.

Anything Short of Rape Doesn't Count

I had much less fun debating right-wing commentators on national TV. After Anita Hill's story first surfaced, I was one of the people asked to discuss the issue of sexual harassment on a wide variety of television shows, ranging from the gravity of the *McNeil-Lehrer News Hour* to the intellectual food fight of *Crossfire*. The half-hour format of that program gave more time than a news show to make points, but only someone who talks as fast as I do had a chance of getting a word in.

I was invited to *Crossfire* in 1993 to talk about ten women who'd reported inappropriate sexual behavior on the part of Sen. Bob Packwood of Oregon. Earlier in the year I'd appeared on the show with host Pat Buchanan, who had since left to run for president. Taking his place was columnist Bob Novak, the same guy who gained notoriety in 2004 for blowing the cover of a CIA agent after her husband criticized the Bush administration. Novak's style was much more aggressive and explicitly hostile than that of his predecessor, who tended to make obnoxious remarks (see the beginning of this chapter) in a quiet voice and low-key manner.

This show aired in the early days of the Packwood scandal, before the smoking diaries surfaced and the senator was forced to resign.[22] Novak tried to make hay out of Packwood being a Republican, claiming women's groups like 9to5 didn't go after Democrats such as Sen. Brock Adams[23] when they were accused of even worse misconduct. I pointed out that many of us did speak out against Adams, who then decided not to run for reelection. I also noted that Packwood was one of the few pro-choice Republicans; women's groups were not happy to see him fall.

"Let's be honest, Ms. Bravo," Novak said, peering out from his protruding forehead and heavy eyebrows. "There's no allegations of sexual intercourse."

"Are you saying if there's no intercourse, there's no harassment and no violation of the law?" I replied.

Novak shifted the focus, complaining that the women in this case had waited so long to come forward. Suddenly I realized how much he resembled the actor who played the police chief in those Inspector Clouseau movies—the guy with the nervous tics who chopped off his finger in a cigar trimmer. I forced myself not to think about it as I reminded him that neither these women nor Anita Hill had "come forward." Instead, investigators came to them. "They said, 'If you ask me, I cannot tell a lie,'" I told Novak. "None of these women had anything to gain from this except scorn and loss of privacy."

This brought a snarl from Novak. He claimed the women in the Packwood case had "accepted" the conduct, which, after all, wasn't such a big deal. Here's how the conversation went:

Novak: "It was not rape, not sexual intercourse."
Me: "If it were your daughter and it wasn't rape but someone pushed her into a closet and tried to lift up her skirt and tear off her undergarments, would it be okay with you?"
Novak: "I think you're overdramatizing what the story said."
Me: "That was what the story said, exactly what I just said."

Novak's retort? "We're going to have to take a break."

I have to say, I liked getting my licks in. But what really mattered was the reaction of 9to5 members in the throes of their own harassment battles. Each time someone from 9to5 appeared on the media, these women let us know how validated they felt. "Even if I don't win a single thing," one woman told me, "it means so much that someone understands what I went through." Public opinion began to shift as well. Right after the Thomas hearings, the majority of people surveyed did not believe Anita Hill was telling the truth. A year later, they did.

Dirty Jokes at the Water Cooler

The *Crossfire* guys were good practice for a confrontation with Bryant Gumbel in 1993 on NBC's *The Today Show*. I'd been interviewed by Gumbel's colleague, Katie Couric, the previous year after the publication of *The 9to5 Guide to Combating Sexual Harassment*, which I cowrote. So when I was invited back to discuss a Supreme Court decision on sexual harassment— only the second such decision in its history—I expected to see a sympathetic Katie again, only to find myself across from Bryant Gumbel. If Katie was known for being perky, Bryant's more often described as prickly, and he certainly was that day. The facts of the case weren't complicated: No one disputed that the boss of the forklift company had a long history of lewd and sexually demeaning comments, or that the plaintiff, Teresa Harris, was offended by them. But the lower court had thrown out the case on the grounds that the behavior hadn't "seriously affected" her "psychological well-being." Fortunately, the Supreme Court ruled unanimously that although sexual harassment may cause emotional devastation, it doesn't have to do so in order for someone to say, "This has gone too far."

Bryant Gumbel was in an uproar, along with the other guest, a member of the Libertarian Party. For Gumbel, the ruling meant men could be fired for telling a dirty joke at the water cooler. I set the record straight, reminding him that the court had laid out strict guidelines for what constituted harassment—the behavior needed to be severe and pervasive and to alter the working conditions of the person making the complaint. Our disagreement didn't end when the segment was over. Gumbel led me into the hallway, where I learned what was really bugging him. A makeup artist at NBC had filed a sexual harassment lawsuit against the network. Among a long list of incidents cited was one dating back four years, involving none other than Bryant Gumbel himself telling dirty jokes to another person while being made up for the show.

"There should be a statute of limitations!" he demanded.

I reminded him that of course, there is a statute of limitations and that he personally would not be disciplined as a result of the suit. "But it would be a good idea to remember that makeup artists and camera people are human beings," I said. "Save the jokes until you're out of their range." As I left him blustering, I noticed Katie Couric giving me a thumb's up from the set.

Toxic Trainings

An important part of our work to combat the impact of the Big Boys was sexual harassment awareness training. I started doing these twenty years ago, when a friend who worked for the Milwaukee County transit company persuaded the union to bring me in to talk to members of the local. Every time she showed up at the dispatch window to get her assignment, the dispatcher shoved a *Hustler* centerfold in her face. She didn't want to turn in a union brother to management, but she was determined to make him stop. Whether or not he changed his attitude after our session, he did change his behavior.

That was the first of many workshops I led in male-dominated settings, although we also trained all levels of employees in a wide variety of workplaces. Those attending were sometimes welcoming, often uneasy, sometimes downright hostile. Once a crew from 9to5 trained every employee at the local sewage district after a number of incidents there. Some people recognized me from media appearances with Melissa Fojtek, a firefighter who had accused the head of the Milwaukee firefighters union, a candidate for mayor, of exceedingly crude behavior, including exposing himself and pointing to a mole on his genitals, insisting that she kiss it. One guy confronted me angrily about our involvement in that case.

"Is it that you think he didn't do it or you think it didn't matter?" I asked.

"So he pulled his dick out," the guy replied. "What's that got to do with being mayor?"

That particular session was probably the most toxic training I've ever been part of. Most people—all men—uncrossed their arms and began to pay attention early on, after they realized we weren't branding all of them as harassers. But one guy sat in the back of the room and droned over and over, "This is such bullshit, I can't believe it," adding disparaging comments about everything from my appearance to what he presumed was my unmarried status ("Feminists are ugly women who can't get a man"). I wish I could say I threw him out after the first two minutes, or that he didn't rattle me. I didn't, and he did. But I finally figured out how to deal with the others. Several men expressed their anger at their female coworkers, none of whom was in the room. I asked the men what they wanted.

"Treat us as individuals," they said. "Don't assume we're all harassers." Fair enough, I said (okay, I yelled). "But what are you doing to stop those who are? Why didn't any of you stand up to the guy who's been insulting me all afternoon? If you treat those women the way you've treated me today, what do you think's going to happen the next time there's a contract dispute and you need to stand strong together?" They heard this (as did many employees who worked in the vicinity of our training room).

That experience helped prepare me for an even greater challenge several years later—training 750 firefighters in Kansas City, Missouri (twenty-one of them female) as part of a court order following a gender discrimination lawsuit. I knew going in that our team of trainers would face resistance, but we had no idea how fierce it would be. Over four weeks, our trainers met twice a day in four-hour sessions with twenty to twenty-five people in each. One of the first groups had made a secret pact ahead of time that no one would speak except for two guys who'd volunteered to torment us. Quickly my male co-trainer and I realized we needed to head them off at the pass. "Time out," I said after the first five minutes. "Clearly you're angry—what are you angry at us for? You don't even know us." One of the designated speakers described an editorial that had appeared in the local paper, declaring it was no longer a noble profession to be a firefighter in Kansas City. The other told about walking into a supermarket in uniform and having a stranger come up and say, "How many women have *you* sexually harassed?"

"I can see why you're angry," I said. "That certainly went too far."

"If you really know that it's just a few assholes who are doing the harassing," one of them challenged us, "then why do we have to be punished? Why don't you just have this training for the assholes?"

"I'm so glad you asked," I replied. "Because you're the ones who can stop the assholes, and you haven't." This was the first time any of them had thought about their role as bystanders. Everything changed after that.

If It Were Your Daughter

We designed an exercise asking people to imagine that their daughter had come to work for the department. "She has the ability and the desire to do the job," I'd say. "No one knows she's your daughter. Are you okay with that?"

Invariably, someone would ask which station she was assigned to. "That one," I'd answer. "The one you're thinking of." (By the time we left Kansas City, we could name those stations.)

Most participants were wary of having a daughter work with "these animals," as several put it. "It'd be okay if people knew she was my daughter," one guy said. "Then no one would mess with her. But otherwise—forget it."

We pointed out the obvious: Every woman there was somebody's daughter. What these firefighters wanted for their own loved ones, they had to ensure for all.

We worked with the union leadership, the fire chief, and the lead women plaintiffs to try to come up with recommendations they would all buy into. I developed role plays that showed the double bind the women were in because of fire-station culture: On the one hand, if they spoke up, they'd be seen as weaklings by coworkers who still didn't universally accept their presence. On the other hand, if they didn't speak up, the harassment would get worse and then, if they complained, they'd be accused of being gold diggers who didn't really mind the behavior but wanted to rake in big bucks. In reality, the women who won in this recent lawsuit didn't get very much—and several didn't win at all. The main issue was not, as rumor had it, sexual jokes, but failure to promote a highly qualified woman, something most people agreed was unfair. In a panel discussion after the trainings, the lead plaintiff acknowledged that all the women wanted was to be heard and taken seriously. "Had anyone met with us and really listened," she said, "we would have dropped the suit."

I persuaded the union leadership and the fire chief to split the cost of a special session just for union officers and stewards. It felt like an AA meeting—one person after another stood up to say how much they'd learned in the trainings and how much responsibility they bore for not stopping the behavior earlier. "We were so busy thinking about our members who were accused of harassment," said one union leader, "we forgot to think about our members who were being harassed." A strapping guy in his forties rose to say the group had to stop worrying about what was popular and start worrying about what was right. As the father of three girls, he said, the training had changed him profoundly. "It's hypocritical for me to preach because I have practiced gender bias," he said (where did he get that phrase, one we never used!). "But what people do is either appropriate or not. It doesn't take a title to stand up and say that. It takes courage and integrity."

Creating a cadre of leaders like this in workplaces all across the country is a difficult task—but one we all need to commit to.

Refusing to Let the Big Boys Win

We also need to stand up to the Big Boys. Many people are aware of the grilling Anita Hill endured during the Clarence Thomas hearings, but fewer know about another battle she was involved in that played before a much smaller audience. A Minnesota state representative named Gloria Segal wanted to raise money to establish the Anita Faye Hill professorship at the University of Oklahoma for the study of race and gender discrimination. Seventy-four chairs had been established previously at the university, all in the same manner: private fundraising of the first $100,000, application to the state for matching funds, approval without debate.

"When this one came up," Hill told me, "my detractors used the opportunity to debate everything—my teaching, scholarship, research, tenure, and my testimony."[24] Bowing to political pressure, the university president backed off his initial approval, despite support from the law school's dean. After Representative Segal died from a brain tumor and a second fundraiser came under attack from the opponents, Anita Hill decided to raise the funds herself. "The money kept coming in, five dollars, fifty dollars—most of it in small amounts. I got more than motivated after the attacks on those fundraisers. I owed it to myself but to them as well to take up where they left off."

Hill gained inspiration from a series of events—three former law students at the University of Oklahoma, all African American women, held a reception and "stood up in a situation viewed as personally hostile for them." In Reno, Nevada, Business and Professional Women—hardly a radical group—passed the hat at a meeting and raised $11,000. "People extended themselves as women, nationally, to transcend political maneuvering by state legislators in Oklahoma," Hill noted. "A whole host of women came together to say, 'You're not going to bully us anymore. Even if you manipulate the process, we're still going to win.'" The chair was established in 1995.

Anita Hill was one of a long line of women of color who have taken the lead in speaking up about sexual harassment. Many of the early lawsuits were filed by African American women, including Paulette Barnes, a government worker whose charge against her supervisor in 1977 led to the first appeals court ruling that sexual harassment was a form of gender discrimination (*Barnes v. Costle*). A forklift operator named Sheila White continued that tradition when she insisted on her right to protest sexual harassment without being punished for doing so (*Burlington Northern*

Santa Fe Railway v. White). In June 2006, a unanimous Supreme Court agreed. Their ruling in her case clarified that retaliating against someone who reports sexual harassment is illegal if the actions "interfere with an employee's efforts" to ensure that he or she is not discriminated against in the workplace.[25]

TRANSFORMING THE MILITARY: THE MILES FOUNDATION

It's hard to think of an institution as challenging to transform as the armed forces. And yet that's exactly what the Miles Foundation has set out to do. "We don't have a magic wand," said the group's executive director, Christine Hansen, herself the daughter of a retired military officer.[26] "This isn't going to happen overnight or by next Tuesday." Still, since its founding in 1987, the group has helped change both awareness and policy about the range of violence—from domestic abuse to sexual harassment, sexual assault, stalking, and trafficking—experienced by women in the military.

"Miles" refers to the name of a 1953 decision by the Army Board of Review which defined "grievous bodily harm." Unfortunately, the Army later failed to recognize violence against women as being different from violence against men or as causing trauma.[27] Hansen's group organized for more than a decade to reverse that. Working with Sen. Paul Wellstone in 1998, the group celebrated passage of an amendment to a defense authorization bill in which for the first time the military acknowledged that interpersonal violence causes more than physical harm and provided for mental health services to survivors. "Senator Wellstone told us this was the first amendment he ever put forth for a defense bill that passed," Hansen said. "He was thrilled. So were we."

In addition to public policy work, the Miles Foundation does extensive education and training, as well as providing direct services to women who have been victims of violence in the military. They also serve as a resource center for reporters, policymakers, scholars, and others. Among the changes they've helped bring about are a clearer definition of sexual harassment, use of "abuse of power" in the definition of sexual assault (victims are predominantly of a lower rank than their assailants) and an expansion of the definition of sexual assault to include "offender known" rape. After February 2004 when Secretary of Defense Donald Rumsfeld described sexual assault as "inappropriate behavior," Hansen said her group and others "raised the roof."[28] A year later, Undersecretary of Defense for Personnel Readiness Dr. David Chu finally made a public statement calling sexual assault a "crime in the armed forces."

Turning Pain into Power

The Miles Foundation has a sister organization known as Survivors in Service United (SISU); *sisu* is a Finnish term that Hansen says means courage, respect, and determination. The nearly 100 members throughout the United States have experienced one or more forms of violence, particularly domestic violence and sexual assault. They give individual assistance to victims in crisis as well as speaking out at public forums and conferences and in media interviews.

For these women, the Miles Foundation provides a vehicle for turning their personal pain into collective action. In 1999, more than 300 survivors worked with SISU and eighty other local, state, and national organizations to put together a briefing paper for Congress and the Clinton administration titled "Improving the U.S. Armed Forces' Response to Violence Against Women: Recommendations for Change." The proposals are being considered by a number of congressional and Defense Department task forces. One key recommendation is a guarantee of confidentiality. "There's been mandatory reporting for domestic violence and sexual assault," Hansen pointed out. Without reporting the incident, victims can't receive needed medical attention—yet many women fear repercussions if they speak out.

A big concern for Hansen and her colleagues is the alarming number of calls they receive about sexual assault from women serving in Afghanistan and Iraq—including a woman assaulted during a scud missile alert. Hansen's group has been working with members of Congress and bringing women to testify in person or in writing to address the problem. In 2005, the defense appropriations bill[29] mandated a number of steps, including clearly defining sexual assault, having services in place, enhancing victims advocate programs, and recommending changes to the Uniform Code of Military Justice. Says Hansen, "This is the first time Congress has mandated and given a date certain for this work to be done."

Hansen realizes her organization has a lot more work to do but feels "the dynamic has changed significantly, in large part because our forces are in harm's way. The fact that members of our armed forces in Afghanistan and Iraq—more than 380 as of August 2005—are being assaulted not by enemy forces but by members of their own unit, makes this what's called a 'force protection issue.' It's been more difficult to get the military to see that 'soldier down' protocol has to be applied. We're still working on that." Those protocols require prompt medical attention to casualties and injured military personnel, including evacuation to a safe environment and medical facilities. Often, Hansen told me, victims of sexual assault remain in the same unit as an alleged assailant. Rape trauma escalates with continued contact.

Holding on to Laughter

Focusing on those who've experienced violence can be painful work. To keep their sanity, Hansen described the "hoo hah" bulletin board they keep, where they place outrageous sayings or snippets of conversation with military personnel or civilian leadership in the military. ("Hoo hah" is the guttural noise marines make when they answer a question.) One of her favorite examples is a conversation she had with a general in Germany who resisted arranging transport to the United States for the wife of a soldier whose beatings four times sent her to a hospital. "This was before September 11," Hansen noted. "He told me, 'Ma'am, don't you understand there's a war going on here?' I took a deep breath and said, 'Actually there is a war going on there, in the home of your soldier; the declared enemy combatant is his wife and two children. You and I are going to change the dynamics of that front line.'

"We laugh at things that would make other people cry," Hansen told me. "We cry as well."

FINAL THOUGHTS: WHY YOU CAN'T SUPPORT WOMEN AND HATE GAYS

In trainings on sexual harassment, even those who learn to be circumspect when talking about women feel free to make jokes and comments against gays. I've struggled to find effective ways to address this. You can tell people some acceptable version of "shut up," but that doesn't teach them anything. Over the years I've found two things that have an impact. First, I remind people that it's nearly always true that someone in the room either is gay or has a loved one who is. That helps quiet most of them. But above all, I talk about how antigay sentiment is rooted in hatred of women. What's really objectionable about the image of gay men, after all, is that they're too much like women. And what's unforgivable about lesbians is that they don't need a man. I link the antigay stereotypes with gender stereotypes, reminding the group that being "like a girl" is the worst insult a coach can hurl at a male player. You'd be surprised how many variations on this I've heard—like the coach who put a tampon in someone's locker to show displeasure with his performance that day. What more striking symbol of femaleness could there be?

I also urge people to think about how rampant this bias is in our society and how it functions to keep people in line. Students use "fag" and "gay" for anyone who's not strictly adhering to the status quo. Even men who use those expressions can relate to that problem.

Students aren't the only target. Gay-bashing is a potent weapon against feminists.[30] Typically opponents try to discredit a feminist activist by hinting that she's not a "real woman," but rather someone who can't stand men (as if a lesbian is any more likely to love all females than she is to hate all males). This creates a dilemma for me. I know that talking about my husband and sons makes me more "palatable" to many audiences. I want them to hear me. But I don't want to play into their prejudices.

My older son Nat taught high school drama and faced a similar problem. When he was student teaching, he took on the gay-bashing so common in his classroom. The students, he realized, assumed he was gay. On the one hand, he wanted them to see that heterosexuals could also object to antigay comments. But if he did that, wouldn't he be saying, "Don't worry about me, I'm straight, I'm fine." The very act of preventing them from marginalizing his objections would reinforce their thinking that being gay was shameful. Nat decided the best way to deal with this was to talk about the dilemma itself. He linked homophobia to gender stereotypes and putdowns of women. Some of the kids paid attention.

I do the same thing with my college students. In her final paper, one woman told me she came from a family that was very conservative. "You've really opened my eyes," she said. "I still have trouble with homosexuality. But one thing you said really made me think, when you talked about gay men being hated because they were like women. How can I buy into that?"

One by one, we have to help people see you can't support equality for women without opposing attacks on gays.

6. NINE TO FIVE: NOT JUST A MOVIE—THE RIGHT TO ORGANIZE

"How would you like it if your mother-in-law slept between you and your wife every night? That's what it will be like for you if we let the union in. And the mother-in-law, the union steward, will be the laziest worker you have, the one with the biggest mouth."
—Martin Jay Levitt, former union-buster, quoting a typical speech to supervisors[1]

When I worked at the phone company in the early 1980s, I was a member of the Communications Workers of America (CWA). Here's what that meant: I got decent pay and health insurance. I didn't have to worry about being fired because my supervisor thought I didn't smile enough or wanted to replace me with someone's nephew. Here's what it didn't mean: that I could fail to show up or mouth off or do whatever I wanted and rely on my union to keep my job. In fact, when I was trained as a CWA union steward, the first thing they taught us was the importance of people abiding by the contract. "If you see someone drinking on the job or starting to be late all the time, step in and get them help," the union president warned us. "If they violate the contract, you won't be able to save them."

The Big Boys would have us believe that unions make it impossible to get rid of irresponsible or incompetent workers and that all they want is to take your money to support fat cat leaders. In reality, unionization brings enormous benefits to women. Nevertheless, only a small portion of the female workforce actually has a union card.

Myth: Unions Aren't for Ladies

In the early days of industrialization, mill owners in New England looked for a cheap supply of labor to run the new mechanical looms. They found it in young, unmarried women recruited from family farms. The "mill girls" were encouraged to see themselves as employed on a temporary basis only, until they could fulfill their true destiny of marriage and motherhood. Ladies interested in reform were urged to focus not on labor associations, but on the home front. A popular book of the time put it this way: "Let her not look away from her own little family circle for the means of producing moral and social reforms, but begin at home."[2] As for money, they were to rely on men to provide.

For some employers, this attitude hasn't changed much. In the spring of 2005, when nurses at Memorial Hospital of Burlington in Wisconsin argued for higher pensions, the head of the hospital told them: "If nurses want good pensions, they should marry well."[3]

Reality: Women Were Always Involved

Despite the advice, women have been demanding "raises, rights, and respect" since the beginning of paid female employment. In the 1820s, "mill girls" in Lowell, Massachusetts, participated in turnouts or work stoppages when the owners cut their paychecks.[4] Two decades later the Lowell Female Labor Reform Association (LFLRA) sprang up, unwilling to "see our sex made into living machines to do the bidding of the incorporated aristocrats."[5] Members weren't asking for the moon—they just wanted their workday to last ten hours instead of twelve. To reach their goal, they used the one political right women had, petitioning the state legislature. In the end, the mill workers had to settle for eleven hours but they also sparked the first investigation into workers' health and safety conditions. (The Big Boys have such charming language to justify their policies. You'll never hear someone say, "Yes, we believe we should have the right to get every drop of sweat out of our workers." Instead, they said limiting hours would interfere with the "freedom to contract"—as if workers had a role in negotiating anything that had to do with their jobs.)[6] And it wasn't just white northerners who stood up for themselves. As early as 1866, newly freed black laundresses in Jackson, Mississippi, organized a union and went on strike for higher wages.[7]

It's true that the first major surge of unions in the late nineteenth and early twentieth centuries developed mainly in the crafts or skilled trades, where few women worked. Typically these "brotherhoods" had little love for their sisters—they saw them as cheaper labor whose hiring would drive down wage levels. Indeed, often they excluded women outright, along with African Americans and many immigrant groups.[8] In 1886, the craft unions came together to form the American Federation of Labor. The group's first president, Samuel Gompers, worried that women employed outside the home "would bring forth weak children who are not educated to become strong and good citizens." By 1910 women accounted for only a fifth of the workforce. Some occupations where females dominated, such as domestic workers, labored under conditions that made organizing extremely difficult.

But that's only part of the story. Many women found themselves in mills or garment shops like the Triangle Shirtwaist Factory, hunched for long hours over looms or sewing machines in rooms that were dark and poorly ventilated, with exit doors literally locked to make sure the workers stayed at their posts. Unions took hold in this industry in the 1910s, and during that decade the number of women union members increased fivefold. Fierce attacks on unions in the 1920s and '30s led to a decrease in membership. But even during that period there were remarkable acts of courage from women. In 1933, for example, 900 African American pecan workers in St. Louis walked out of seven factories owned by the same man, demanding equal pay and treatment with white women workers. The owner tried to divide the women by offering the whites a raise if they'd go back to work. Instead, 1,500 black and white women marched to City Hall. They won all their demands.[9]

In the mid-1930s, the Congress of Industrial Organizations emerged and engaged in extensive drives among both skilled and unskilled workers, women as well as men. During the decades that followed—the very time when the women's movement has been described as being "asleep"—women workers were taking on unfair employers and energizing labor unions.

Look Who Wasn't Sleeping

Many people have heard of Mother Jones, the feisty organizer of coal miners who coined the phrases, "Pray for the dead and fight like hell for the living," and "Don't mourn, organize." But how about Myra Wolfgang? Luisa Moreno? Dollie Lowther Robinson? We don't learn in school or even in most women's studies courses that in 1937 Wolfgang, at the age of twenty-three, planted herself in the aisle at a Detroit Woolworth's to launch a sit-down strike of sales clerks and counter waitresses; she went on to become an international vice president of the Hotel Employees and Restaurant Employees Union (HERE). Luisa Moreno held an equivalent post in the Food, Tobacco and Agricultural Workers starting in 1941, after years spent organizing Mexican pecan shellers in Texas and cannery workers in Los Angeles. In 1937 Dollie Lowther Robinson earned six dollars a week for seventy-two hours of operating a mangle (a machine to press clothes) at the Colonial Laundry in Manhattan. The strike she led of the 300 mostly black women there helped bring tens of thousands of laundry workers into the Amalgamated Clothing Workers of America. Robinson later became education director of the union's Laundry Worker Division.[10]

Wolfgang, Moreno, and Robinson were just three among many women who risked arrest, beatings, and defamation to gain dignity and decent working conditions during the decades when the women's movement was supposedly dormant. During the 1930s, more women than men joined unions. Their number jumped to 3 million during the war, when "Rosie the Riveter" forged steel, built tanks, and performed other tasks left vacant by men fighting overseas. Yes, those Rosies were bumped aside when the men came marching home—but many of them, and other women as well, were hired on elsewhere, serving food, answering phones, selling and typing and cleaning and doing all the other jobs that by then were dominated by females. And they continued to join unions and participate in strikes (like the 1947 telephone walkout, when picketers carried signs saying "The Voice with a Smile Will Be Gone for Awhile").[11]

By 1956, the percentage of union members who were female was 18—double what it had been before the war. What had changed was not just that more women were employed, but also that unions paid more attention to the occupations where women worked.

Myth: Unions Only Want to Take Your Money

If women are attracted to unions, they shouldn't be, according to the Big Boys, who claim unions are "outside parties" that have only one purpose for existing: "The union can guarantee you nothing except that it will take money from you and perhaps take you out on strike."[12] Employers, usually with the help of expensive outside consultants, harp on what the unions will take away—dues money—and trade away—"whatever it takes to win costly little plums for themselves."[13] After all, the consultants claim, negotiating is just horse trading and inevitably requires giving something in return.[14]

Reality: The Union Advantage

So what did all these women see in unions? For starters, higher pay and benefits. The numbers speak for themselves:

- Pay: median weekly earnings are 28 percent higher than their non-union counterparts—and for women, that figure is 34 percent.
- Pensions: 73 percent of union workers have guaranteed pensions, compared to only 16 percent of nonunion workers.
- Health insurance: 92 percent of union workers have access to job-based health insurance—the figure is 68 percent for nonunion workers.

Paid sick days, paid vacations, supplemental income during unemployment—all of these are benefits much more common among union employees than the rest of the workforce. That's true across "collars"; today more than half of unionized women are in white-collar jobs.

Deidre May is a good example of someone whose life improved dramatically when she joined a union. I met May in 2001, when she became a leader in 9to5's Poverty Network Initiative in Milwaukee. She'd struggled to support herself and her five daughters in one low-paying job after another, often cleaning offices and hotel rooms. Then she became a member of the Hotel Employees and Restaurant Employees Union.

"Before," May told me, "I was at the mercy of working part-time jobs, temporary jobs which did not assure me any kind of benefits or guarantees."[15] She wanted a way to support herself and her family while attending a four-year college. Now the union calls her at least once a week, often more, to serve food at a convention or other big function at one of the downtown union facilities. May described working at a reception for those attending the GMO, a major golf tournament in the Milwaukee area. She was assigned to work in one of eleven tents, along with four other servers. The tent had 850 people; the five servers split the 13 percent gratuity on $21.95 per plate. "Each of us in the union jobs made $485 on top of $4.50 an hour. Management had temps working those jobs, also. They made $8 an hour flat. That was it."

In previous jobs, May felt "locked down to a certain amount. If you get a raise at all, it might be 20 cents or a quarter a year—that's not making a big difference. In the union, we get automatic raises."

The union also means "you're protected," May said. "If you're scheduled to work at a particular hotel and they cancel the function, you're guaranteed at least four hours of pay. If one of my daughters is sick, I can turn down a job without penalty." This was a huge contrast to the many times she had lost her job when her youngest daughter, who has diabetes, faced some emergency. May particularly likes the union grievance process. "If you're fired unfairly, you get retro pay plus you're back on the job and the supervisor is reprimanded." For May, the issue of dues is simple: "You pay union dues so you have someone to fight for you when your voice isn't loud enough."

Deidre May makes sure she uses her own voice as well. "Ever since I got involved with 9to5," she told me, "I've been aware that I have rights and I have a voice. When I first started working through the union, I heard management demanding that people do this and that. I'll stand in the middle of the room and tell them, 'Say Please and Thank You. You want to be treated with respect—so do we.' No one has ever pulled me aside."

Recently May was able to bring her oldest daughter, Gabrielle, into the union as well. Gabrielle had been working at a fast food restaurant making $7.50 an hour. "They'd tell her she has to go off the clock [working without having the hours count] because they didn't want to pay overtime," May said. "With my job, if you work nine hours, you get your regular pay plus overtime for that one day."

Changing Lives

Like Deidre May, Linda Chavez-Thompson, first woman to be executive vice president of the AFL-CIO, says the union movement changed not only her life but that of her family as well.[16] Growing up as the daughter of cotton sharecroppers in rural Texas, she'd never heard of labor unions. "For my family," said Chavez-Thompson, "good wages, and health insurance, and disability insurance, and pensions were as far from us as the moon and the stars. I worked for 30 cents an hour hoeing cotton when I was ten-years-old and by the time I was nineteen, my pay went up to a grand total of $1.50 an hour. I knew it was wrong. But I did not know a thing about unions."

The future labor leader's biggest dream as a child was to be a clerk at Sears, "so I could work inside all year round and get away from the hard physical labor on the farms." Eventually she did find an "inside" job, as a secretary for a laborers' construction union. "I saw what a union could do to get people out of poverty," she said, and soon helped her father get a construction job in the city of Lubbock and join the union. "All of a sudden, he was making more money in one week than he could make in an entire month on the cotton farm and he had health insurance and he was treated with dignity and respect on the job. His life and mine have never been the same."

More than a Paycheck
Unions don't just represent a bigger paycheck for women. "Good pay and benefits are not enough," says Chavez-Thompson. "Women are also concerned about working family issues such as sexual harassment, pay equity, paid family leave, and flexible work hours—and unions have taken the lead on those issues, too." She noted that flexibility bargained by the union is unique for two reasons: "Representatives of working women are actually at the table when they are shaped. And these benefits, once bargained into contracts, cannot be taken away on a whim."

Consider rights for pregnant women. These didn't begin in 1978 when the law required it—decades earlier, unions began demanding such rights and winning contract provisions ensuring them. Since pregnancy wasn't "developed by women for their entertainment," as one labor feminist put it, unions argued that it should be viewed as a "social function" and involuntary unemployment deserving of income support.[17] The American Federation of Labor (AFL) and the Congress of Industrial Organizations (CIO) supported federal legislation in the 1940s and '50s to broaden social insurance programs to include temporary disability benefits, including for maternity leave. Given the lack of progress at the national level, they also initiated various state measures to cover pregnancy under either unemployment or disability systems. The legislation didn't get very far, but labor leaders saw the need to fight for a *floor* of protection for everyone and then use collective bargaining to win bigger gains. Later on, unions brought a wave of lawsuits to end discrimination against pregnant women, and, after the disastrous Supreme Court decision on "pregnant people" in 1976 (see page 246, note 3), they spearheaded the successful campaign for the Pregnancy Discrimination Act.[18]

Not surprisingly, the Families and Work Institute in New York found that union representation is one of the strongest predictors of good work and family benefits.[19] Companies with 30 percent or more unionized workers were far more likely than nonunion companies to provide the following: paid time off to care for sick children (65 percent compared to 46 percent);

fully paid family health insurance (40 percent compared to 8 percent); temporary disability insurance (87 percent compared to 66 percent); and pensions (79 percent compared to 40 percent).

Childcare is another example of pioneering work by unions. That tax credit for childcare expenses on your income tax form (or your parents') originated with the CIO. Even though the 1954 legislation creating the credit allowed only a small amount to be deducted, it represented a huge step forward because it recognized that women are "breadwinners as well as bread makers," and gave legitimacy to the use of caregivers.[20] Unions also pioneered innovative childcare arrangements for their own members. Beulah Compton, a Seattle waitress and union leader whose husband abandoned her and their two daughters when she was only twenty-three, promised when she ran for union office in 1953 to provide childcare for afternoon and evening meetings. Not only did she follow through, she arranged for an older former waitress to be on call for emergency childcare.

We hear a lot today about childcare support from best practice companies. In fact, the Amalgamated Clothing and Textile Workers Union (ACTWU) established a network of childcare centers in the 1960s which made them the biggest private-sector provider of childcare at the time. Some of the most innovative work in this area has been done by the New York Union Childcare Coalition, which in the 1990s successfully lobbied the state legislature to add hundreds of millions of dollars for childcare to the state budget.

Fair Treatment

Some unions have little to brag about on the issue of gender, having pigeonholed women into lower-paying jobs and resisted efforts to change the pay structure. But women who made advances against pay inequity usually did so because of their union. In 2003 in the nation's capital, for instance, female custodians in the House and Senate fought and won an Equal Pay Act case; even though their work was the same as or similar to that of male custodians, the women earned a dollar an hour less. Delegate Eleanor Holmes Norton noted that the women would have "faced an almost impossible task using the rules for bringing and sustaining an EPA class action" had they not had representation from the American Federation of State, County and Municipal Employees (AFSCME).[21] Back in 1945, labor groups joined with women's organizations to introduce the first federal equal pay law. The following year, 200,000 women were among

United Electrical strikers who helped shut down seventy-eight plants across the country; equal pay was a key demand. Unions also spearheaded the lawsuits that laid the groundwork for revaluing women's jobs in a number of states (see Chapter 2).

For many women, the union signified the only way to escape sexual intimidation from unscrupulous foremen. A female worker at Midland Steel gave this explanation for why she joined the United Auto Workers (UAW): "When you belong to a union, the foreman can't screw you. Last month my foreman asked me to go out with him, and I told him 'to hell with you, Charlie. I know what you want.' He got mad but he didn't try to spite me. He knew damn well the union would be on his neck if he did."[22]

While homophobia remains a huge problem within the labor movement as in society at large, some unions have led the way in fighting antigay bias. An early victory came in 1975, when the Graduate Employee Organization (GEO), Local 3550 of American Federation of Teachers at the University of Michigan, won protection against discrimination based on sexual orientation. They encountered significant bias. "One conservative regent said, 'If we do this, there'll be naked men running after sheep in the hallway,'" explained Andre Williams, a current union activist.[23] "But the union knew how to run picket lines." After narrowly making it onto the strike platform, this provision was one of the first settled. Thirty years later, the GEO led the way for rights of gender identity and gender expression, winning contract language after a one-day walkout. As a result of the union's activity, the University of Michigan is moving to make all its health care inclusive for transgendered and transsexual individuals.

Myth: Unions Are Outmoded Because of Growth in Professional Jobs

Antiunion spokespeople maintain that unions have outgrown their purpose. The growth of professional jobs renders unions a thing of the past, they argue, a holdover of a working-class United States that has simply disappeared. For skilled workers such as nurses, librarians, or supervisors to join a union would be "unprofessional."

Reality: Low-Wage Jobs Are Growing the Fastest

There are two big problems with this argument. First of all, the Bureau of Labor Statistics says seven of the ten occupations with the greatest projected growth through 2012 will be in what are now low-wage, service jobs:

retail sales, customer service representative, food service worker, cashier, janitor, wait staff, nursing aide, and hospital orderly. Many of these jobs pay less than $18,000 a year.

And let's not forget that employees in professional jobs have a lot to gain from unionization as well. Consider the example of Karen Springborn Emerson, trained as a nurse in the 1960s at the Milwaukee County School of Nursing. "We got one week break a year," she told me, "and demerits for having goldfish that died in the dorm."[24] Fifteen years later, she was working the 5 to 11:30 shift at St. Francis Hospital when the nuns sold the enterprise to a business group. The new owners began to reorganize in ways that Emerson and her colleagues saw as bad for patients and bad for workers.

"I said, we need a contract," Emerson recalled, "something stable to build on. We need a union." The administration's response? "Whenever we complained about wages, when they eliminated housekeeping and had us clean floors and stock shelves—things that took us away from our patients—they threw 'professionalism' in our faces. Later when I met with people at the Labor Council, steelworkers, pipe fitters, I realized they were all professional and skilled, they knew how to do their job. To [the hospital administration,] professionalism meant 'shut up and behave.'"

It took six years, but the nurses eventually won a contract with the Wisconsin Federation of Nurses and Health Care Professionals. "The union means we have control," Emerson said. "In the contract, we have safety language, language about nursing duties versus non-nursing duties. We can concentrate on our patients. We nailed down standards. They can screw up our health benefits, but those key issues cannot be revoked."

Now a widow with four children, Emerson was eager to share her story after coming home from a twelve-hour night shift. "I'd rather pay my union dues than pay my electric bill," she told me. And then she related a conversation with her brother, a dentist who is staunchly antiunion. "I asked him, 'What do you think the American Dental Association is? You pay dues. You set standards. That's what we do.' He was speechless."

Myth: Companies Like Wal-Mart Can't Unionize and Still Offer Low Prices

One priority area for the labor movement is organizing Wal-Mart and stopping the "Walmartization of America" that forces other employers to drive down wages and benefits. Opponents of unionization argue that Wal-Mart wages are competitive. Besides, pay the workers more and you'll destroy the low prices consumers love. Wal-Mart itself ran a two-page ad in the *New York Review of Books* in April 2005 insisting higher wages would mean raising prices and that would "betray our commitment to tens of millions of customers, many of whom struggle to make ends meet."

Reality: Try Costco

Unfortunately for Wal-Mart, there's another big box discount store that offers low prices while paying a decent wage and being open to unions. Costco workers earn an average of $17 an hour, 42 percent more than the average wage at Wal-Mart's Sam's Club; more than four in five workers at Costco are covered by health insurance, compared with less than half at Wal-Mart.[25] How can Costco do it? The big savings come in turnover costs—a mere 6 percent a year at Costco, compared to 21 percent at Sam's Club. (It also helps that Costco's CEO has a salary of $350,000 a year, much less than the nearly $23 million taken home by Wal-Mart CEO Lee Scott in 2004.)[26] Lest you think Costco is a do-gooder employer who doesn't care about the bottom line, profits per employee there amount to $13,647—Sam's Club figure is $11,039.[27]

Who pays for Wal-Mart's low wages? We do. The company's pay scales have forced tens of thousands of its workers onto food stamps and Medicaid at a cost to taxpayers of billions of dollars. Walmartwatch.com estimates U.S. taxpayers pay $1.5 billion subsidizing Wal-Mart Medicaid costs alone—that's 15 percent of Wal-Mart's $10 billion in profits last year.

Speaking of which, did you know that five out of the ten richest people in the United States are members of the Wal-Mart–owning Walton family? This rarely gets raised when the Big Boys proclaim low wages are necessary for low prices. How about lowering the profits?

Myth: Union Membership Down Because Unions Are No Longer Relevant

No one can dispute that overall numbers for union members have plummeted, even as the percentage of union members who are female continues to climb.[28] In 2004, only 12.5 percent of working Americans were union members—13.5 percent of male workers, 11.3 percent of female—down from more than a third of all workers fifty years ago. According to the antiunion Web site, Union Free America, "This is just one more indication that the working people of America are rejecting unionism."[29] Unions, the argument goes, simply aren't relevant for most workers' lives.

Reality: The Numbers Are Down Because of Downsizing and Union-Busting

Claiming that unions are irrelevant for women implies that corporations are women friendly. If by chance you started with this chapter and need a reality check, please see Chapters 2, 3, 4, 5, 7, and 8. Still, if the union advantage is so great, it's fair to ask why so few workers are organized.

Here's why: because downsizing and offshoring have wiped out millions of jobs, especially in manufacturing industries. And because the law is so weak and employers as a group have so fiercely opposed organizing.

The National Labor Relations Act (NLRA) established the right of employees to organize in order to negotiate collectively with their employer over wages, benefits, and working conditions. Among other provisions, it outlawed a number of tactics used to break unions—including spying on and intimidating workers. But, as former union-buster Martin Levitt revealed, the Big Boys simply turned to a new group of experts in "union avoidance" to find "more subtle techniques" for the ones that were prohibited.[30] Besides, the law never included serious penalties. In effect, it tells employers, "You'd better not interfere with an organizing drive—and if you do, we'll be really disappointed in you."

Kate Bronfenbrenner, director of labor education research at Cornell University, found that employers illegally fire union supporters in 31 percent of organizing campaigns.[31] That translates to 20,000 workers illegally fired or disciplined every year. Penalties are so meaningless employers have little to fear from violating this or other parts of the NLRA. As one consultant told his audience, "You got to remember you only lose once. What happens if you violate the law? The probability is you will never get caught. If you do get caught, the worst thing that can happen to you is you get a second election and the employer wins 96 percent of second elections. So the odds are with you."[32]

Employers can force workers to attend closed-door meetings to hear antiunion propaganda—and 92 percent of private sector employers do so when faced with a union drive.[33] Nearly four out of five also require—force might be a better word—supervisors to deliver antiunion messages in one-on-one meetings with workers. Rather than spending money paying a decent wage, employers dish out enormous amounts to outside consultants to wage antiunion campaigns. Martin Levitt points out that union organizers are able to talk to workers only after they've heard "eight hours' worth of the other side, sometimes accompanied by threats, sometimes by tears."[34]

I remember handling a call from a woman who worked at an answering service. Someone had mentioned the idea of a union; no one had approached a particular local or talked to a union organizer. Yet the owner got wind of it and told the women he'd shut the place down before he'd let them unionize. Sounds illegal, right? It is, but apparently more than half of private sector employers—seven out of ten in manufacturing—make similar threats. Not surprising considering that the law provides for no fines or other monetary penalty for employers who violate this provision.

For decades after passage of the NLRA, it wasn't uncommon for employers to recognize the union if a majority of workers signed cards authorizing that union to represent them in collective bargaining. Employers may still decide to do this—but today most will not. Even if every single worker signs an authorization card, employers can demand an election, giving management time to utilize the intimidation methods described above. As the executive director of Human Rights Watch put it, "Legal obstacles tilt the playing field so steeply against freedom of association that the United States is in violation of international human rights standards for workers."[35]

Squashing Democracy

Say you make it through all these hoops and win your union election. Nearly half the time, employers manage to avoid negotiating a contract. Levitt describes how he spent twelve months stalling and obstructing contract talks at a nursing home in Sebring, Ohio, known as Copeland Oaks. "The law imposes on management and a newly elected union a 'duty to bargain' for twelve months, and no more," he wrote. "I figured I could jerk off the union for a year, no problem."[36]

An Oregon professor's detailed comparison of labor law and the standards of democratic elections in the United States reveals how shockingly unfair the situation is: "The unequal access to voter lists; the absence of financial controls; monopoly control of both media and campaigning within the workplace; the use of economic power to force participation in political meetings; the tolerance of thinly disguised threats; the location of voting booths on partisan grounds; open-ended delays in implementing the results of an election; and the absence of meaningful enforcement measures—every one of these constitutes a profound departure from the norms that have governed U.S. democracy since its inception."[37]

Some obstacles are also created by certain unions or union organizers—

preying on female members or potential members, ignoring women's specific work or life circumstances, blocking the way or failing to make room for women in leadership. And unions, like every other institution in our society, have had their share of outright corruption. We need changes within the labor movement, but above all we need to strengthen labor law.

FEMINIST SOLUTIONS

We can't attain the democratic standards our country says it stands for unless we remove the multiple barriers for workers who want to organize. That means employers who violate the National Labor Relations Act need to know there'll be hell to pay. Some measures that would help are laid out in the Employee Free Choice Act, a bipartisan bill cosponsored by Sens. Edward Kennedy (D-MA) and Arlen Specter (R-PA) and Reps. George Miller (D-CA) and Peter King (R-NY). These include:

- Letting workers decide without employer interference, by requiring employers to honor what's known as "card check." This allows certification of a union as the bargaining representative once a majority of employees in an appropriate unit have signed authorization cards. Some state and local governments have voluntarily instituted card check provisions for their employees; all employers should be required to do so. Until that time, we should work to have government bodies adopt neutrality or "labor peace" resolutions, ensuring that public contractors will not interfere in organizing campaigns; in exchange, unions often agree not to call strikes that might disrupt needed services.

- Removing barriers to a first contract, by having a mediation and arbitration process. If the union and employer aren't able to reach agreement after 90 days, either party should be able to take the dispute to the Federal Mediation and Conciliation Services (FMCS). If the FMCS isn't able to bring the two sides to agreement after 30 days, the dispute would go to mandatory arbitration.

- Imposing stiffer penalties for employers who violate the law, including triple back pay for employees who are fired or discriminated against during an organizing campaign or a drive for a first contract. Employers who willfully or repeatedly violate employees' rights in such campaigns should also face a civil fine of up to $20,000 for each violation. Civil rights violations allow for punitive damages—these should as well. Temporary restraining orders should be placed on an employer found to be violating the law during a campaign.

Making Unions More Women Friendly

It's no mystery what would make unions more women friendly. Female union members have already pointed out the changes they need, and some unions have implemented one or more, although few offer the full range of supports:[38]

- Change practices: Schedule meetings at convenient times and places; keep them short and to the point. Bargain for paid release time for union activities, so activists can still have lives outside of work and union activities. Offer reimbursement for expenses (such as phone calls and travel costs). Provide childcare activities that are fun and meaningful for kids.

- Change focus: Target the kind of workplaces where women are concentrated. Take up issues women care about, such as flexibility for family care, equal pay, and an end to sexual harassment and other degrading treatment.

- Change hiring and promotion training: Go beyond lip service by offering mentoring and training opportunities to increase women's participation in better paying jobs and leadership roles. Go out of the way to find qualified women organizers. Set goals and timetables for making the union staff and leadership bodies resemble the diversity of union members.

- Change culture: Rather than trying to get female activists and organizers to adapt to the existing culture and be "more like the guys," look for ways to change the culture to be more welcoming to women and any other group that has been underrepresented among union leadership. Culture means "attitudes, behaviors, practices, events, rituals and customs."[39] Meeting in a bar because that's where you've always met sends a message about how women and their kids are valued. Include separate space for women (and other groups which have been underrepresented)—caucuses or committees, places people can feel safe to raise concerns, give each other support, exchange strategies. Be sure these structures have full sanction from the union and are a way to bring women's issues into the mainstream of the organization, rather than pushing them off to the margins.[40] Strong prohibitions against sexual harassment or exploitation have to be accompanied with meaningful training and real consequences for anyone who violates the rules.

Transforming union culture is the most important and the most difficult change. For a long time, unions and many nonprofits relied on staff to work grueling schedules to get the job done. Here's the good news: What women need unions to do is exactly what unions need in order to survive. Having a structure that is less top-down and more democratic, that really listens to and energizes the members and makes it possible for them to be involved, is the key to building a powerful movement.

Just as in the workplace, the changes we want aren't a favor to women—they're a better way to run things.

Making Unions More Worker Friendly

We also need every union to champion the public policies this book lays out—to be leaders in the fight against sexism, racism, homophobia, and any form of oppression. Back in the 1940s, Revels Clayton, an African American leader of the Marine Cooks and Stewards Union, laid out the links: "If you let them red bait, they'll race bait. If you let them race bait, they'll queen [gay] bait. These are connected—that's why we have to stick together."[41]

Making the labor movement worker friendly requires an insistence on ethical practices and a fair salary structure for all staff. Unions should model the policies they fight for in the workplace—including family leave policies for women and men, and benefit packages that cover domestic partners in everything from health care to pensions. And they should leverage pension funds to demand change in how employers treat workers and the environment, rather than to build personal fortunes for select leaders.

Above all, the labor movement needs to develop what one activist calls a "compelling vision," a vivid picture of what we're fighting for and how to get there.[42] Rather than competing in turf fights, unions need to band together to organize Wal-Mart and other low-wage employers. Less talk of "buy American" and more focus on genuine internationalism will help stop the pillaging of Third World countries by multinational corporations and at the same time halt the treatment of U.S. workers as disposable commodities. That means collaborating with unions in other countries for joint organizing campaigns.

TAKING ON THE BIG BOYS

Some Big Boys have accepted unions as a way of life, and in a number of cases, union-management collaboration has led to exciting breakthroughs.[43] Unfortunately, employers who boast of making unions "partners" usually limit the union's role to choosing among limited options—how many to lay off and when, which benefits to cut and how. Profits, executive salaries and perks remain off-limits in these conversations. And for most Big Boys, unions are a thorn in the side to be prevented at all costs. *Catastrophizing* and *demonizing* are the dominant themes, interspersed with *patronizing* efforts to separate women from each other and from their male coworkers.

9to5's History with Unionizing

Early on, the founders of 9to5 in Boston decided to experiment with a sister organization that would be part of the union movement. Too often members would organize, research issues, get petitions signed by coworkers, meet with the boss, and he'd say "I'll get back to you"—and do nothing. Or, management would make an accommodation for one worker but refuse to change policies in general. "We said, 'There ought to be a law that forces them to talk with us instead of just ignoring us,'" explained 9to5's cofounder, Karen Nussbaum. "Then we found out there was a law—the National Labor Relations Act." Collective bargaining meant workers could have an ongoing voice in what happened on the job; a contract was much stronger than a vague assurance.

Nussbaum and her colleagues "didn't quite trust that the unions out there would be a place where our members' needs would be met and their leadership recognized. So we decided we needed to create our own union." In 1975, they launched Local 925 in Boston in partnership with the Service Employees International Union (SEIU). Five years later, the initiative expanded nationwide. SEIU agreed to honor 9to5's organizing vision while offering financial resources and support. For the next twenty years, District 925 operated as a national local within SEIU, organizing in a number of cities and maintaining offices in Boston, Cleveland, Cincinnati, and Seattle.[44]

When I first joined 9to5 in 1982, some thought that District 925 the union would replace 9to5 the association altogether. That never happened. Many clericals weren't in a position to join a union. Maintaining the association allowed women to be activists wherever they happened to live or work. We wanted women to know about the importance of unionization. But we also believed in the importance of collective action in general—especially in order to change public policy, which would help millions, and to identify effective business practices. Having a working women's organization helped us influence the labor movement while developing a bridge between labor and women's groups. And it was an effective way to provide leadership skills for both nonunion and union women. So 9to5 and District 925 developed side by side. The two groups worked together on several initiatives and always felt a strong bond, but they were separate entities, each with its own board, finances, strategic plans, and methods of organizing.

The Big Boys didn't see it that way.

"Union-Free" Consultants Hold a Seminar on 9to5

I'd had a small taste of antiunion campaigns when I lived in Baltimore and a group of us at the hospital tried to organize. But I hadn't expected to run into this at 9to5. First of all, we weren't a union and didn't engage in collective bargaining. At the time, our sister organization, District 925, had opened an office in Chicago but had none in Milwaukee and no plans to expand there. Imagine my surprise when I opened the mail one November day in 1982 and found a flyer titled, "9to5—More than Just a Movie: How to Keep 9to5 Out of Your Office," sponsored by a "union-free consulting firm" called Management Resources Associates (MRA). MRA had forgotten who opens the mail. Some secretary simply sent it on to us.

At the time, our chapter was only a few months old. We had two or three dozen members, no money, no staff (I volunteered one day a week). An environmental group, Citizens Utility Board (CUB), let us use their office. Our total assets consisted of a telephone and an answering machine. Why did MRA consider us a danger? Because a *Milwaukee Journal* reporter had written a feature about our group, albeit in the "women's pages," complete with a giant photograph of Dolly Parton telling off her boss.[45]

We wanted to picket the seminar, but they were holding it at a hotel in the boonies on a workday morning. Instead, we decided to pay the $50 fee for me to attend. I had a feeling the hosts might recognize my name, even though I hadn't been identified in the news article (I was working as a temp and feared being fired if my involvement were known). So I signed up as "Leslie Miller" (my middle name and Larry's last name) and listed my occupation as "consultant." If I managed to get in and no one heard from me within half of an hour of start time, other leaders would call a press conference for that afternoon.

Since the *Milwaukee Journal* at the time was an afternoon paper, I decided to give a scoop to Lois Blinkhorn, the reporter who'd written about 9to5. We ran into our first snag: Blinkhorn's editor wanted her to get a quote from the MRA. That would tip them off, I warned—they'd close the seminar to the public and to the media. And that's exactly what happened. Blinkhorn was turned away, but because I'd prepaid, I got in. MRA staff in the registration area eyed me suspiciously—I think they feared I was a competitor who would try to lure potential clients. Indeed, I was busy scanning name tags, which listed company as well as name; I recognized most of the large corporations in Milwaukee.

As sixty-some people settled around tables in the meeting room, the MRA executive told us about the call from Lois Blinkhorn. "We've been holding these union-free seminars for years and the media has never written about them," he proclaimed. What better proof of the power of 9to5 and the importance of this session (and presumably of hiring *his* firm to stave off the danger)! That was the first of many moments where I had to resist the urge to guffaw or stand up and respond. An outburst would feel great but it would also get me thrown out, and I was on a mission to learn exactly what these guys had to say. I grasped my pen and stuck to writing down every word I heard.

Sherlock Holmes Uncovers Our "Secret"

The first speaker was a lawyer who proceeded to "unmask" 9to5 as a union front. Exhibit A, displayed via transparency: our chapter letterhead. Exhibit B: the letterhead of District 925 (they were virtually the same). I didn't know whether to be amused or insulted—why would groups hiding their relationship adopt such similar names! Never mind that Lois Blinkhorn's article about the organization—and all our literature—contained a detailed paragraph on the association with District 925. The speaker then launched into a warning about the seriousness of this unionization threat. "I've been predicting for decades that clericals would organize," he said, "and I've been wrong each time. Not this time." What made 9to5 so dangerous, he explained, was that it combined the "militancy" of the labor movement with the personal approach of the women's movement. I sat up a little straighter in my plush meeting chair.

Next the MRA executive launched into a scenario to describe how

9to5 wormed its way into a business. "First they find out some dirt on you—and that's pretty easy," he said, alluding to a number of current corporate scandals. 9to5 would train employees to make demands on the boss, hoping he wouldn't respond. When, inevitably, the employer proved to be unresponsive, 9to5 would show up "and start handing out union cards." Once again, I had to bite my tongue.

The speaker then pulled out all the myths about how unions prevent employers from getting rid of workers, however lazy or unfit. I was eager to share my training as a union steward, but that would have to wait for our press conference.

As I suspected, MRA had sent someone to one of our meetings—the speaker quoted me twice—but the gathering he described was somebody's fantasy. Those attending, he insisted, were not allowed to state their full name nor the name of their employer. They'd have to stick with something like "My name is Sue and I work at a bank." (We'd only had a few meetings, but we always started by going around and saying our full names and where we worked.) "However," he noted, "if you stick around for the coffee klatsch at the end of the meeting, you can find out if anyone from your company is there."

A hand shot up from another table. "If they're really a union," the attendee asked, "isn't it illegal to send spies to their meetings?" The MRA leader was prepared: "For this purpose, they're not a union, so it's not a problem."

No Comment

My favorite part of the seminar was the advice to participants about what to do if 9to5 got some dirt on their employer. "No matter what it is," the MRA spokesman said, "just say 'No comment.' Anything you offer in your defense will just make you look worse."

The edition of the *Milwaukee Journal* with Lois Blinkhorn's piece on the seminar, announcing that I was in attendance, hit the street before the session ended.[46] All the major media outlets sent representatives to our press conference, back in the much-less-fancy conference room of CUB's office building. I summed up what I'd heard and offered simple counteradvice: "Rather than worrying about keeping 9to5 out of your office, focus on cleaning it up."

The reporters asked a variety of questions. One said he would be contacting MRA—did I have any idea what they would say? "I just paid

$50 to find out," I told them. "They'll tell you, 'No comment.'" And so they did.

Standing Up

One of my favorite stories about taking on the Big Boys was an action that lasted only a few minutes but had an enormous impact. It was led by Harriette Ternipsede, a woman who joined 9to5 in 1990 when she heard about the organization's campaign against electronic surveillance. As a reservation agent at TWA in Chicago, Ternipsede and her coworkers were essentially tethered to their desks, having to punch in one code each time they logged on to their computer and a second when they plugged in their headsets. The late 1980s and early 1990s were the beginning of "this call may be monitored for quality purposes." Agents were expected to follow a script to the letter, and managers began to listen in.

"They monitored us to see if we used their phrases," Ternipsede said, "and also to see if we were using the most efficient methods of typing in information. The problem was, they kept changing the software." The workers couldn't keep up. Detailed logs charted how many callers each person spoke with and for how long. "They even kept track of how many minutes you spent in the bathroom," Ternipsede told me.[47] "Any time not on the phone was called 'unmanned time.' We would get call after call with no breathing space. Every second was money to the company. If they lost too much time, you'd get a reprimand." To the workers' amazement, managers even listened in to workers' conversation *between* calls. Ternipsede called that "a big point in our fight to get a union."

Ternipsede and her coworkers had joined the International Association of Machinists and Aerospace Workers, but had yet to see a contract. "Everyone was really down in the dumps, really fatigued," said Ternipsede, a rail-thin woman who started working at TWA back in 1960. "They were sucking the blood out of us." During this time, she spoke to a number of reporters covering 9to5's campaign against such intrusive monitoring. One day after she described her work setup, a reporter asked Ternipsede whether the workers ever got to stand up. "I realized that we never did, not in either sense of the word," she said. She'd organized a support group of about twenty women clerks. A few days after this conversation, they decided to hold a stand-up. Here's Harriette Ternipsede's description:

> Since we were not allowed to leave our desk, we devised a situation

where at a given hour many of us would stand up at our desk. We never stopped working—our headsets were on, we were plugged in, each of us held a keyboard in one arm and typed on it with the other. We just stood for a few minutes, but that drove management wild. They told us we couldn't stand up anymore. The action gave us unity and a good feeling. We could hold up our heads. It sounds like a very small thing, but our working conditions were pretty dismal. We had to react. Despite what they said, we did the stand-up several times. They never knew when we'd stand up again, and what that would mean the next time.

The women did win a contract and some improvements in their working conditions. Because the women had stood up, "management had to sit down with me," Ternipsede said—she'd been elected chairperson representing some 650 workers. "Because we had union representation they had no choice but to cut back on the more odious things they did."

"These Are Our Phones"

For the Big Boys, monitoring workers was never about efficiency or quality—it was about control. I once debated the issue with the head of the U.S. Chamber of Commerce and a representative of the airline industry on the Chamber's cable TV station.[48] First they claimed monitoring was really an issue of "fairness" for workers, a way to "remove arbitrariness from supervision." That's a good goal, I argued, but urged them to do a better job of hiring and training managers, rather than spying on the workers. "Spying is what we do to the enemy," I said.

And then came one of those rare moments where the Big Boys simply tell the truth. The Chamber leader leaned over and said something to this effect: "Ms. Bravo, has it ever occurred to you that these are our phones and our companies and we can do whatever we want?" Exactly, I responded—which is why workers need their own voice at work.

Ternipsede and her coworkers inspired me to write a novel (as yet unpublished) called *Standing Up*. It's about four friends who work at an airline call center in Milwaukee and give each other support to change their lives at home and at work. My fantasy is that the book gets published and then pockets of women in cities all across the United States begin having stand-ups and winning changes at work. We'll read about them in the paper: "Today in Pocatello, Idaho, eight support staff at a trucking company held a stand-up for one minute to protest the lack of sick pay. The owner had no comment."

AN INVISIBLE WORKFORCE MAKES ITSELF KNOWN: DISTRICT 925 IN CINCINNATI

Organizing clerical workers means working among women who may have little experience with unions or activism. This was certainly the case when District 925 organized at the University of Cincinnati in 1988. Debbie Schneider was the president of the Cincinnati local and later directed the national organization.

"The University didn't run a nasty, brutal, private sector antiunion campaign," Schneider told me.[49] "They didn't fire people or even try to buy them off." Instead, special consultants designed a "constant pounding of letters" to workers warning of dues, strikes, corruption, and loss of flexibility. "You'll lose your autonomy, your ability to be an individual, the relationships you have," the letters said. "You could get time clocked." The administration tried to exclude many clericals on the grounds that they were all "confidential" employees. In non-academic departments like the hospital and medical center, "they would make pitches that unionizing isn't professional," said Schneider. "They didn't try that on the academic side because the faculty had a union."

According to Schneider, the workers "weren't persuaded by any of the arguments, but they were intimidated. They got the message that this, the biggest employer in the city, didn't want a union. The university would get its way. All they have to do is say, 'This isn't our way' to scare a certain number off." The union lost the first election by twenty-nine votes.

Two years later District 925 tried again and this time they won, having created a manual for workers exposing management strategy and how to respond to it. As usual, the union then had to fight for each contract. According to Schneider, the administration would say, "There is no more money. The only way to give you more money is to take it from students." They combined this declaration with demonizing and hardball tactics. The main reasons clericals stayed on their jobs despite low pay was a generous sick leave policy, free tuition for their kids, and good health benefits. In each of the first three contracts, management threatened to take these benefits away.

The tactic backfired. "People who were generally mild-mannered became furious when they tried to take their family benefits," Schneider said. "Management thought they would make people regret having a union. Instead, they made people think, 'This is meanest employer in the world, we're so glad we have a union.'" Many people who hadn't joined before signed up. The workers' slogan was "Whatever It Takes," captured on buttons that read WIT.

During the first contract, District 925 held small strikes lasting one hour or one day. "We wanted to show people you could go on strike and come back to work and still have a good relationship with students or patients, coworkers," Schneider said. For the second contract in 1992, they first tried a number of tactics, including rallies with community people, prayer vigils, and what Schneider calls "guerrilla faxing. We'd tape page upon page in a big banner, write in marker, 'Must we strike?' and fax it to the board or the lawyer's office. It tied up the fax." The workers also did actions around health and safety issues, including a "wall of pain" and a number of petitions. And they conducted a ballot vote on whether workers wanted to keep sick days. Workers had to cast the ballots in person at the union office, and were urged to write on the back what ailments they'd use sick days for.

"There were lines and lines in hallways," Schneider said. "They got to see each other and others got to see them en masse." When the university refused to pay the union's team for the time spent in bargaining, as they did for other unions, people made continuous phone calls saying, "Let our people go."

Getting Heard

Finally the union decided to hold a three-day strike. They began pulling people out of their offices in the administration building at 11:00 A.M. in the morning, starting with the eighth floor. That group would go down to get their colleagues on the next floor and so on, until they were a large and raucous group. "People were really pissed at the administration," Schneider said. "We wanted them to have an outlet for that and to feel the numbers." Because the campus had so many entrances, having small groups trying to block entrances couldn't keep people out of campus. "It was not our goal to keep people from going to classes," Schneider explained. "Our point was to show strong defiance of these concessions." Two auditoriums at opposite ends of campus each filled with 400 workers.

The administration had said they were short of funds and that's why they had to take the benefits away. So the union leaders said, "Let's see if we can find the money." They took people to buildings where lavish expenditures had been made. "Workers were marching through those buildings with whistles and noisemakers, with the press in tow," Schneider said. "Afterwards people said, 'I can't believe I did it.' For a workforce that's always invisible, it was very powerful to make a big scene."

Later, the two large groups came together for a rally. Schneider said the university leadership was furious. "They had cops videotaping every single thing. The women had on their nice work outfits with sneakers. The university couldn't believe they'd cause such disruption." Administration lawyers went to court to prevent large gatherings. The union had anticipated this and changed tactics the next day to groups of twenty-five, then groups of four stopping delivery trucks.

"We won [the contract fight] all three times," said Schneider. "Other unions did take concessions; we never did." Best of all, women who had no activist background found themselves making speeches, creating chants, giving press interviews, engaging with students, and speaking at congregations and community organizations.

"Lots of people surprised themselves," Schneider said.

FINAL THOUGHTS

Most of the time, the Big Boys make the rules, and they change them when it's convenient. We desperately need some checks and balances—and that's precisely what good unions provide. Women in unions gain higher compensation and greater security. But perhaps above all, they gain an ongoing say in how their work is valued and how they are treated on the job. Women need unions—and the union movement needs women involved at every level in order to revitalize and reform itself.

7. WORKING OTHER THAN NINE TO FIVE: PART-TIME AND TEMPORARY JOBS

Memo #1: Employees in this company may now choose to work part time.
Memo #2: Employees who choose to work part time will no longer be
eligible for certain benefits, including health insurance, vision coverage,
dental coverage, and life insurance.[1]

In the early days of Milwaukee 9to5, I worked as a word processor for a large engineering firm. My assignments were exactly the same as the rest of the staff. So were my hours. My skills were among the highest in the office. Yet the other word processors—including someone hired after me—were paid at least twice as much as I was. My employer was not violating any law.

The other women were permanent employees; I was a temp.

I was hardly alone in this predicament. Paying less to part-time and temporary workers is one of three legal forms of discrimination remaining in the United States labor market.[2] Not only is such discrimination permitted, the Big Boys encourage it. And if the majority of people affected happen to be female, well, so be it. After all, they *choose* to work these jobs—and look at all the flexibility they gain.

Or so say the Big Boys.

Myth: Temporary Employment Brings Women Variety, Flexibility, and Good Pay

According to the American Staffing Association (ASA), the trade association for temporary agencies, temp jobs can be a great opportunity for working women. They provide variety and flexibility for someone who "[doesn't] have time for the routine 9-to-5 workday" and wants to "choose where and when she works." Training seminars can sharpen skills and "contribute to career development." For those seeking permanent employment, temporary assignments give an opportunity to check out different companies and select just the right match, or to "prove [yourself] as an invaluable employee."[3] As for pay, some temporary workers earn more than their permanent counterparts. ASA boasts that "most staffing companies offer health insurance as well as vacation and holiday pay, and many offer retirement plans. Virtually any temporary or contract employee who wants benefits can find a staffing firm that offers them."[4]

Reality: Temp Jobs Are Often Unequal

I know from my own experience that temp jobs can come in handy, tiding you over while you take care of a family member or, in my case, solicit grants and donations for a nonprofit job. If a position is temporarily vacant because of an employee's new baby or surgery or sabbatical, a temp might be the perfect fill-in. I've had friends who used temping to try out an employer, and at 9to5 I hired people on a temporary basis to try them out as well.

In short, temporary jobs can be terrific—provided they're equitable and voluntary. The problem is, often they're neither. I certainly didn't appreciate earning so much less than my coworkers in that engineering firm. Say "flexibility" or "permanent job" to many temps and they'll either laugh or scream. When I met Jennifer, for example, she'd worked more than two years as a temp for the New York phone company known as Nynex. Because she wasn't a "regular" employee, Jennifer was eligible for none of the company's widely hailed family friendly policies. She had no vacation, no sick time, no holidays—and a daughter with a chronic health condition. Ramona became proficient as a file clerk in a Milwaukee hospital during the eleven months she worked there as a temp. The day the job was posted as a permanent position, she applied—only to be told she wasn't eligible because the company wanted to hire "from within." Peggie temped for more than ten years because she couldn't find permanent employment. During that time she worked stints of three years each at IBM and Coca-Cola. Her annual income was less than $12,000 and she had no benefits. In order to pay medical and dental bills, Peggie went without a car for two years. "Even though I'm always working," she told me, "I live in poverty."

Then there were the women in the Wisconsin Works or W-2 program who were routed to temporary agencies in order to get them off the welfare rolls. Equonne's story is typical. I remember how straight she sat in her chair as she told a reporter about her assignment of taking inventory at local stores. Although the temp agency promised full-time work, most weeks she worked only two days. "The W-2 agency told me I can't quit the job until I have another or I won't get any benefits," she said. Despite the fact that she couldn't support herself on these wages, she was denied any supplemental cash assistance. The reporter asked Equonne what kind of job she wanted. "I'd like to work on a computer," she said, spreading out her fingers above an imaginary keyboard. She'd asked repeatedly to be allowed to take a twelve-week clerical training course. The W-2 agency refused.

I know many stories like these. And I also know the statistics. In 2004, median weekly earnings of temp workers were $384 a week, 35 percent less than regular workers. Only 5 percent of temps get health-care insurance from their employer,[5] and just 10 percent get a pension (compared to two-thirds of regular full-time employees). Being paid less than full-time and permanent workers doesn't just mean lower pay—often it amounts to poverty wages.[6]

Even highly skilled workers find themselves classified as temps and therefore cut out of benefits. In 1999, a class-action suit against Microsoft resulted in a ruling that the software giant had unlawfully denied "permatemps" stock options and other benefits available to Microsoft employees. Not to worry—the temp industry came up with a solution. Ed Lenz, spokesman for the ASA, assured employers that it wasn't illegal to draft language in company benefits plans explicitly excluding temp workers. Microsoft had just failed to take that step.[7]

Reality: Temp Jobs Are Often Unfair

Pay and benefits don't tell the whole story. In 2000, 9to5 conducted employment testing at twenty-five temp agencies in Milwaukee. Two pairs of white and black testers outfitted with tape recorders and similar résumés applied for entry-level jobs.[8] Here's what they found: While some agencies do a good job with training and placement, nearly two-thirds of the agencies tested engaged in illegal or unfair practices or both. In a follow-up study, six of ten agencies were guilty of specific instances of race discrimination—practices such as offering employment to the white job-seekers at the time of application and again during a follow-up call, while telling black testers the same day that nothing was available. One agency staff told a white tester she "didn't look like factory material" but "like she belonged in an office setting" and offered her a position as a clerical for $8.50 per hour. When the tester indicated she couldn't type, the interviewer told her, "That's okay, you can learn as you go." The black applicant at the same agency was told there were no openings. Another interviewer asked a black tester whether she was "a nice person and wouldn't fist fight."

Given the fact that African Americans are twice as likely as whites to work as temps, that finding was particularly alarming. And discrimination wasn't limited to race. One interviewer informed testers that "higher paying jobs are for men only." She then called over to another staff person, "What do we have available for women?" Female testers were routinely asked whether they were married and had kids; males applying at the same time were not. An interviewer at one agency complained about a woman on her staff and announced she was "about to terminate [her] because of her pregnancy." Turns out the woman had called in to say she had complications and couldn't work that day. Applicants were typically asked questions about health status before a job offer, in violation of the Americans with Disability Act.

The practices our testers encountered weren't all illegal; some were just unfair. A surprising number of agencies had partnerships with check cashing establishments where workers were required to pick up their check; they didn't have to cash the checks there, but many workers wound up doing so and paying the check-cashing fee. Several agencies demanded that once hired, temps would have to take any job—whatever the wage, wherever the position was located—or be terminated. "Some employees need to be at work before the buses start running," one staff person said. "If for any reason they are not there, they will be terminated. You can't call in later in the day and say, 'My boyfriend died' or 'My kid's in the hospital.'"

From 9to5 members and callers to our hotline, we heard other examples of outrageous practices—temps who were paid at a lower rate than was quoted at the time of hire, given a different set of tasks than those described, given inadequate safety training or equipment, sent on an assignment they couldn't get to and then denied unemployment on the grounds that they "voluntarily quit." One woman was told, "You speak English—you don't have to do heavy lifting." Temps complained of being sent to what seemed like a great assignment—only to find it meant crossing a picket line and replacing striking workers. Immigrants and other low-wage temps commonly face charges for transportation—and here's the rub: You have to take—and pay for—the company van, even if you could get to the site much more cheaply on the bus; the van arrives early at the worksite but you aren't paid for the waiting around time. Temps told us stories of being held hostage at work, having to stay overtime because the van wouldn't come until after hours. I remember a woman named Anna who worked at a print shop. "I was very ill," she said, "plus the machines were down so there was no work. I repeatedly called the agency, but they wouldn't pick me up. The company insisted they come. So they finally sent a bus." Anna was charged $75 for that trip; the money was taken out of her check. "They never told us that could happen," she said.

Day labor employees face the most abysmal conditions. Listen to Maria Flores describe the time the agency took her and other workers to a gum factory:

> Upon arriving there, instead of a factory, it was a huge, dirty cellar. The bathrooms and everything was incredibly dirty. But the most incredible thing was to have to pack candy without anything hygienic covering our hands. To think how many children were going to eat these candies, because they were packed very beautifully, without knowing who packaged them. I worry as a worker, but also as a mother. But the worst was that we arrived at the day labor agency at one in the afternoon to work. They would take us to the worksite at two o'clock, and we would start at three thirty and end at twelve midnight, without the right to a break—not even a bathroom break. We arrived home at one in the morning. It didn't matter to the drivers. Sometimes it was raining and raining and they just left us there, even though they charged us for the ride.[9]

Temp by Any Other Name . . .

Some firms lease workers to an employer. That means if you want a job with XYZ Corporation, you're told to go to LMN Leasing and they'll get you a position. Problem is, you're likely to earn less and have less job security than a regular XYZ Employee. Moira Casey explained how this worked. In 1987, she began clerical work with Arco in Anchorage, Alaska. Even though she did the same work as regular Arco employees, she got the job through an agency and was classified as a leased employee, receiving lower pay and fewer benefits than her coworkers. In 1991, she transferred to the Prudhoe Bay area. Until she was laid off eight years later, she worked two weeks on and two off, flying back and forth in Arco's jet. While she was gone, a regular Arco employee worked her shift. Moira Casey received training and supervision from Arco employees, and she ate and slept in Arco facilities. Yet "Arco treated us like second-hand citizens," she said. "While the company enjoyed huge profits, we got the shaft."[10]

At least Moria Casey knew what her status was. When I headed a U.S. study team on nonstandard work put together by the Philippine American Foundation, we heard testimony from a woman named Jamiela. She told us she was working for NBC News in New York when she spotted an opening for the *Dateline NBC* program and applied. After getting the job, she noticed that the signature on her paycheck changed, but figured that was just a change in payroll companies. Then Jamiela began to have a conflict with her supervisor. She tried to use the NBC grievance procedures—and only at that time did she find out that she was not, in fact, an NBC employee but an employee of Kelly Staff Leasing. She was referred to a Kelly representative in Los Angeles who knew nothing of the conditions in Jamiela's office and was unable to be of any help.

The American Staffing Association advises employers to turn to leasing as a way to boost profits. "Employee leasing—in which you turn over your work force to a professional employer organization that leases your employees back to you—can save you substantial cash on employee benefits," the ASA's Bruce Steinberg told entrepreneur.com.[11]

If temping isn't a panacea for women, how about part-time work?

Myth: Women Choose Part-Time Work to Achieve Balance

Polls show that many people would like to reduce their working hours, especially to manage family responsibilities. More and more employers offer part-time options and count these among their family friendly policies. They point to the surge in part-time jobs, particularly among women, as evidence that employers are accommodating the wishes of mothers.

Reality: Many Have No Choice

I know lots of people, especially women, who do want reduced hours on the job. But not all part-timers work a shorter schedule by choice.

This problem first hit home for me in 1985 when I called a woman named Linda Williams. Milwaukee 9to5 was holding a phonathon to raise money for health insurance for our part-time staff. "How great," Linda told me. "I wish I could contribute." Turns out Williams's husband had walked out on her and left her to support their three children on her own. Despite lots of skills and a college degree, she couldn't find a full-time job. So she spent forty-five hours a week working three part-time positions, one of them at a health care facility—none of the jobs offered health insurance. Not long before we spoke, Williams had suffered a heart attack at the age of thirty-eight. She didn't tell me much about the actual attack, but her children later showed me a diary entry describing that night, how she tried to convince herself it was merely indigestion though she was in excruciating pain and sweating so hard she had her son drag a fan over to her chair. Like many people who are uninsured, she dreaded going to the hospital, either for fear they wouldn't treat her or fear of the cost. She hung on until morning and went to see her doctor, who informed her she'd suffered a massive heart attack and needed triple bypass surgery.

Linda Williams was one determined woman. She'd researched federal funding for the uninsured, and she'd even found a doctor who was willing to perform the surgery pro bono, but she couldn't find a hospital that would allow him to do so. Our 9to5 chapter held a press conference to publicize her plight. Lots of good things followed: A local hospital agreed to allow the surgery; the surgery was successful; Williams found a full-time job with health insurance. Problem was she owed $20,000 to the anesthesiologist and radiologist and fourteen other hospital personnel who'd treated her. So she took a second part-time job in order to pay a little something every month on those bills. She was on that second job when she suffered another heart attack and died, the day before her forty-second birthday.

I'm no cardiac expert. Williams was significantly overweight. Maybe her heart was so damaged, nothing would have helped. Still, all that stress from running from job to job, from being uninsured, from worrying about those bills, surely didn't help.

Linda Williams's case may be extreme, but many things about her situation are unfortunately quite common. Few people realize that the category where women made perhaps the greatest advance over the last few decades—70 percent of new entrants—is moonlighting. We're now nearly half of all people who hold more than one job—and nearly a third of those women work two or more part-time positions.[12] Some economists estimate that most of the growth in part-time employment from 1970 to the mid-1990s came from involuntary part-timers who would prefer full-time jobs.[13] The figure would be much higher if we counted women who want to work full time, but reduce hours because they can't find or afford adequate childcare.

I've met women at all levels who describe themselves as involuntary part-timers. Some, like Denise, have been on welfare. Denise got a job cleaning rooms at a hotel. Several times a week she was sent home or had her hours cut because the hotel didn't have enough guests the night before. She wound up working twelve to fifteen hours a week but couldn't get any cash assistance to supplement that because she was classified as "employed." Her childcare provider required her to pay the full amount, even when she was able to bring her children home early.

Others who long for full-time jobs have PhDs. An astonishing majority of all teachers of college credit courses in the United States are not regular employees.[14] When I met Michelle Kelly in 2000, she was teaching art history at North Seattle Community College. She taught all four quarters, one class less per year than a full-time teacher, and earned $15,000–17,000 a year. To make ends meet, she always worked one or two additional jobs as well as creating and marketing her own artwork. Michelle spent hours commuting by bus because she couldn't afford a car, and she was on a waiting list for low-income housing. "Some months my parents, who live on Social Security, help me with groceries," she told me.[15]

And then there are employers like Wal-Mart, who intentionally increase the number of part-time hires—or shorten hours of those already working—in order to cut workers out of health or pension plans.[16]

Reality: Part Time Often Brings a High Penalty

Linda Williams was hardly alone among part-time employees in having no health benefits. Fewer than two in ten part-timers receive health insurance from their employer, compared with two-thirds of full-time employees.[17] Many are low-wage workers like Julia, who had four jobs—driving a school bus, delivering newspapers, working with the Girl Scouts, and selling Tupperware. None of the jobs had benefits. "I had to make hard choices about supporting my kids instead of spending time with them," Julia said. "Now I'm laid off two of my jobs. All I can find are more part-time jobs without benefits."

Health insurance isn't the only benefit part-timers often lack. To qualify for the Family and Medical Leave Act, for example, you have to work at least twenty-five hours a week. That means many part-time workers find themselves out of work when they take time off to give birth. Tracy, for example, worked half-time as a clerical in New York. She lost her job after giving birth because she had some complications and needed one more week off than the six (unpaid) her employer offered. The employer refused. You might think she'd be eligible for unemployment insurance (UI), but like most states, New York equates UI eligibility with willingness to work full time. Someone who has chosen reduced hours for family care reasons, for example, and who is laid off but willing and eager for a new part-time job, can be shut out of benefits while she searches for one.

The good news is that more companies are discovering the value of quality part-time options. I did a report highlighting fifteen such employers in Wisconsin. By quality, I mean a chance to work fewer hours at an equivalent hourly pay rate, at least prorated benefits and paid time off, and equal access to training and promotional opportunities. That could mean working a shorter week, sharing a job with someone else, gradually increasing hours after returning from leave, or gradually cutting hours when phasing into retirement. Smart employers do this not as a favor to women or to parents, but as a better way to do business. "[Not paying benefits to part-timers] may save some money in the short-term," said Deb Palmer of Thrivent Financial for Lutherans, a benefit organization based in Appleton, Wisconsin. "But in the long term it doesn't provide a good value because of increased turnover and lack of internal knowledge. If you treat people as full time but just at reduced schedule, they end up being more committed to the organization."

Finding these model employers, however, proved to be a much bigger challenge than I expected. Many employers I had to rule out from the start. Some had no part-time options; others had them but not on an equitable basis. Jane works as an engineer at such a company—a large organization that always lands on the "best places to work" lists. She's grateful she was able to reduce her workweek to thirty hours and she loves her job. But benefits for part-timers are very limited. "Health insurance has a significantly higher premium," Jane said. "Vacation and sick time are cut in half regardless of hours worked per week. I lost tuition reimbursement and paid maternity leave. Holiday pay was just eliminated. I've been promoted three times, but now have hit the limit [of advancement opportunities]."

There were employers I wanted to include who took themselves off my list. One HR representative described two division heads who were job sharing. I was delighted, because I couldn't point to many examples at such a high organizational level. A few days later, the woman called back to tell me I couldn't include this in the report. "Other division heads might get ideas," she said. Another company had been recommended by a union representative who'd helped bargain quality part-time options. Turns out her bargaining unit had them but the other two units didn't—and top management didn't want them to get ideas either. A third employer had been bought by another company after our interview; the new management wasn't keen on calling attention to this particular employment practice.

Reality: Women Choose Fewer Hours, Not Lower Pay

And then there's the issue of pay. Part-timers earn 15 percent less per hour than full-time workers with similar education, skills, and experience.[18] I've never met anyone who wakes up one morning and says, "Gee, I'd really like to earn less money and have fewer benefits." Putting up with a penalty is hardly the same as choosing it.

You're probably asking, isn't this illegal? Turns out no law says that if you and I do the same work for the same employer, we have to get the same base pay (unless we can show the part-timers are overwhelmingly female and the full-timers overwhelmingly male).[19] Part-time employees may spend less time on the job, but most work full time every hour they're there. Dave Adam, vice president of corporate finance at Johnson Financial whose schedule is 80 percent time, put it this way: "My boss would say I accomplish as much or more as some full-time employees. You come in more refreshed to tackle what's in your inbox. The benefit to the employer is a dedicated employee who can focus on the effort at work." Dave Adam, by the way, works at one of the companies I highlighted and does receive equitable compensation, including full benefits. He told me he's inspired others at the company to have a more balanced life: "My supervisors on occasion will say, 'I had a chance to do X, I thought about the Dave Adam approach, and I ended up taking my daughter on a ski trip instead.'"[20]

Myth: Free Agent Nation

Some see the growth in nonstandard or contingent workers—those who don't work full time in permanent positions for a particular employer—as an exciting phenomenon, the result of rising demand for independence. These new workers are "free agents"—job-hopping, tech-savvy, fulfillment-seeking, self-reliant, autonomous employees.[21]

Reality: Independent Contractors Get Short-Changed

It's not surprising that many people long to be their own boss, even if they don't want to run a business and employ others. What is surprising is how little protection these folks get. Independent contractors and freelancers aren't protected by any labor or employment statutes, including antidiscrimination laws. If you're hired as a freelance court reporter and then a lawyer or client makes a vulgar advance, you can complain, but you can't file a complaint. Likewise, you may find yourself having much less control than you anticipated. Kelly, a freelance court reporter in Florida and mother of one, had gone fifteen years without benefits when we got her testimony for the Philippine American Foundation report on nonstandard work.[22] She worked "on call"—which meant she had to report for duty when her agency told her to, often on short notice. She got no paid vacation, pension benefits, or paid sick days. She also wasn't told what time she'd finish work each day, so she worried constantly about whether she could pick up her son. Kelly's pay was relatively good, but she said she was earning the same as she did a decade earlier.

Employers who hire independent contractors save a bundle. They don't have to pay workers' compensation, unemployment tax, social security, or any health, vacation, or other benefits. They don't have to provide any family leave. Minimum-wage and overtime rules don't apply. Not surprisingly, some employers see this as a handy little category and apply it generously, whether or not the individuals in question actually meet the legal criteria. Here's what the law says: To be classified as an independent contractor, you have to control the "means and manner" by which you do your job. Think of a caterer who works for many clients. Clients determine what they want served, but the caterer is in charge of all the details. And the caterer can turn down an assignment for any reason. Yet an alarming number of people—from clerical workers to salespeople to grocery store delivery staff—are classified as independent contractors even though they work for the same employer for years and for no one else, take direct supervision from that employer, do their job on that employer's premises, and perform functions traditionally performed by the employer's own workers.

Consider this trick: Some employers take their current staff, utter the magic words, and poof—the former employees are now independent contractors, doing exactly the same job but without coverage from employment laws. We're not just talking low-wage workers. This has happened to broadcasters, technicians, writers, and many others.[23] While it may often be illegal, the enforcement of state and federal labor laws is usually insufficient to prevent it.

Who's the Boss?

Here's another variation of calling people who work for you something other than your employees and treating them differently: the category of "contract workers." Large manufacturers or other employers (think Company A) may subcontract various pieces of the job to an assortment of smaller employers (let's call one Company B). Company B may be a fly-by-night operation that hires workers, often immigrant women, at low wages, works them overtime and refuses to pay extra, or skips out altogether without paying wages and reinvents itself as Company C. The workers know they're creating a product for Company A and appeal to the owner for their wages. "Sorry," Company A says, "we're not your boss. You'll have to go after Company B." Which, of course, no longer exists.

Intentional Shift in Staffing Strategy

How did it happen that one set of workers could labor side by side with regular employees and receive considerably less compensation? Laws protecting workers were devised at a time when the dominant mode was full-time, permanent employment. (Some groups, of course, especially African Americans and immigrants, were left out even then.) But in recent decades, the lack of requirement to treat nonstandard workers the same as regular employees has turned into an *incentive* for employers to hire more workers in part-time, temporary, and contract positions or to *reclassify* their current staff. Guess what happens when employers move staffing costs from the "labor" line item to something like "purchasing"—it looks like productivity has gone up, driving stock prices up.[24]

Staffing strategies that used to characterize only low-wage sectors such as farmwork and garment sweatshops are now being applied in areas such as high tech and finance.[25] Employers who want to treat workers fairly then face an unfair advantage. To reverse this trend, we need to *remove* that advantage and create a level playing field.

FEMINIST SOLUTIONS

The starting point for our solutions has to be equal pay for equal work, regardless of the total number of hours worked or employment status of those who perform it. For part-time workers, that means equal base unit pay and at least prorated benefits, and equal treatment under the law. Treating part-time workers differently should be acknowledged as discriminatory. Current provisions excluding part-timers from coverage under the Family and Medical Leave Act and unemployment insurance, among others, must end. We must also enable everyone to work full time if they want to by increasing flexibility of work hours and public involvement in dependent care (see Chapter 3).

Reduced hours will work only when employers change their corporate culture as well (see Chapter 3). Barbara Wankoff, human resource director at the accounting firm KPMG, told me how important it was that employees working reduced schedules get a clear message from the top urging time off be genuinely free of work.[26] "It's just as critical there's not another message coming out the day before or after saying, 'Make sure your chargeable hours are up,'" she said.

Other nonstandard workers such as contract workers, leased employees, and the like, should not be discriminated against in pay, benefits, working conditions, or rights on the job. To extend this protection to temps requires several changes. First, we have to limit the amount of time someone can be classified as a temp before being offered a permanent job. Temps should be just that—someone filling in for another person temporarily unable to work, or carrying out a genuinely short-term project that can't be done by regular staff. We also need to regulate the temporary and leasing industry in order to eliminate bad actors. Agencies should be licensed and bonded. If they provide transportation, usage should be voluntary; the vehicles must be safe and fees must be limited. Temps must be allowed to turn down assignments for just cause and to collect unemployment when they are unable to find full-time or part-time work. The Office of Federal Contract Compliance Programs (OFCCP) should include numbers of temp workers in the affirmative action plan of government contractors. And we have to prohibit the practice of temp agencies supplying replacement workers to companies whose employees are on strike.

Role for Government Agencies

We need to end misclassification of workers as independent contractors by a combination of tighter definitions,[27] greater enforcement, and stricter penalties. The key distinction should be proof that the individual really is in business for her or himself. In addition, contract workers need protection.

The individual for whom a worker ultimately performs a service must be held responsible for that worker's fair treatment, even if an agency or contracting firm serves as an intermediary between employer and employee.

These changes mean greater funding for the appropriate government agencies, including the Department of Labor, EEOC, and OFCCP. The Occupational Safety and Health Administration (OSHA) needs to be expanded so that an employer responsible for a worksite maintains a safe working environment for all workers at the site, regardless of who pays them.

TAKING ON THE BIG BOYS

9to5's involvement with nonstandard workers goes back to the 1980s. Given the disproportionate percentage of women among part-time and temp workers and our role in advocating flexible work options, we had to make sure these jobs were equitable—and we suspected and then documented that they were not.[28] The Big Boys mainly *minimized* the problem, downplaying any disparities or writing them off as "tradeoffs." When we challenged that view and identified solutions, we ran into plenty of *catastrophizing* and *demonizing.* Our strategy, as usual, was to involve those affected, show the dimensions and the consequences of the inequity, point to solutions while winning some concrete improvements, and build power to win more.

Stacked Decks in the Stacks

In 1987, one of our members in Milwaukee came in to talk to me about her job. A short, energetic woman in her forties, Nancy worked as a circulation aide in the library. Circulation aides did most tasks performed by library aides—checking books in and out, shelving them, keeping materials in order. Except unlike library aides, they weren't in the union, they earned minimum wage, they were allowed to work only part time, and they had no benefits of any kind—no sick days, holidays, vacation days, and certainly no health insurance. The position was a prerequisite for becoming a library aide; Nancy had tried several times to move up, but with no success. Our research showed that the position was originally created to give young people of color a foot in the door to city employment, but that goal had long since gone missing. Many circulation aides were women like Nancy, far from teenage years, white as well as African American, helping to support families.

On Valentine's day in 1988, two months before the mayoral election, our 9to5 chapter presented the city with a Heartless award for unfair treatment of these part-time city workers. (We'd invented this award in 1983, when a member with pelvic inflammatory disease got a call in her hospital room from her boss. "I was going to fire you for excessive absenteeism," he said, "but I've found a mistake in your work, so I'm firing you for that." Her doctor was in the room at the time. "I can't believe anyone could be so heartless," he said. Neither could we—and we decided to drop in on the guy at his office, media in tow, to make the presentation.) Then-alderman Tom Donegan dressed up as the missing-a-heart Tin Man to accept the award on behalf of the city and share his concern. Also attending was John Norquist, a candidate for mayor. Norquist pledged that if he won the election, he'd look into the problem.

Norquist did win, and to make good on his promise, he appointed me to the Library Board. Some governance positions, such as the Milwaukee Sewerage District Board, pay a stipend of several thousand dollars. The Library Board is not in this category; they don't even pay for parking (and they certainly don't wipe out fines for overdue books). But I did get to raise the issue of the part-time workers and was hard at work with circulation aides and the union to formulate a solution when I got a phone call from the mayor's chief of staff, a man named Carl Mueller, to set up a one-on-one meeting.

Anyone familiar with politics knows that mayors typically have a division of labor among staff to relate to various community organizations. As soon as I got this call, I checked with 9to5's liaison, Eloisa Gomez, to see if she knew what Mueller wanted to see me about. She hadn't even known he wanted to meet with me. That raised a red flag. I spun out an elaborate fantasy in which the chief of staff called me on the carpet for bringing too much attention to this circulation aide matter and ordered me to desist or be fired from the Library Board. It was unfathomable that anyone would think I'd go along with that. And yet, amazingly, this is exactly what Carl Mueller said. In my fantasy, I was impressively cool and collected during the conversation. In real life, I had my arms and legs crossed so tightly against my body and my brow so furrowed, Mueller immediately figured out that the meeting wasn't going to go as planned.

"You seem upset," he said.

My body language may have betrayed me, but I was able to give the response I'd imagined: "Does the mayor know about this meeting?" Mueller asked why I was asking.

"If he is aware of it, I'm calling a press conference to denounce you both," I said. "If he isn't, call him immediately and then send me a formal apology." Mueller began one of those fancy back-pedaling maneuver politicians like so much. I wasn't buying it.

A couple days later, I received a handwritten note saying, "Believe it or not, I greatly enjoyed our conversation and I suspect you did as well." I never heard another word against my work on the circulation aide issue. Those in the position got a raise; it was no longer a required stepping-stone to the library aide job.

We also worked with members of Congress, starting with then-congresswoman Pat Schroeder (D-CO) in the 1980s and more recently with Sen. Ted Kennedy (D-MA) to draft legislation prohibiting inequity in pay and benefit rates for part-time workers. The issue has taken on new interest because of the number of professional women—and some men—who want to reduce their hours (see Chapter 3). We won't see large numbers making this change as long as employers send out memos like the ones at the beginning of this chapter, granting permission for part-time hours with one hand and stripping those jobs of benefits with the other.

Demanding Fairness for Temps

In addition to part-timers, 9to5 was concerned about abusive practices for temps. This organizing also began in the 1980s and has taken many forms: outreach, support, training, public education, legislative efforts, coalition-building, direct action, and research. By far the most innovative and effective research we did was the employment testing described earlier (see pages 151–53).

For a long time, housing groups have sent pairs of people of different racial or ethnic groups to a place for rent or for sale to see if they were treated differently, in order to expose discrimination and go after offending owners. We read about a nonprofit in Chicago that had tried something similar with hiring and immediately recognized this as a method we could use with temp agencies.[29] Testers who were carefully trained to be thorough and objective could shine a light on the illegal and unfair practices we were hearing about from our members in Milwaukee. We also wanted to link these problems to a serious flaw in welfare-to-work programs that allowed administrators to fob participants off to temp recruiters and declare them "employed" and ineligible for any cash assistance.

We knew the testers would uncover problems, but even we were surprised by the extent of what they found. As the daily logs started coming in, we approached Chester Bailey, the district director of the EEOC, to see if he'd hold a joint press conference with us when we'd completed the project and written up the results. Bailey had been extremely responsive to a 9to5 member who was paid less by a temp agency than men in the same job (see Chapter 8). He'd expressed interest in going after bad actors and encouraged our testing project. At the time, employment testing was controversial. The question was whether testers had "standing" to bring a complaint. Some EEOC staff argued that if you weren't really looking for a job, you couldn't be considered discriminated against. Bailey disagreed. The issue for him was simply whether or not an employer had violated the law. (Later that year, the U.S. Court of Appeals for the Seventh Circuit affirmed that employment testers do have standing, as the Court had earlier ruled in a case involving housing testers.)[30] When the report was ready, 9to5's organizer, Linda Garcia, arranged the press conference in front of the EEOC's bright blue building in downtown Milwaukee. Bailey made it clear that he would go after temp agencies if formal complaints were brought: "Testers subjected to employment discrimination can file claims with the EEOC," he said, "and seek monetary damages if they can prove discrimination."

In the end, we didn't have the resources to focus on conducting more testing and bringing complaints. Instead, we used a combination of training for some temp agencies and direct action against others to drive home the message that unfair treatment had to end. We also held "Know Your Rights" workshops for temps; organizers rode buses and took short-term temp jobs to distribute materials in English and Spanish. We persuaded the Workers Rights Board in Milwaukee, a group of clergy, public officials, and other leaders, to hold a hearing on temp jobs. Members of 9to5 and a local immigrant rights organization testified about their experiences; a representative of the American Federation of State, County and Municipal Employees linked the problem to budget cuts that axed union jobs and replaced them with lower-paying temps. In all these endeavors, we continued to work with reporters to expose problems and call for clear standards for the industry.

Temps Shall Not Be Scabs

One abuse we targeted was temps being assigned to replace strikers. In February of 2003, the workers at a Tyson plant in Jefferson, Wisconsin, walked off the job. These are the folks who make the pepperoni you may eat on pizza. The company wanted a big bag of concessions, including a four-year wage freeze, a cut in starting pay from $11 to $9 an hour, and a two-week cut in vacation time for highest seniority workers. The workers and their union, the United Food and Commercial Workers International said, "No way." Support for the strikers in Jefferson was so strong that many local businesses, schools, and others refused to buy pizza with Tyson pepperoni on it. Company executives had a hard time finding scabs in town. So Tyson hired a temp agency known as QPS Staffing to ship them in—including some parolees referred to QPS by the State Department of Corrections.

Working with the union, we held a series of demonstrations at QPS headquarters in Brookfield, Wisconsin, right outside Milwaukee. Just before Thanksgiving, for instance, a group rallied in the cold while a state legislator presented QPS president Scott Mayer with a "Gobbler Award." Nancy Thrasher, one of the strikers, summarized the demonstrators' purpose: "QPS's bosses will eat turkey with all the trimmings, courtesy of the money they have gobbled up by supplying strikebreakers to Tyson. Meanwhile, working families like my own wonder where our next meal will come from." The strikers were particularly moved by statements from 9to5 members who were themselves temp workers in need of jobs but who pledged never to find one by scabbing. "I've worked temp jobs for eight years in order to support myself and my children," Tiffany Harris told strikers earlier that year.[31] "Right now I'm out of work and really need a job. But I would never take one crossing a picket line. Places without unions feel they can do whatever they want to do because there's no one overseeing what's going on." She added that the enemy in this situation shouldn't be the temp workers "who may feel they have very little choice to support their families," but rather QPS, and called on all workers to "stand together and support each other in the fight for better working conditions for all of us."

We weren't able to stop QPS from sending scabs to Tyson. But we did get State Senator Tim Carpenter to introduce legislation that would prohibit such a practice. And as a result of the heat on QPS, the agency soon had a smaller pool to work with. After the union approached Governor Jim Doyle, the State Department of Corrections announced that parolees would no longer be referred to QPS Staffing. Doyle issued a statement saying individuals "can make their own choice on whether or not they can work at Tyson, but we're not going to have the State, in any way, encouraging people to cross a picket line and work there."

Connecting the Dots

To develop a serious campaign for fairness for nonstandard workers requires a coordinated national effort. Over the years, we kept track of other groups interested in the issue and began to build a network that eventually became the National Alliance for Fair Employment (later changed to the North American Alliance for Fair Employment when some Canadian groups joined) or NAFFE. The Alliance, which began with more than twenty member organizations and grew to more than forty, announced its formation in May 2000 with a press event at the National Press Club designed to connect the dots about this staffing trend.

The media had run stories about various aspects of the contingent work experience, without tying any of them together. Articles about the UPS strike called attention to the inequities of part-time work. The Microsoft case made public the existence of permatemps denied benefits enjoyed by regular workers. Other stories disclosed individual cases of contract workers winning back pay from the primary employer after a subcontractor underpaid them. We wanted to link these separate situations in order to demonstrate that they were all part of a deliberate shift in employment strategy with serious consequences for U.S. workers, affecting people at every level.

The launch event included release of a report and announcement of poll results. Pollster Celinda Lake found that three in five Americans knew a contingent worker or had been one themselves and thought they were getting shortchanged, working with no job security for no or low benefits.[32] More than two-thirds of the respondents believed it unfair to pay contingent workers a lower rate than regular workers doing the exact same job. The poll had political implications: Six out of ten respondents said they were more likely to vote for a candidate who supports legislation to stop unfair treatment of contingent workers. Lake called this "an understandable finding, when one in four of those surveyed with permanent jobs worry they could wind up becoming a contingent worker."[33]

Our speakers that day ran the gamut from low-wage day labor, temp, and contract workers to a UPS part-timer, a professor, and a highly skilled computer programmer. One by one they approached the mike to tell their stories of fighting unfair treatment. Michael Dunn, a lanky father of seven, had lost his job as a production supervisor after nineteen years in the New Mexico oil fields. He came to Chicago to care for his ailing parents, then found himself jobless and homeless. "I wound up doing day-labor for a temporary employment agency, taking home $25 a day from minimum-wage jobs after I paid the bus fare," Dunn said. As part of the Chicago Coalition for the Homeless, he helped shut down two day labor agencies operating outside the law. Tracy Jones proudly shared how she and 9to5 had taken on the gender discrimination of a temp agency in Milwaukee. Siaka Diakite delivered groceries in New York City. In soft and halting English, he described how his employer wrongly classified him and his coworkers as independent contractors and paid them less than minimum wage, until the National Employment Law Project sued for back wages and recognition that the grocery store was the workers' key employer.

Lillian Moriskey spoke next. A long time 9to5 member, she'd worked for twenty-one years handling packages part time for UPS in Cleveland and was part of the 1997 Teamsters strike that narrowed the pay and benefits gap between full- and part-timers. "People don't have to juggle two or three jobs anymore," Moriskey said. "The agreement gave us back our lives."

The last two speakers reminded the audience that professional status doesn't offer automatic protection. Peter Salama, a Microsoft permatemp, worked with WashTech in Seattle in its suit against the computer giant's denial of benefits to thousands of employees. And Larry Kaye, a part-time professor at the University of Massachusetts and member of the Coalition of Contingent Academic Labor (COCAL), described how he tried to handle his diabetes without health insurance while teaching multiple courses yet earning only $12,000 a year. After COCAL organized a campaign on campus, part-timers won full medical, dental, and pension benefits and a floor of $4,000 per course.

Competition Doesn't Require Discrimination

I represented NAFFE at the event, reiterating our message that paying nonstandard workers less violates the basic American principle of equal pay for equal work. "These are the unseen faces of a New Economy in which seven in ten employers have let permanent employees go and replaced them with temporary hires, and more plan to do so in the future," I said. Given that two-thirds of firms expected to increase their contingent staff in the next five years, we called for action by government, unions, businesses, and workers to provide greater protection and rights.[34] Among our proposals was a code of conduct for temp agencies, creating a set of standards for the industry based on equity, honesty, and fair treatment.

The press clubroom was filled with our supporters, but also with media representatives from the *Washington Post*, Scripps Howard, National Public Radio, and others. One reporter asked me if the conditions we were calling attention to weren't just a fact of life as U.S. employers compete in the global economy.

"It's a choice," I replied. "Investing in workers is also a choice. If employers said, 'Sorry, we need to cut costs in order to compete, so we're hiring women and people of color and paying them less,' we'd say that's illegal. It should also be illegal to hire part-timers or temps for less." I pointed out it was already illegal to misclassify people as independent contractors or leased employees in order to pay them less, or to deny responsibility for the actions of subcontractors.

Temp Employers React

Predictably, spokespeople for the American Staffing Association reacted to NAFFE's proposals with hosannas for the "flexibility" and "opportunity" provided by temp work. Within the industry, ASA worked to discredit NAFFE as a pawn of organized labor whose main objective was unionizing all temporary workers. Only a few months before our NAFFE launch, the National Labor Relations Board had ruled that temp workers could be considered part of a single bargaining unit along with regular employees, a most unwelcome change for the temp industry (and one that a majority of Bush appointees on the Labor Board overturned five years later).[35] In their European operations, the big agencies were accustomed to unions and regulations as a fact of life. Yet these same employers were determined to stop any advances by labor in the United States.

A few unions had targeted employers who relied on significant numbers of temp workers. But for the most part, temp workers are transitory and scattered, a difficult base for union organizers. NAFFE and the labor movement were more interested in stopping the use of temps as scabs, along with a wide range of equity issues and the implications these had for general living standards.

To move forward, we needed to break the ASA's stranglehold on its member groups. Early in our work, in the summer of 1998, I had approached someone I knew at Manpower, Inc., to discuss having that agency sign the NAFFE Code of Conduct. Over lunch at a posh restaurant, this woman raved about the code and declared that Manpower already followed each of the proposed practices. "I see no reason for them not to sign," she told me. But when I tried to follow up, I got a cold shoulder for four weeks and finally a voicemail sent on a Saturday morning, informing me that Manpower could not sign because that might bring "negative attention" to the industry. "Abusive practices bring negative attention," I said in my return voicemail. "Let's talk." I couldn't get a meeting. Years later, this woman explained to me that her boss had put the kibosh on our talks. "Why would we meet with 9to5 and the AFL?" he said.

I found myself back at Manpower in June 2001 when a videographer hired to shoot a sexual harassment video for their staff recommended me to write the script. I was directed to meet with Executive Vice President Terry Hueneke, who would be the face of the agency in the video. "Forget the video," he told me. "I want to talk about NAFFE." Hueneke was dismayed that in every article about abuses in the temp industry (and there were lots of them since NAFFE's founding), reporters always mentioned that Manpower was (at the time) the nation's largest employer. "If you're tired of seeing that link," I said, "sign our code of conduct and join us in raising standards in the industry." Hueneke had another proposal—that we come up with an agreement of our own. At that point I brought in a team from NAFFE to conduct negotiations.

Tracy Jones, the former temp who now worked for 9to5, was part of that team. Every time Hueneke touted various Manpower policies, Tracy shared abuses she'd experienced and heard about from other temps. We brought in an ethics column from the *New York Times*, in which a temp recruiter asked what to do about the "common occurrence" of employers calling temp agencies and asking for whites only or males only. "It's not enough to say you have effective practices," I told Hueneke. "Manpower has a responsibility to help raise standards for the industry as a whole." Talks dragged on for months. Hueneke left and was replaced in these sessions by the new Executive Vice President Barbara Beck. From time to time, CEO Jeff Joerres joined in. Manpower wanted NAFFE's seal of approval; NAFFE wanted Manpower to stand up to the ASA. We were at a stalemate.

Eventually we did reach agreement on a dozen key points, including no use of temps as strikebreakers. Turns out Manpower had once lost a big contract with AT&T because they wouldn't provide temps ahead of time to be trained to work during a strike. Both sides realized we diverged on many points (such as the use of permatemps). We couldn't get Joerres to hold a public event with NAFFE about this document; he didn't want to look too cozy with us. And we weren't in a position to monitor Manpower's behavior. But we shared an interest in driving out the bad actors like Labor

Ready Inc., the United States' leading provider of temporary manual labor to light industry and small businesses, and creating meaningful standards for the industry. NAFFE has been able to point to this agreement and demand that other agencies follow suit.

GARMENT WORKERS TAKE ON
JESSICA MCCLINTOCK

Earlier I wrote about workers who get hired by Company B to perform work for Company A, only to have Company A deny any responsibility if Company B cheats or disappears. Beginning in 1992, a dozen Chinese immigrant workers took on such an employer and, against all odds, won their fight.

The employer was Jessica McClintock, a company that manufactures the pricey Gunne Sax brand. I first heard about this struggle from a woman named Young Shin, executive director of Asian Immigrant Women Advoctes (AIWA) in Oakland. We were both part of a delegation brought to Beijing by the Ms. Foundation in 1995 for the Fourth World Conference on Women. Young and I bonded over talks about her twin daughters, then age five, and dinner at a Korean restaurant near our hotel.

Here's what I learned: McClintock contracted the sewing of Gunne Sax dresses to a small operator known as Lucky Sewing. Every day the immigrant seamstresses turned out sleeves or collars or some other piece of the fancy dresses. They routinely worked six to seven days a week, ten to fourteen hours a day, often below the legal minimum wage, without any benefits. Sometimes they would go weeks without getting paid. Then one day McClintock pulled the contract from Lucky Sewing (she'd started sending work to lower-wage Mexico). The subcontractor's owners declared bankruptcy and laid the women off. At the time they were owed $15,000 in back wages. The women approached AIWA to see what options they had.

Young Shin and her colleagues wanted the seamstresses to see exactly how much they were being exploited. They trooped out to a fancy shopping area in San Francisco and walked into a Jessica McClintock boutique, where five of the women examined a green velvet, off-the-shoulder dress they'd made with their own hands: price tag $175. Then they calculated what each had been paid for her piece. It added up to a paltry $5.

"I felt a pain in my heart," said Fu Lee, "because we sew for so little and (the dress) was selling so high out there. And even that little amount, we didn't get it."[36] She and the other women decided to become involved in what became the historic Garment Workers Justice Campaign, a model for antisweatshop organizing.

Step one was a direct appeal to Jessica McClintock, a woman who'd made a public commitment to social responsibility and supported anti-AIDS work. In an open letter in September 1992, AIWA asked the manufacturer to pay the back wages. They also organized a public support rally for the twelve women and began to reach out to a broad grouping of labor, religious, women's, student, and community organizations. McClintock refused responsibility.

AIWA belonged to several national networks, each involving a variety of partners. Leaders contacted these allies, as well as students they knew at college campuses around the country. The campaign spread. Members launched a boycott against Jessica McClintock, demonstrated at McClintock's boutiques and the stores selling her goods, held community hearings with elected officials. The City Council of Berkeley and the Alameda County Board of Supervisors voted to endorse the campaign. With pro bono aid from a PR firm, AIWA developed a sophisticated media strategy, beginning with an ad in the October 26, 1992, *New York Times* titled "Let Them Eat Lace," and culminating in CBS's *60 Minutes* segment called "Behind the Seams" on December 11, 1994. AIWA staff and volunteers conducted research on all aspects of Jessica McClintock, Inc., which had taken in $145 million the previous year.

One striking element of this campaign was the active involvement of the seamstresses. "It was not easy for these women to stand up for their rights," Young Shin explained, citing fear of blackmail and loss of jobs.[37] "But once they realized the unfairness of the system, and with so much public support, they were empowered to demand their rights as women and as immigrant workers." From seeking back pay for themselves, the immigrant seamstresses set a larger goal: a new standard of corporate responsibility that would protect the rights and dignity of all workers employed by subcontractors.

AIWA planned activities around the women's schedules. In addition to demonstrating and meeting with policymakers and reporters, the former Lucky Sewing workers attended literacy classes along with other immigrant workers who assembled electronic products and cleaned hotels and office buildings. Together they organized events for families in the community, wrote and distributed newsletters in their native languages, gave testimonies about working conditions, and attended gatherings with ally organizations. Sometimes wearing masks to conceal their identity, the women told the public what it was like to sew those dresses in sweatshops decorated with signs warning workers against "loud talking and going to the bathroom."[38]

Eventually the Department of Labor got involved—after an embarrassing mistake of including McClintock on its 1995 "Fashion Trendsetter" holiday bulletin. In 1996, Labor Secretary Robert Reich announced an agreement between the company and AIWA. Jessica McClintock, Inc., donated money to establish a garment workers' education fund for workers to learn their rights as well as a fund for Lucky Sewing workers. The manufacturer also agreed to sponsor scholarships for students and garment workers; provide garment workers with bilingual state and federal publications on fair labor standards; establish a hotline for workers to report labor violations; and explore with other groups alternative methods for worker wage protections.

The fight for corporate responsibility continues. But AIWA and the seamstresses gained enormously in the process. They helped create hundreds of new activists and developed a campaign model for many other organizations. Perhaps above all, they inspired untold numbers of immigrant women—they, too, could learn their rights and gain some measure of justice. As Young Shin put it, the Garment Worker Justice Campaign "demonstrated that immigrant women, demanding justice together, can shake down the mighty garment industry."

FINAL THOUGHTS

"Paper towel employees." That's how a woman I know once referred to herself and other temp workers. "We're disposable," she said. "They use us and throw us away." Some may see the growth of nonstandard workers as a glorious "free agent nation." But if you're low-wage, or female, or nonwhite, or noncitizen, or all of the above, you're much more likely to relate to the paper towel analogy. A nation that values equity and fairness can and must do better.

8. WHAT THIS NATION REALLY THINKS OF MOTHERHOOD: WELFARE REFORM

*America . . . subsidizes births among poor women, who are also
disproportionately at the low end of the intelligence distribution. We urge
. . . that these policies, represented by the extensive network of cash and
services for low-income women who have babies, be ended.*
—Charles Murray, *The Bell Curve*[1]

When I was a kid, my father used to tell a riddle that drove me crazy. It
went like this (you'll know from the amounts how old this story is): Three
salesmen ask a hotel clerk for a shared room. "That'll be thirty dollars," says
the clerk. Each man chips in ten bucks. Minutes later, the clerk realizes
he's made a mistake—the room costs only twenty-five dollars. He gives
the bellboy a five-dollar bill to take back to the men. On the elevator, the
bellboy ponders how to divide the five among three people. He decides to
give each man a single and keep the remaining two dollars himself.

"Okay," my dad would say, "how much did each man pay?"

"Ten dollars minus one dollar is nine dollars," my sister and I would
answer, huddling together. After the first time, we knew what was coming.

"How much did they pay altogether?"

"Twenty-seven dollars."

"And how much does the busboy have?'

"Two dollars!" By now we'd be shrieking.

"Twenty-seven plus two is twenty-nine. Where's the other dollar?"

My sister and I scoured the entire hotel for that dollar, but we never
found it. I still remember the day we figured it out—you had to *subtract* the

two dollars from twenty-seven to get the actual price of the room (twenty-five), rather than *adding* the two dollars and comparing that to the incorrect price.

In the process, I learned a really important lesson: If you don't frame the problem correctly, you can never get the right solution.

This is just what happened with the disastrous experiment known as welfare reform.

Misdiagnosing the Welfare Problem

In 1996 Congress passed the Personal Responsibility and Work Opportunity Reconciliation Act to "end welfare as we know it." Our political leaders defined the problem as women who "didn't work" and were "dependent" on taxpayer dollars. The solution: Require the women to work; any job would do. The measure of success would be reducing the numbers on the welfare rolls. The fewer people receiving assistance, the greater the success— regardless of the actual income level or well-being of those who left.

There was, of course, another way to frame the problem: Many mothers whose jobs were undependable and who lacked any other support had no choice but to endure the indignity of public assistance in order to take care of their families. The solution: Value the work of caregiving, reform work to pay a living wage and be flexible for family care, solve the health-care crisis, invest in childcare and education, tackle the root causes of domestic violence. The measure of success would be reduction in poverty and improvements in the living standards and stability of families.

What led the politicians to that first formulation? Almost without exception, those who voted to "end welfare as we know it" had never known welfare—or hunger or poverty or severe economic hardship.[2] Most had never even met an actual welfare recipient. In one fell swoop they ended the nation's commitment to poor children based not on their own experience or research or any sound data. Instead, they relied on the stereotype of welfare recipients as irresponsible women who refused to get a job—as Tommy Thompson put it, "these women [who] won't do their end of the deal by working."[3]

As for opportunity, the Personal Responsibility and Work Opportunity Reconciliation Act created plenty, but not for women and their children. It brought career opportunities for the politicians and a windfall for private contractors. And for some of the Big Boys, the new law represented the prospect of a steady supply of cheap labor.

Myth: The Welfare Queen

The central figure in this drama was the welfare "queen," a stereotype that is all-too-familiar: She starts collecting as a teenage mom, cruises in a Cadillac, pops out babies to haul in bigger bucks, spends her food stamps on drugs or hands the stamps over to her boyfriend so he can spend them on drugs. Too lazy to work, she passes the day watching soaps instead of her kids. She's never held a job. And she's black. Her lifestyle is bankrolled by huge amounts of taxpayer dollars.

Or so we were told. History tells a very different story about who's on welfare, why, for how long, and for what reason.

A little background is instructive. The public assistance program called welfare, formally known as Aid to Families with Dependent Children (AFDC), dates back to 1935. Its purpose was "to release from the wage-earning role the parent whose task is to raise children."[4] Taking care of kids, in short, was thought to be a job. The intended beneficiaries were almost exclusively mothers, but not *all* mothers trying to raise kids on their own. As journalist Jason DeParle points out, divorced and unmarried women were largely excluded, and in the South, so were most blacks.[5] "Southern members of Congress controlled the presiding committees," says DeParle, "and made sure the law did nothing to interfere with the South's supply of cheap field labor."

Things began to change in the 1960s. By then Congress had made it easier for widows to receive more generous Social Security benefits. A combination of the War on Poverty, high unemployment, and welfare rights activism led to greater access for many of those previously excluded, although states were still free to determine their own payment levels. By the time welfare reform was enacted nationwide, nearly four and a half million families were receiving AFDC. As DeParle points out, "while the program once conjured a West Virginia widow, it now brought to mind a black teen mother in a big-city ghetto."[6] The welfare queen stereotype began to take hold.

Reality: Undependable Work

When spinmeisters work their magic, facts tend to fall by the wayside. Here's a look at the real story. At the time welfare was "ended," the racial breakdown of those receiving AFDC was about 40 percent white and 40 percent black.[7] The majority of families on welfare consisted of a mother with one or two kids.[8] Contrary to the image of lazy soap watchers, 70 percent of women on welfare were employed or looking for a job.[9] They were *cyclers* (on and off welfare) or *combiners* (people who combined work and welfare because they earned so little, they qualified for assistance). According to a study of six Midwest states by Northern Illinois University, only 6.3 percent of AFDC recipients had never worked; only 3.4 percent were under eighteen.[10]

A big part of the problem was the lack of jobs, even during good times. For every entry-level job in Wisconsin in 1996, there were 3 jobseekers, 7 for every such job in Milwaukee. Change the description to a living wage job and the numbers shot up to 18 jobseekers per opening in Wisconsin, 45 to 99 in Milwaukee.[11] I remember stories on TV showing hundreds of workers camping out and standing in line for hours when some manufacturer announced job openings. How did the politicians tune that out?

As for the cost and value of welfare, consider these numbers: At its peak, AFDC accounted for only 1 percent of the federal budget. Welfare checks did not approach the poverty level in any state in the United States, even combined with the value of food stamps. In 1992, for instance, the average total of a grant plus stamps fell nearly $4,000 below the official poverty line.[12] Not a very royal life.

Some women undoubtedly were guilty of welfare fraud. But when the press tried to track down the prototypical welfare queen, a Chicago woman Ronald Reagan claimed used eighty different names to collect $150,000 in benefits, they found she didn't exist.[13]

As for actual welfare recipients, what were they doing during the times they were on AFDC? Mostly, they were working. They just weren't getting paychecks for that labor, because they were caring for their kids. For the Big Boys, "taking care of children is real work" (as White House Director of Communications Karen Hughes indignantly noted after Teresa Heinz Kerry claimed that Laura Bush never held a "real job")[14]—except when it's done by women who are poor. Whether in the home or in paid jobs caring for other people's loved ones, caregiving is consistently devalued by those in power in the ways they count most—status and compensation.

Reality: Needing Time to Care

Anyone who's spent time among women receiving welfare has known people who wound up on AFDC because they were a good mother or daughter or niece. Clarence Thomas's sister, much maligned by him in a 1980 speech to conservative Republicans as someone who "gets mad when the mailman is late with her check—that's how dependent she is,"[15] in fact was taking time off her two minimum-wage jobs to care for *their* aunt, who'd had a stroke. Lack of leave or flexibility drove many women to public assistance when a loved one fell ill.

Women on welfare mostly found it humiliating.[16] But for low-wage workers ineligible for unemployment insurance, welfare was how you made do when you got laid off. For those unfamiliar with the law or unable to afford a lawyer, it was also where you turned when you got fired—including for being pregnant. For many, it gave a way out of violence, an end to dependence on a man who caused harm.[17] To some it represented a way to get health insurance for a kid, or to avoid having to leave young children home alone. And for others, it was simply the only way they could eat and feed their families.

Some women, of course, signed up for welfare simply because they could. It was one among many sources of income, none sufficient on its own. Some welfare recipients abused their children or were addicted to drugs—just like some middle-class and wealthy people. But the Big Boys painted them all with the same "bad mother" brush.

A Typical Story

Consider the case of Lalease Thurman in Milwaukee. Thurman spent time on public assistance after she left her emotionally abusive husband, the father of her three children. Ask her about the Personal Responsibility and Work Opportunity Act (or about almost any topic, for that matter) and you'll hear how eager she is to take responsibility for her family. She just wonders when the "work opportunity" part kicks in.

"I'm a great mother and a great worker," Thurman told an audience of 600 in a Milwaukee church, her kids clustered proudly in front of her.[18] "I just want a good job." What does a good job look like? She'll list the key criteria: It pays a decent wage, it isn't too far away, you won't be fired if you have a sick kid. Thurman would like to be able to use her many skills, including a two-year secretarial services degree and courses in early childhood development. She'd love opportunity for growth. But she's willing to work hard and above all, she wants to be able to support her family *and* care for them.

Not so long ago, Lalease Thurman could have found employment at one of the area's large manufacturing firms, several within an easy bus ride from her home in the central city. The jobs were unionized, paid well, and had benefits. Today most of those plants are empty shells, surrounded by shuttered small businesses. African American women like Thurman were usually the last hired and hence first laid off as the city saw the loss of 83,000 manufacturing positions over the last forty years—nearly half of those since 1989.[19]

The jobs that replaced them? Mostly nonunion, part time, low pay. At the time of her testimony, Thurman was working at a big-box retail outfit in an outlying area. Her workdays and shifts, usually 12–8 P.M. or 1–9 P.M., changed frequently and sometimes without notice, making childcare arrangements for her three kids problematic. Often she was scheduled to work forty hours, but because her status was part time, she received only limited benefits.

To get to work, Thurman rode two buses an hour and a half each way. Sometimes the bus was late, but no matter—her boss would mark her with a violation of attendance rules, known as an "occurrence." Sometimes the kids were ill, but like most low-wage employers, hers wasn't sympathetic. "When my kids are sick, if my dad's not home, they usually have to stay home alone or go to school sick," Thurman told me. "I write notes to the teacher asking if they can put their head down and get extra homework to make up for not participating in class. I don't have a whole lot of choices."[20] She requested to work full time on the day shift so she could get medical benefits. But due to attendance problems, she wasn't eligible to go full time.

One night her childcare provider showed up drunk. Thurman wasn't about to leave her kids in that situation and called in to work. But because the absence didn't involve a doctor's note, her boss assigned double absence points, pushing her over the limit. She was let go.

Every day she traveled to that job, Lalease Thurman agonized over the evenings away from her children. By the time the second bus dropped her off after work, the kids were usually asleep. "If I stay home when they're sick," she told me, "my employer calls me a bad worker. Because I can't help with their homework, the school says I'm a bad mother. And if I have to go back on welfare, I'm considered a bad role model."

Of those voting for the 1996 end to welfare, the best intentioned believed a low-wage job would be the entry point to a ladder of success. In fact, the available jobs had few rungs on the ladder and these had footholds more slippery than a Milwaukee winter sidewalk.

Myth: Dependency on a Handout

"Ending the cycle of dependency" is the mantra of welfare reform, as illustrated by the Clarence Thomas quote about his sister. The question is, Who's dependent on whom?

New York Times reporter Jason DeParle followed three Milwaukee-area women over seven years to gauge the impact of welfare reform in Wisconsin. In the process, he traced a relative of two of the women back to the sharecropping system in the Mississippi Delta. Sharecropping, says DeParle, had "only one theme: The need for cheap and abundant (in this case, black) labor. . . . Perhaps nowhere was the prosperity of the white elite as dependent on perpetuating a large black underclass."[21]

Reality: Dependency on Cheap Labor

What do you know, welfare reform turns out to have the same driving force (or at least the same result)—reliable, you-don't-have-to-search-for-it, they-won't-raise-a-fuss-about-it cheap labor. Tommy Thompson, then governor of Wisconsin, said as much to a gathering of restaurant owners in 1988; excerpts of his address were broadcast on public radio.

At the time restaurants and other low-wage employers were having trouble finding enough people to work at minimum and near-minimum wages. What about the law of supply and demand?, you might ask. If employers can't find workers at the going rate, they'll have to pay more. This is how the market's supposed to work—unless the supply side can be manipulated. Instead of encouraging a pay adjustment, Tommy Thompson told his pals not to worry about how they'd fill those slots. Welfare reform, he assured them, would solve the problem. He was designing a program which would turn out to be the precursor to reform on the national level, one that demanded "work first"—or in plain language, "work or else." Women would be required to take a job, in most cases the first one offered. So much for the marketplace.

Angie and Jewell, two of the three women DeParle writes about, "succeeded" in moving off welfare under Thompson's plan. The problem was, their success amounted to finding low-wage jobs. They were still poor. They still had trouble paying the bills and scrounging up enough food. They needed to double up to afford housing. But unlike before, they were unavailable to their children, who suffered the consequences. Angie's four children all ran into problems, according to DeParle. The youngest, Darrell, suffered from unexplained seizures which a friend of Angie's thought might be "psychosomatic, a lonely boy's bid for attention."[22] Von, who did the best academically, finished his freshman year in high school with a grade point average of 0.2. His older brother, Redd, dropped out of school after failing ninth grade twice and began thinking about selling drugs, saying, "I'm tired of not having no money." Kesha, the firstborn, had a baby at seventeen and left school. Jewell's son, Terrell, began cutting school and hanging out with what his mother considered the wrong crowd.

Angie, Jewell, and Opal, DeParle's third subject, had been on welfare for long stretches of time. Even if the average stay was two years or less, some people seemed to linger. Research shows that half of those long-term recipients had significant problems that could interfere with working, including severely limited cognitive abilities, depression, medical disabilities, and cocaine use (Opal fell into this category). Multiple problems were not uncommon.[23] Forced work would not cause these situations to improve.

For most women on welfare, in short, the problem was not "dependency," but the fact that employment and other systems like education, mental health, and substance abuse treatment were undependable, and that caregiving was not considered to be work.

A genuine system of reform would address all these problems. The one we have operates as if they didn't exist.

Why the New System Was Doomed to Fail

The program that replaced AFDC is known as Temporary Assistance for Needy Families, or TANF. Tommy Thompson, promoted to secretary of Health and Human Services under George W. Bush, proclaimed TANF the "greatest social policy change in this nation in 60 years."[24] And that it was, if by "great" we understand scale as opposed to value: The dismantling of the safety net was unprecedented. No longer would mothers (or fathers) raising children automatically be supported if they found themselves on their own and without sufficient income. States had the option of limiting assistance to two years; none could provide it for longer than five. In addition, for the first time, states were allowed to hand over the job of implementing such a program to private, for-profit agencies.

Ask the women who'd had to use public assistance and they'd tell you in a heartbeat that the system needed reform. But their wish list grew out of a clear goal: They wanted out of poverty.

Those who designed welfare reform had a different goal in mind. At best, they saw work as uplifting. At worst, they wanted a captive cheap labor force and a scapegoat—if taxpayers could focus their anger on the welfare queen, they might be less demanding about their own falling wages and rising health-care costs. Almost all who voted for "ending welfare" sought political capital by pandering to popular prejudice. Ending poverty, a path to decent jobs—these weren't part of the picture for most of those politicians.

Not surprisingly, TANF (and its precursor in Wisconsin, Wisconsin Works or W-2) failed to build in a method to track those who moved off assistance. The policymakers assumed that anyone no longer on the roles was employed, and that employment was an end in itself. What if the jobs turned out to be low-wage, too few hours, unpredictable shifts? Not a problem to Jason Turner. He's the guy hired by Thompson in 1993 to redesign the welfare program in Milwaukee. As DeParle points out, "Turner's fascination with welfare began in a place where it didn't exist—the leafy precincts of Darien, Connecticut,"[25] when he happened to read an article in *U.S. News and World Report* about the growing number of people who "didn't work" and instead received "government charity." The news floored him. Jason Turner was twelve-years-old and attending prep school and he'd found his mission in life.

Later he would describe his belief in the power of work, no matter what kind, by asserting, "It's work that sets you free." (DeParle notes that Turner apparently didn't realize he was quoting the motto on the gates of Auschwitz.)[26] The architect of W-2 had no illusions about the quality of the jobs available to those receiving welfare. In fact, Turner told a gathering in Milwaukee, he modeled W-2 on the lives of low-wage workers.[27] If those women couldn't get a day off when their kids were sick, by golly, neither would anyone on W-2. If they had to scramble to figure out childcare for an evening shift, why should W-2 participants expect anything different?

Never mind that in the past those same low-wage workers had AFDC as a safety net between jobs.

Reality: Free Work

Turner and others extolled a feature of W-2 called "Community Service Jobs" or CSJs (known as workfare in other places). Typically CSJs were supposed to provide valuable work experience and skills to someone with little work history. Women would receive their W-2 grant rather than a wage, but in return they'd become more marketable.

Meet Venez Blackman, who in 2004 spent ten months working a CSJ in the emergency room of a major hospital in Milwaukee. At the age of thirty-four, Blackman has a high school diploma, some college courses, lots of workforce experience, and lots of spunk. She turned to W-2 "as a last last LAST resort"[28] after being laid off and seeing her unemployment payments run out. She'd already tried various temp jobs but needed something more reliable to support herself and her eight-year-old son.

Once on W-2, Blackman was required to attend various classes on job readiness. "They tell you, 'Don't talk slang or wear hootchie shorts to the interview,'" Blackman told the state's head of the W-2 program, "stuff I already knew. They don't ask you what your career goals are or get to know you as a person." Everyone seemed to be assigned to a CSJ regardless of work experience.

"The only reason I took that CSJ was that I thought it would lead to a job," Blackman insisted. But month after month, despite good reviews, hospital personnel said they just weren't hiring. They got ten months of free labor and Venez Blackman got ten months of time on her welfare clock—the amount of time she could receive W-2, which now had a lifetime limit of two years.

Shocking? Wait until you meet Jackie Caruso, also a veteran worker who ended up on W-2 after a layoff. Her CSJ was at McDonald's (how's that for community service!), where she was supposed to receive managerial training. "I never got past the cash register and fry maker," Caruso said.[29]

Many TANF recipients did find jobs, although they didn't always last very long. Gena Mitchell worked at a large postage meter company in Savannah, Georgia. She described a revolving door of hiring black women who'd been receiving public assistance—either welfare or, as in Mitchell's case, Supplemental Security Income (SSI) for a son with a medical disability.[30]

During the job interview, the personnel manager encouraged Mitchell to talk about her family situation and then offered sympathy for her son's situation, asking how Mitchell managed and whether she received any assistance from the government. "When I told them I got SSI," Mitchell explained, "she gave me what she said was a routine form that allows the government to know they will be employing someone with a very ill child. Only after I was fired did I find out they got $3,000 for me—that form got them a tax credit." Gena Mitchell also found out the company that year hired and fired 740 black women, most former welfare recipients, to get those tax credits. For each recipient hired, the company got the tax, no matter how long they kept them on.

"A manager named one Friday Black Friday, because everyone they let go was black," Mitchell said. "Most blacks weren't making the target. No one could. The whites didn't either but they weren't fired except when they were caught defrauding the company or looking at porno on the Internet."

Reality: Welfare for Business

Hmm, handouts of cash as entitlements, with almost no monitoring or accountability. Sounds like conservatives' descriptions of welfare. Except the recipients in this case are profit-making and often highly profitable enterprises.

In Wisconsin and many other states, the freebies extended to for-profit social-service agencies overseeing the TANF contracts. Many who left the welfare rolls under their watch didn't actually find jobs. Not to worry. Agencies were rewarded for lowering the number on welfare regardless of whether those "welfare leavers" were better or worse off. Wisconsin's program was set up with what was known as a "light touch"—translation: If they don't ask, we won't tell. Agency staff was to respond only to what applicants specifically requested. If someone didn't know to inquire about emergency housing assistance, for example, she shouldn't receive any information on that program, even if she were eligible and her chances at success would be enhanced by it.

The profit motive provided an ugly added attraction to deny people aid. It also meant that a much bigger chunk of the funding got swallowed up in administrative costs than was the case under AFDC. Peruse the Milwaukee press and you'll find headlines of huge executive salaries, financial mismanagement, corruption, and graft associated with W-2 agencies. For all the talk about cheating by welfare recipients and the need for stronger enforcement, most of the scandals involving the W-2 agencies brought no action or a mere slap on the wrist during the Thompson administration.[31]

Reality: Inadequate Work Supports

Everyone knew low-wage jobs in themselves couldn't provide a decent living. And most decision-makers had figured out that you couldn't expect women to work if their kids didn't have someone to watch them. As a result, work supports such as food stamps, childcare assistance, health-care programs, and the like were built into TANF.

But the shortsightedness about employment extended to work supports as well. Many women who are eligible for childcare subsidies are not taking advantage of them because they can't afford the co-payment. Fifty dollars a week seems like a dream payment to many parents, but for those earning less than $15,000 a year, it's a lot of money. A corporate manager encouraging employers to hire more women off welfare told me the story of a group of bakery workers in Detroit brought in to work the midnight shift. The owner of the bakery was quite pleased with the former welfare recipients' work ethic and competency. But he was puzzled by one thing: Every time they had a break, the women would go out to the parking lot, even when it was bitter cold. Turned out their kids were sleeping in the cars.

Others eligible for subsidies but not using them cite a lack of eligible providers in their community, or a lack of trust in the quality of care. These women would like to give the subsidy to a relative, but often these grandmothers and aunts aren't certified as childcare providers, and therefore are disqualified.

One Step Forward, Two Steps Back

One problem for parents who do use the subsidies is losing them just when they begin to earn more money—but not enough money to pay for childcare on their own. Tina Orth, for example, was earning $10.49 an hour at a Milwaukee bank when she learned she was no longer eligible for childcare subsidies. She had to move her child to a different, less expensive care provider, one who proved unreliable on enough occasions that Orth lost her job. She was unable to collect unemployment because at the time, trouble finding childcare was not a valid consideration for eligibility. Finally she got another job—and was written up by the *Los Angeles Times* as an example of a success on Wisconsin's W-2 program. The article failed to point out that Orth was earning $7.50 an hour, working part time with no benefits and no flexibility whatsoever. She had to take four buses to get her daughter to childcare and herself to the job. Not surprisingly, the job didn't last long.

As for parents of children with special needs? Many of them have developed expertise and special skills caring for these children. They could be paid to take care of someone else's disabled child—but not their own.

Lack of quality care has a big impact on a parent's ability to stay employed. It also has an impact on kids' ability to learn and feel safe and be healthy. A Boston teacher described the connection between children's educational achievement and their parents' job situations. "The [children] don't see much of their parents. A lot of these people could only get jobs at night . . . so kids come in without signed permission slips or homework [done]."[32] A Milwaukee teacher told me, "I've never seen so many children coming to school sick because their parents couldn't get permission to take off work."[33]

So how are things going in the post-welfare world? Some women got decent jobs, just as they had under AFDC. Given the limits on access to education, however, most welfare "leavers" who are employed are stuck in low-paying jobs. Half or more are still living in poverty, a greater number than before in extreme poverty.[34] More of these children are among the nearly 4 million middle school kids (and 40,000 kindergarteners) described as being in "self care"—that means they're home alone.[35] Many states have long waiting lists for childcare. Families may not be lining the streets, as some envisioned—but many are squeezed into housing where they double and triple up with relatives or friends. One grandmother told me how her daughter spent the night in the emergency room with horrible stomach pains. After hours of tests, the doctors told her the diagnosis: "You're starving." The woman hadn't wanted to ask her mother, who was already providing shelter and food for the babies, for anything more for herself.

The architects of welfare reform did achieve their goal of cutting the rolls—but they didn't save taxpayers money, especially given administrative costs and profits to private agencies, and they certainly didn't enhance the quality of life for most former recipients. Because they misdiagnosed the problem, their solution was doomed from the start.

FEMINIST SOLUTIONS

Solving the problem of welfare requires different premises, goals, and strategies from those the Big Boys used. For starters, the real objectives have to be ending poverty and supporting families. Given that most women end up on welfare because of problems with employment, the focus should be reform of *work*. Specifically, that means decent pay, flexibility for family care, universal health care, and quality childcare. Women moving off welfare, like all workers, need the right to organize. Workers earning low wages need greater access to income supports, but above all, we need to raise the wage floor. Improved transportation systems are crucial—but creating jobs where people live, and affordable housing near outlying jobs, are even better solutions.

Any program to end poverty will target ways to create family-supporting jobs, as well as education and training aimed at linking people with such jobs. That requires careful partnerships with workforce investment programs and with technical and four-year colleges. It will also involve more on-the-job training and courses delivered at worksites on released time.

Supporting families means valuing the work of caring for family members. For those with infants or short-term emergency care situations, the answer is sufficient and affordable leave (see Chapter 4)—and a safety net of public support for those who need it. Those tending to a disabled family member should be able to receive pay for providing that care at the same level the state pays a private care worker. If the caregiver is able to work part time, equitable treatment for part-time workers will help (see Chapter 7), but some people may need supplemental assistance if those wages falls short.

Enlarging the Caregiver Tax Credit and making it fully refundable for those without a taxable income will also help, as well as having Social Security cover years spent out of the workforce to care for a family member. These tax policies are ways to acknowledge that all the tasks involved with raising kids or nursing a sick loved one do, in fact, constitute work and should be supported by a society that values families.

The safety net that remains must be reasonable, humane, and inclusive, without time limits, and without excluding immigrants. Rather than assuming abuse, it will seek to help each person be successful. The program will take the advice of people who have known welfare firsthand. "Address the whole person," Venez Blackman urges. "We just want opportunity. Don't assume I'm going to make bad of an opportunity when you haven't given me one." Coaching and meaningful choices will accommodate most people.

For agencies providing service, states will have to ensure accountability related to effective outcomes. That means requiring a high bar for training that speaks to people's actual skills, health, and life situations. Once people are ready, it means demanding placements in good jobs and monitoring agencies carefully to make sure those standards are met.

For such changes to work, they must be linked to reform in other systems. Given the close association between domestic violence and women needing assistance, welfare reform needs to go hand-in-hand with efforts to end violence and foster equality in personal relationships (see Chapter 9). Child support programs must be strengthened—but they also have to help fathers find meaningful work, not just send them to jail, especially if they happen to be nonwhite.[36] Real economic development that slashes poverty, small class sizes and other educational reforms that increase graduation rates, greater access to higher education and to treatment for mental health problems and addiction—these and other changes will reduce the *need* for assistance.

Raising the Wage Floor for Everyone

Still, more is needed to guarantee a decent wage for all workers. The following public policies would help:

- Adjust and index the minimum wage. In the last forty years, the minimum wage—what FDR described as "a fair day's work for a fair day's pay"—lost nearly a third of its value. Rather than fighting every so often to tweak the rate, we need to adjust it to make up for all the lost value and then index that amount to annual cost of living increases, as is done with Social Security.[37]

- Adopt the concept of living wages and community benefit agreements. More than a hundred localities have passed some form of a living-wage ordinance or a community benefit agreement. The most meaningful require contractors and employers who receive public dollars to hire community residents and pay a wage that brings people at least to the official poverty level. The jobs that are created should also provide flexibility for family care.

- Develop a self-sufficiency standard for each locality. Many experts have recognized that the official poverty level underestimates family costs and should be replaced.[38] Rather than a one-size-fits-all number, women's groups have been developing self-sufficiency standards.[39] This calculates how much money working adults need to meet their basic needs—including transportation, taxes, child-care—without subsidies of any kind, factoring the cost of living and working according to family size and geographic location.

- Strengthen work supports like the Earned Income Tax Credit (EITC). The EITC, a refundable amount from the federal government and some state governments to those who pay little or no taxes because their earnings are so low, should be maintained and improved—a better phase-out system, for example, so that getting a raise doesn't result in a loss of income, and higher benefits for families with more than two children.

- Provide universal health care. We have to find a way to provide insurance for all, regardless of where they work. A nation as wealthy as ours can no longer afford to see health care as a "fringe benefit" rather than a right. Until we succeed, we need to ensure that low-wage employers provide insurance or pay their fair share into state funds, rather than having taxpayers subside billions of dollars in health-care costs for Wal-Mart and its ilk.

- Stop using public dollars to entice private corporations. A West Bend, Wisconsin, business leader sued his county board for approving a $4 million payment to an outdoor-gear showroom. "This is America," he said. "If they want to build a store there, God bless them. But it shouldn't be built with taxpayer dollars."[40]

- Remove incentives for companies to move offshore: Globalization may be a fact of life, but we don't have to give incentives for companies to ship jobs overseas. At the least, Congress should remove tax breaks—estimated at $7 billion[41]—for U.S. companies that operate overseas rather than at home.

This isn't an exhaustive list. Among other things, we need to make pensions portable and protect Social Security; increase support for public higher education and job training; promote global "fair trade" agreements that contain meaningful and enforceable labor and environmental standards; implement a progressive tax policy, replacing the current one that favors corporations and the rich. Working together, we can create the entire package of reforms. But we must start by acknowledging that achieving justice and equality requires systemic, institutional change.

Finding the Funds

How to pay for all this? As I've written elsewhere in this book, ending corporate welfare would go a long way toward making these changes possible (see Chapter 3, page 55.) Civil rights leader Ralph Abernathy used to ask why, if the United States could pay millionaires not to grow food, it couldn't afford to help poor children eat.[42] We have the means. We just need the political will—and political leadership that doesn't squander billions of dollars on irresponsible military ventures or contracts to cronies made with no competition and no monitoring.

Let me be clear—I'm not against welfare for business. I just feel it should come with eligibility requirements and accountability. Directing tax credits and other public dollars to needy businesses who create jobs in underserved communities, for example, or who offer targeted job training and other such programs, can be a good idea. But any such incentive programs must require that the dollars have a direct impact on workers and the community. A feminist future will put an end to cronyism and decisions dependent on campaign contributions.

TAKING ON THE BIG BOYS

In the past, the main focus of welfare activists had been better treatment and greater access for people needing assistance. Leaders of the welfare rights movement felt betrayed by those who favored forced work schemes as the way to "reform" the system.[43] While 9to5 addressed issues of fair treatment and the value of caregiving work, we knew that most women on welfare also wanted to be able to earn a living. We targeted the need to reform *work* so that it could be a way out of poverty rather than another form of poverty. We carried out this organizing on many fronts––public education, direct action, research, and media campaigns. In the process, we took on Democrats as well as Republicans and people within the movement as well as bureaucrats. Nearly two decades later, we're still waging the struggle—but with some successes under our belt.

How We Got Involved

How did a working women's organization become so involved in welfare reform? 9to5's focus dates back to one blustery Milwaukee day in 1986. The board of the Milwaukee chapter had scheduled a discussion about women on welfare who were taking clerical training at ITT one floor above us. Like much good networking among women, we'd gotten to know them in the bathroom; the two floors shared a narrow ladies' room with three stalls and one sink which happened to be right next to our office. The trainees seemed to love the program and especially liked the network of support they built with each other. But the instructors told us that many of the trainees wound up losing their jobs not long after they found them. Their network ended as soon as they graduated. They needed ongoing support and coaching on things like how to deal with conflict or what to do if they had no job description or whom to tell if the boss put his hands on them. ITT's instructors lacked the time and know-how to fill the gap.

Around a nicked conference table, seven 9to5 board members began brainstorming a project to address this. And the stories spilled out. A young white woman had been on AFDC when her daughter was born. An African American woman in her early forties said she'd had to go on welfare when she lost her job some years earlier. Another had a sister in the same boat. That night the board realized there wasn't a bright line separating women on welfare and low-paid "working" women like 9to5's members. Helping the ITT women hang on to their jobs was a logical extension of our mission.

We designed a Job Retention Project that soon was replicated by 9to5 chapters in Cleveland, Atlanta, and Los Angeles. More women on welfare got involved with 9to5. By the time Tommy Thompson's reform efforts began to wreak havoc in Wisconsin, we were speaking out.

And that undermined a chief tactic of the Big Boys. In addition to *minimizing* the problems of women living in poverty, they counted on *demonizing* those who needed assistance To make that work, they tried to *compartmentalize* women who needed to be allies—pitting "welfare women" against "working women."

It doesn't take a political genius to realize that welfare reform can't be explicitly marketed as a guaranteed supply of cheap labor. How much easier to seize the old welfare queen stereotype and shape a PR strategy around that! Tommy Thompson acknowledged to a reporter that welfare reform was "a fantastic campaign issue." Turns out his chief welfare reform architect, Jason Turner, was also his point man on election polling.[44]

Bipartisan Contempt for the Poor

The Republicans weren't the only ones making hay out of welfare as a campaign issue. It was, after all, a Democrat who not only signed the Personal Responsibility and Work Opportunity Reconciliation Act but bragged about doing so. President Clinton says his own life experience shaped his thinking. He told a reporter that watching his mother get ready for work every day "no matter what the hell was going on" gave him "a sense of pride and meaning and direction."[45] To his credit, he first called for more than just cutting the rolls: two years of education and training followed by meaningful Community Service Jobs with no time limits, all on a voluntary basis. Yet politics quickly shaped the program into one with little or no emphasis on education, severe time limits, and requirements to accept any job no matter what the consequences on children's well-being. Clinton got on the bandwagon of describing welfare checks as coming out of "taxpayers' hides."[46] Making sure the Democrats presided over welfare reform seemed to have become an end in itself.

Unlike some women's organizations based in Washington, DC, we never had faith that a chat with Leon Panetta, Clinton's chief of staff, would turn the president away from the disastrous path to which he'd committed himself. 9to5 continued to speak out and rally and make public our criticism. I did attend a meeting of women's leaders in 1996 with Panetta and Bruce Reed, Clinton's point person on welfare. The surly Reed was adamant about the political necessity of some drastic change. I sat next to Panetta, who cast his sorrowful eyes on the packet of stories and facts and figures I'd marshaled. They might feel they could count on women's vote, I told him, but many low-wage women fall into the "undecided whether or not to vote" category. If they didn't see the Democrats as any different from Republicans, why would they bother? Panetta claimed he cared. Donna Shalala, then-secretary of health and human services, said she pleaded. Some staff even quit. But Clinton stood his ground.

We knew we were in for a long fight.

Reframing the Debate

Experience told us that the most effective way to stop the demonizing of women on welfare was to have them tell their stories. Early on we arranged for members with direct experience of welfare to speak at congregations and community groups, sharing how they wound up on welfare and what they wanted for themselves. Whatever the audience expected, it wasn't Kerryn Laumer, a white woman with bright eyes talking about having to go on welfare when her mother was diagnosed with ovarian cancer and Laumer promised she wouldn't have to die alone. Afterward she could find only temp jobs with no health insurance. The congregants hadn't expected Denise Torres, mother of three who had work experience and training certificates, but no job. Our speakers tore away stereotypes and linked their stories to values most Americans share: that work should pay, that it shouldn't jeopardize kids, that people should be allowed to care for family members *and* have ways to support them. We urged congregants to contact their legislators. These efforts helped win some early victories—ending "bridefare" (paying women on welfare "bonuses" if they married) and "learnfare" (sanctioning parents whose children were truant), and preventing the W-2 grant amount from being subminimum wage.

I repeated the women's themes in a 1997 debate on W-2 sponsored by the public radio station in Milwaukee.[47] My opponent was Andy Busch, director of the Welfare Policy Center of the Hudson Institute, a conservative think tank. I expected someone fierce, but Busch looked like a young lacrosse player—rosy checks, curly hair, mild manner. Still, he didn't deviate from the conservative playbook. He opened with "personal responsibility," describing W-2 as "encouraging parents to exercise their fundamental responsibility to provide for their families." This was going to be easier than I thought. I countered with facts and stories of how many women wound up on welfare *because* they were responsible parents, and how hard it was to provide for a family when you earn poverty wages.

Busch moved on to "opportunity." He was especially proud of the Community Service Jobs, a way for women to learn new skills and get valuable job experience. I told the audience about a woman I'd met whose CSJ was at a county building cleaning toilets and scrubbing floors. "I've been cleaning toilets and scrubbing floors all my life," she said. "What kind of training is this?"

So much for patronizing—Busch immediately shifted to demonizing mode: "Work is not always fun," he declared. "It involves sacrifice." Still referring to the woman who had objected to the lack of opportunity offered by her custodial CSJ, he went even further: "There are people who work in those jobs who pay taxes that have gone to support parents who thought they were too good to do jobs like that." After audible gasps from many people in the room, he tried to say he was "just being provocative"—but he'd made his point.

I prepared to take him out: This woman, I reminded him, like most on welfare, had been working and paying taxes much of her adult life. Her problem wasn't the custodial work but the fact that she wasn't being paid—unlike the county workers who labored alongside her. Blaming women on welfare, I pointed out, aims to "shift people's focus from the real problem: 'Why can't I pay my rent or be home when my kid is sick?'" Rather than assuming work has to be degrading, our goal should be universal reforms that would help everyone gain decent jobs and care for their families.

I liked besting this guy. But convincing the fifty people in the bookstore and the listeners to public radio would never be enough. We had to reach a wider audience, and we had to reach policymakers.

Demanding Accountability

To allow more women to share their experiences, a large community coalition demanded public hearings at times and locations where women on W-2 could speak. The state finally agreed to hold such a hearing in Milwaukee in March of 2001, after a rash of news stories about problems in the program. Those were precipitated by the efforts of then-state senator Gwen Moore, who'd requested an audit of W-2. (Moore, a former welfare recipient who went on to become the first woman and African American elected to Congress from Milwaukee, had tried everything to stop W-2. The original plan, which called for requiring women on assistance to work for subminimum wage, was introduced at the same time as another pet project of Governor Thompson, a new baseball stadium in Milwaukee. Still short one vote for the stadium, the governor brought in baseball legend Hank Aaron to try to win over Moore. "They're gearing up for a return to slavery," she told Aaron, "and you want to talk to me about baseball?" Thompson then called her to his office. "What do I have to do to get your support?" he asked. Moore's response: "Take W-2 off the table." She could hear the governor hollering long after she left the room.)[48]

One of the W-2 agencies highlighted in the audit was a private outfit called Maximus. In addition to misspending hundreds of thousands of W-2 dollars feting lobbyists and campaigning for contracts in other states, Maximus had a tidy side business, a temp service named MaxStaff. They weren't prepared for one Tracy Jones, a single mother who wandered into a job fair at the agency and was told they had a position for her. Turns out the job was through MaxStaff. Jones would be paid $7 an hour to pack boxes for a large furniture store out in the exurbs. As the only woman in her department, Jones, a powerfully built woman who'd worked temp jobs for years to support herself and her son, was dismayed when she discovered the men she'd trained were making $8.13 an hour. When she went to her supervisor to demand an explanation, Jones was assured the men were paid the same rate she was. The next morning, a supervisor leaned into the van about to shuttle Jones and her coworkers to the warehouse and delivered this warning: Talking about salaries could lead to termination. What management didn't know was that Tracy Jones had been a union steward and knew how to do her homework. She had pay stubs from some of the men in her pocket, along with the phone number for the EEOC. Shortly after she filed a gender discrimination complaint with that agency, Jones was let go for "problems in her performance."[49] She began to speak out, and soon got involved with 9to5, who launched a campaign against Maximus.

Our staff and other groups organized dozens of women like Jones to attend the March 14 hearing at the Martin Luther King Center. But when we showed up, the small auditorium was already packed with spokespeople for the W-2 agencies and their various subcontractors, all of whom were allowed to speak first while the TV cameras were still present. Just when some of the W-2 participants began to testify, a fire alarm pierced the room. Everyone bundled up and hurried outdoors. A second alarm sounded shortly after we filed back in. They weren't the only false notes that day.

To an ever-dwindling audience, the women described their experiences. Anita Fleming, mother of two preteens, talked about her community service job "packing things into boxes." Fleming told us she'd never spoken in public before, but you'd never know it to hear her describe being injured with a hernia on that assignment. "I had the statement from my doctor that I needed to have surgery," she told the panel. "Employment Solutions [another W-2 agency] still took my money away." The W-2 participants' demands were simple: training, meaningful work, due process, and respect.

Fleming and the other women we'd brought were frustrated; some were furious. "They pulled those alarms themselves to keep us from being heard," one told me. On the plus side, they'd found each other and a way to stay connected. The state agreed to set up a citizen advisory panel. We insisted on having two women on W-2 be part of that process. One small change at a time, we managed to make some progress—more money for childcare and kinship care (usually grandparents), an end to the "light touch" approach (see page 184), increased staff for oversight in the Milwaukee region. Our coalition also persuaded a majority of the legislature that W-2 participants should be able to spend at least fifteen hours a week in technical training; Governor Thompson vetoed the measure.

Still, the day of unfettered profits for W-2 agencies was over. While Maximus got only a token fine, we'd opened the door to a larger issue of accountability for the agencies. Maximus closed down their temp agency. Employment Solutions, also charged with financial mismanagement, decided to leave the welfare business. Today under a Democratic administration, the state department responsible for W-2 is planning major revisions in what it demands of agencies and how it monitors performance.

A New Wrinkle: Jobs Don't Last

On the national level, I coauthored a research report that helped show the problem was not dependency but jobs that were undependable. Together with the Radcliffe Public Policy Center, 9to5 interviewed 350 people in Boston, Denver, and Milwaukee about how low-income parents manage work, family, and their children's education.[50] The parents (all living below 200 percent of poverty), employers, and teachers we interviewed had many different views, but they all agreed that low-wage work couldn't sustain a family and made it hard for parents to stay employed—whether or not that person had been on welfare. Although 40 percent of the parents interviewed were paid more than $10 an hour, nearly seven in ten grossed less than $20,000 a year. One in four earned less than half that. Only two percent owned a home; 37 percent sought donated food at some time during the previous year. More than half had no regular access to a car.

The income finding surprised us. Our study had stumbled onto a reality overlooked by most welfare reform advocates: what sociologists call "job churning." That means losing your job and having to get another one—for these women, mostly because of family care reasons. What we documented was the disastrous impact that has on kids—shuffling through a hodgepodge of caregivers after school, staying up late or being awakened because a parent had to work second shift, missing important appointments for health or learning problems, spending long hours home alone, dealing with evictions and school changes when a parent got fired.

In addition to media interviews on the report, my coauthor and I went to Washington in March of 2002 to brief congressional staff. Here was the tricky part: Many of those we visited were legislators who had voted for the 1996 law abolishing the old welfare system. They didn't want to say they'd voted wrong. On the other hand, they did agree that work should pay. Our message was that work can't pay if it doesn't last, and it can't last if it harms kids. We told them what the women had told us: "I want to be a role model for my son," one woman put it. "But he sees how stressed I am, how poor we are, how little time we have together. What kind of lesson is that?"

We also brought with us a 9to5 pamphlet called "Welfare as WE Know It: The Case for Reforming TANF."[51] In it our members with experience in the system shared their stories—and their proposals for solutions. 9to5ers across the country used the booklet with their elected officials to ask for their support.

Our work helped win backing for a number of measures to improve TANF on a national level, including greater support for education and training, more experimentation with programs that let low-income parents stay home with an infant, more funding for childcare. Because of our members, moderate Democrats like Sen. Herb Kohl in Wisconsin and even Republicans like Sen. Ben Nighthorse Campbell in Colorado became vocal in calling for more childcare support. The progressives didn't prevail, but they were able to keep more punitive policies from being passed.

As I write this book, the Bush administration holds the purse strings and continues to dole out huge amounts of money for cockamamie schemes like abstinence education and marriage promotion.[52] Author Barbara Ehrenreich pointed out the fundamental flaw in that strategy: Since most people marry within their social class, poor women would have to be bigamists and marry 2.3 poor men at once in order to break out of poverty.[53] Ask Lalease Thurman or Venez Blackman or any of the other women we've worked with and they'll tell you what they want: "Caps and gowns, not wedding gowns." They'd be delighted to find a good mate, but most of all, they want to be able to support and care for their children.

Hurricane Katrina made visible to many Americans the layers of poverty and racism that most policymakers have failed to acknowledge, much less address. Whether and how this nation accepts responsibility for changing that situation remains to be seen. But any plan that doesn't include the solutions outlined above will fail.

"STAND WITH SISTERS FOR ECONOMIC DIGNITY"

Getting the attention of Congress is always a challenge. In September 2002 a group called the National Campaign for Jobs and Income Support not only got Congress to pay attention—they knocked their socks off. They did this not with a rally or hearing or fax-in or call-in day, but with a thirty-eight minute cultural performance on Capitol Hill, professionally directed and choreographed, starring nine women who were now or once had been on welfare.

The campaign represented a coalition of more than 100 organizations (including 9to5) in forty-plus states, spearheaded by the DC–based Center for Community Change (CCC). LaDon James, a CCC staffer, came up with the idea for the skit. "I wanted to figure out a more creative way to get the message out," she told me, "a way to hit the hearts and guts of many people who hadn't taken the time to understand the plight of women on public assistance."[54] James turned to playwright Gwendolyn Hardwick at NYU and songwriter Tiye Giraud, She found the cast in New York, where the campaign had several member groups. Four groups—We Make the Road by Walking, ACORN (Association of Community Organizations for Reform Now), FUREE (Families United for Racial and Economic Equality), and Community Voices Heard—each contributed two people for the skit, which now had the title "Stand with Sisters for Economic

Dignity." LaDon James saw herself as the coordinator, but when the women discovered she'd been on welfare herself, they insisted she join them as a performer.

The nine women met weekly at one of the various organizations, which took turns providing childcare and food. First order of business: sharing stories, two each week. "These women, all single mothers, were used to being marginalized and not listened to," James told me. "Now they had a forum to speak to their peers. As we discussed our struggles—what brought us to public assistance, our dreams and aspirations, what we thought we were going to get through public assistance versus what we actually got, how we had to fight to get what we were entitled to in the first place—the women found they had even more commonality than they knew." The support spilled over to friendships that lasted long after the performance.

Dramatizing the Burdens of Poverty

Playwright Gwen Hardwick did more than listen to the women's stories. She fleshed them out by asking questions such as "How did you feel when you applied for assistance?" and then urging the women to show her how they would express those feelings with their bodies and facial expressions. The skit opens with the women dragging their chairs, hunched over, breathing hard in and out. "You're hearing the burden women have to bear," James explained.

Tiye Giraud created a song based on what the women talked about and named it "Caught Up in the WEP of Deception"—referring to the notorious Work Experience Program in New York that required people to perform work in exchange for their welfare benefits. Actors Danny Glover and Tim Robbins lent their support. Senators Paul Wellstone and Patty Murray agreed to host the performance for members of Congress and their staff on September 18.

Tyleatha Samuels, one of the participants, described what it was like to get up in front of the packed room: "I'm two paces away from Danny Glover and he's looking at me right in the face," Samuels said. "It was nerve-racking but also moving. I could identify with each one of the women's stories. Being beaten—I've been in a relationships like that. Trying to get food stamps and they're not giving you enough. Wanting to get an education, a better job, wanting to do better for your family."[55] At one point in the performance, Samuels, who uses a cane because of arthritis in both knees, let out a scream as she described going into a welfare office to get help. "They tell you you're going to get some experience, and then they want you to clean the street for $68.50 every two weeks. You're already getting the short end of the stick by not having enough job training—like you need any more setbacks than what you already have."

I asked what it was like learning how to perform. "Tim Robbins said Hollywood came to Washington," Samuels replied. "But you didn't have to do that much acting—you were living your own life." The women shared the painful indignities they'd experienced. One woman was sexually and physically assaulted by her husband in front of her children. Others were forced to give up high school or college in order to take the make-work jobs, some without proper childcare. They breathed together and belted out a song written for the skit: "Caught up in the WEP of deception, we're trying to save our lives. Make-work no benefits, work no advancement, work no way to get out of this enslavement. There's got to be a better way to do this. Stand with a sister and help us make a difference."

CCC had arranged for other women from member groups around the country to come in for the event. One of the performers threw out the question: "Will you stand with a sister to help make a difference?" Actors Glover and Robbins answered, "Yes!" Then one by one these other women stood up, identified themselves as being on public assistance and said, "Yes," they would stand with a sister.

"There wasn't a dry eye in the place," James said. "It definitely created a buzz on the Hill—no one had done something so creative."

Calling on Policymakers to Step Up

In addition to what the experience meant for the women involved, James believes it had significant results, "Senator Murray set up a meeting with the other women senators where the performers could come back and talk about why TANF is a women's issue. They felt compelled to step up. We forced people not to ignore the issue and gave leverage to work being done in communities because of the bubbling effect this story had. The song stuck in people's head and forced them to think about it." James believes the performance helped influence passage of the bipartisan plan in the Committee on Finance. The video has continued to influence students of social work in universities across the country.

"We helped educate a broader constituency, tap into places we weren't able to get into with our usual modes of operation," said James. "People who saw this firsthand or on video, down to our consultants, were able to reflect back on their childhood or other experiences and connect with those women. That's the power of culture and the arts."

What did it mean to her personally, I asked? "I was the one that cried the most," she said. "To reflect on where you came from, the obstacles you've faced, brainstorm with other women who are going through it to come up with solutions is really powerful. Some things I had put on the back burner because they were so painful, I was forced to reflect on because of this process. It made me a stronger person."

FINAL THOUGHTS: MOVING BEYOND PARTIAL SOLUTIONS

Many good people have focused their attention on implementing work supports, measures like the Earned Income Tax Credit that help supplement low wages. As long as women's work is undervalued and workers lack real power, we must maintain and expand such supports. But they're a *tactic*, not a strategic solution. Our goal is to raise the wage floor, and that's where we must direct our main energies.

I remember being invited to a focus group some years ago by an early proponent of the EITC. He asked a dozen low-income women what method they'd prefer for receiving a wage subsidy (directly in their paycheck, at the bank when the check was cashed, or once a year as a tax return). The woman standing next to me thrust her arm in the air. "I work hard," she said. "Why can't I just have a decent wage?"

Those who live in poverty, disproportionately female, want exactly the same thing everyone else does—to support themselves and their loved ones with dignity, to work hard and be valued accordingly. They deserve nothing less.

9. REVALUING WOMEN'S WORK
OUTSIDE OF WORK

[I]t is women, more than men, who want to have children. So is it not unfair of them to insist that the men share heavily in the child rearing? . . . If quantity of family time matters more to women, it is unfair for them to impose that value on their husbands. And regarding domestic chores, most men aren't as concerned about a tastefully decorated and sparkling clean home."—Marty Nemko, columnist for the American Conservative Union[1]

People often equate feminism with "allowing" women to do work associated with men. But feminism also means valuing work associated with women, including raising children and creating a home. As we have seen in earlier chapters, this is impossible without changing the way business does business. But truly valuing women also requires changes on the home front.

The Big Boys tell us that the private sphere is where women in the United States have made particularly impressive progress. Laws have erased all traces of women's inferior status in relationships. Even women's work in the home is no longer a burden, thanks to technology and men pitching in.

The truth? The glass may not be half empty, but it's a long way from full.

Myth: Equality in Marriage

Nowhere have the signs of progress been greater for women than in marriage, according to the Big Boys' view of the world. Husbands and wives in this country are now equal partners in marriage and divorce. As a result of marital property laws, patriarchal privilege is a thing of the past. What's his is hers and vice versa.

Reality: More Rights Not the Same as Equal Rights

Before someone blasts me for ingratitude, let me acknowledge that the progress has been huge. No longer are wives considered the property of their husbands, prohibited from owning anything or leaving an abusive marriage or making key decisions concerning their children. Women—by law, at least—don't have to fork over their earnings to males in the family. Their husbands can't legally beat or rape them, and rape is no longer seen as an offense against the father or husband whose property is damaged. I'm thankful courts stopped using the definition of husband and wife as one person, meaning "the very being or legal existence of the woman is suspended during her marriage, or at least, is consolidated into that of her husband."[2] All these forms of domination described the status of American women in 1848, when a group of women and male allies gathered in Seneca Falls, New York, to sign a Declaration of Sentiments concerning women's rights. Activists fought hard for every change, usually state by state. Many states hung on to "head and master" laws—husband has final say over household decisions—until the 1970s. Marital rape didn't become a crime in most places until the 1980s.

Still, more rights aren't the same as equal rights—and rights on paper, as we have seen, are often a far cry from rights in real life.

Not So Happily Ever After

In recent decades, the laws governing marriage have seen welcome progress. Most (but not all) states now have marital property provisions, granting that any items acquired during the time of marriage are jointly owned by both spouses. But the Big Boys have found ways to limit the impact of these laws—money is money, after all. So let's get the facts straight. First, marital property refers to *assets*, not *income*. That means that a wife who has sacrificed her career to do the family caregiving and therefore earns less upon returning to work, or who works in an undervalued female job, is not automatically entitled to any share of the future earnings of her ex-mate. The notion that a man's earnings and degree belong to him, regardless of his wife's sacrifice in making them possible, is the key reason men's standard of living increases after a divorce, while women's declines—so much so that 40 percent of divorced mothers wind up living in poverty.[3] Even in cases where a woman is awarded "maintenance," judges usually base the amount on her immediate need—as if she were a charity case—not on the value of her caregiving over the years. Awards are typically low and temporary. Most judges responding to a survey agreed with this statement: "A wife's alimony is based on how much the husband can give without diminishing his current lifestyle."[4] Or as one Georgia family law judge put it, "[A]limony is like feeding hay to a dead horse."[5]

Laura's story is not uncommon. She worked in a marketing position while her husband Steve finished his law degree. The couple agreed they wanted to start a family and that Laura should stay home for the first few years. Steve spent long hours at the office, seldom showing up for his kids' special events. Over time he became more and more distant and verbally abusive to Laura, who decided she wanted a divorce. With the kids in school, Laura was prepared to go back to work full time, but had to settle for an entry-level job paying less than $40,000 a year—considerably less than she would have earned had she not taken time for parenting. Steve's annual income had reached nearly $200,000. Declaring that Laura "makes enough for herself" and that the kids would get child support, the judge ordered no alimony. Steve also was entitled to half the value of the house; Laura had to sell it in order to give him his share. "I couldn't afford the mortgage anyway," she said.

Some states have begun to address the problem by revising their laws to consider factors such as "periods of unemployment" as a result of performing "domestic duties"; "contributions to childcare"; "impaired earning capacity"; or "lost income capacity."[6] Unfortunately, the existence of these statutes doesn't guarantee a thing. Settlements are still in the hands of judges, many of whom disregard such provisions out of ignorance or bias.[7]

This isn't the only problem with marital property laws. What most state statutes require is not an equal but an "equitable" division of property. Only a handful require a fifty-fifty split. Oklahoma, for instance, allows a man to keep all of his stock options after divorce; Connecticut requires a couple share only their debts. As for the rest of the property, the definition of "equitable" is up to those judges.

Wisconsin law presumes a fifty-fifty split, says Amy Shapiro, a family law attorney in Milwaukee, "but that's not written in the statute. [The standard] is often not taken seriously. Only in a 40-year marriage where both parties are retired do you really get to fifty-fifty. If it's a 15-year or

10-year marriage, that doesn't happen." Shapiro described seminars she's attended with as many as five judges on a panel: "Each of the judges is presented with the same facts, but you get five different answers. One will say, 'I don't know if this case warrants maintenance.' Another will say, 'It should be fifty-fifty.' You never know what you're going to get."[8]

Reality: Double Standard Still Applies

Women also are hurt by double standards about adultery. No-fault divorce laws now in most (but not all) states eliminated the need to charge a spouse with cheating in order to end a marriage. But in many places, adultery on the part of the person needing spousal support—usually female—still serves as grounds to deny any alimony whatsoever, even if the liaison happens *after* the couple breaks up. As for the sexual practices of the person liable for maintenance—usually male—that's irrelevant in the eyes of most judges.

Consider my friend, we'll call her Evelyn, in South Carolina. Evelyn's husband, think of him as Nigel, is a wealthy doctor. Nigel was able to focus on his medical practice because Evelyn worked while he finished training and then raised their four children and took care of all the household details, as well as the charity work and entertaining that boosted her husband's status. Twenty-five years later, Nigel announced he wanted a divorce so he could date younger women. The couple separated and agreed it was okay to see other people, as long as they were discreet in front of the children. Nigel soon acquired a girlfriend and began, not so discreetly, to live with her. He balked when Evelyn demanded her fair share of things like his pension and their vacation home. One day Evelyn got a call from Nigel's lawyer: Go along with his version of the financial settlement or they'd take advantage of the adultery law—South Carolina considers the couple married until the divorce goes through.

"Threatening that he had 'evidence' of adultery was bad enough," Evelyn told me. "What hurt more is realizing that he doesn't value what I've done for the last twenty-five years."[9]

South Carolina isn't the only state that applies the term *adultery* to relationships after the end of the marriage. In Georgia, for example, alimony can be reduced or terminated if the recipient has a live-in lover, no matter how many years after the divorce.

And then there's the pesky problem of child support. Although child-support payments have crept up in recent years, in 2001 only 52 percent of divorced mothers received the amount ordered; among unmarried mothers, the number was closer to 32 percent. As a *New York Times* reporter put it, "Fathers' rights groups have a tall order explaining those statistics, convincing judges—and the country at large—that if fathers skip town, or refuse payment, it's a function of how unfairly family courts treat them rather than the very reason that the courts treat fathers the way they do."[10]

Myth: Women Have the Upper Hand in Custody Cases

Divorce isn't just about property and money; decisions also have to be made about child custody. And there, the Big Boys maintain, the courts clearly favor women. A number of men's rights groups have sprung up, largely in response to what they see as unfairness in this arena. The organizations typically have names that include words like *equity* and *rights*. (A Louisiana group chose the acronym "FORCE—Fathers on Rights for Custody Equality.") One man told a reporter he felt like "a second-class parent" whose ex-spouse had been permitted by the system to stifle his freedom. "It's as bad as slavery," he said.[11]

Reality: Women Still Face Major Obstacles

I know of cases where men have been treated unfairly in court. I know loving divorced fathers who have to fight for their visitation time. I certainly know men who want to provide economic support for their children and can't find a job, yet keep being pursued by child support enforcers while wealthy dads waltz through legal loopholes. I also agree courts shouldn't assume that women are always fit parents or must be the primary caretaker. Most kids benefit by having both parents prominently in their lives.

But when the Big Boys say women have the upper hand in custody decisions, they make a mockery of the enormous obstacles many mothers face. Take the issue of stereotypes. Judges often interpret even a small amount of involvement from men as exceptional interest in their kids— after all, they're doing lots more than their fathers did. By the same token, women doing less than their mothers look bad, even if they're carrying most of the load. "Dads showing interest get a lot of what they want," attorney Amy Shapiro told me. "Judges want to encourage dads; they don't care about their past behavior."

Men in high-powered jobs?—good providers. Women in similar jobs?—neglectful mothers. Cases like that of Marcia Clark, one of the prosecutors in the O.J. Simpson case, spotlighted the problem of women being sued for custody if their jobs are too demanding, regardless of what contortions they may go through to spend time with their kids. "Like all moms," opined an article in the *Detroit News* at the time, "Marcia Clark can't have it all."[12] Sharon Prost, former chief counsel for the Senate Republicans, lost custody of her two children to her husband despite the fact that she spent more time with them than he did. The judge ignored a teacher's praise for Sharon Prost as a "surrogate room mom" while commenting favorably on her husband's sporadic involvement in school activities. "[H]er devotion to her job and/or her personal pursuits often takes precedence over her family," ruled the judge—who awarded her a mere six days of visitation a month.[13]

Today states have three ways of deciding custody. Many require joint custody. That may mean the children go back and forth from one parent to the other, but not necessarily—more likely, it means the divorced parents have equal rights about decisions regarding the kids. Other states grant custody to the parent deemed the primary caregiver. Still others use the standard "the best interest of the child." The problem is, judges may decide that the parent who can provide greater income is, in fact, the better bet for placement. Attorneys advising fathers in custody fights point out that judges "prefer good neighborhoods to bad, permanence to transience, houses to apartments . . . ownership to renting, large quarters over small."[14]

Men understandably don't want judges to presume that women love their children more or are entitled to custody simply because they gave birth. However, not everyone who clamors for joint custody wants to spend more time with his kids. Some simply want to pay less money. Consider this observation from Dr. Mary Duryea, director of Family Court Services in the Alameda, California, Superior Court: "[Y]ou overhear people in the hallway saying, now, how many days [of custody] do I need to get before my child support obligation is reduced?"[15]

Researchers at Harvard and Stanford found that joint physical custody often turns into a primary-custody situation, with the mother taking greater responsibility—but receiving less child support under the so-called equal arrangement.[16] A group called the National Congress of Fathers and Children is trying to enshrine this situation in legislation. They've endorsed a bill to exempt fathers from paying any support when joint custody is granted—even though children may actually reside in their father's home only a third of the time.

Fatherhood Trumps Past Abuse

Perhaps the greatest concern in custody decisions is the frequent disregard of a man's abuse of his wife. My twin sister, Dr. Lynne Bravo Rosewater, is a psychologist who specializes in work with battered women. People say that a woman should just leave a man who beats her; if he won't shape up, she should get a divorce. But certain experts who get involved along the way often complicate matters—especially if the batterer says he wants custody of the children. In such cases, both parties are evaluated with a personality test known as MMPI (Minnesota Multiphasic Personality Inventory). Typically, the batterer describes the domestic situation in more positive terms than the abused wife. "If you say things are better than they actually are—what's known as a 'fake good,'" my sister said, "there's no penalty in the validity of the MMPI test when it is computer scored. Batterers, who minimize the reality of the beatings they inflict, are seen as 'normal,' while battered women, who are confused and fearful, tend to look disturbed. The husband says, 'I should have custody, my wife is nuts.' That argument gets a lot of women to back off divorce proceedings."[17]

My sister reminded me that if you're in a violent situation, "your children are always at risk." Studies show half the men who batter women also hit their kids.[18] The urge to protect the children may lead a woman to get out of an abusive relationship—but it also may make it more difficult to leave. Some years ago Lynne was involved in such a case. A woman who was being beaten by her husband, a major in the armed services, fled the state with her kids because their mental health was deteriorating as a result of his physical and psychological abuse. (The guy's job was to interrogate prisoners; in addition to brute force, he was a master at mind games.) The woman took her children for treatment to a psychiatric hospital in another state. As soon as she left, her husband went to court to get the kids back. The psychiatrist in charge wrote a letter warning that returning to that situation would be detrimental to the wife and to the children. Okay, the judge ruled, the wife didn't have to come back—but the kids did.

"Of course, she came back, too," my sister said. The major's violence quickly escalated. "Batterers are terrified of being needy," Lynne explained. "An abuser grows to hate his victim because he fears she will abandon him. And when she does leave, he expresses that hatred in ever more dangerous ways." Afraid for her life, the major's wife ended up killing him. She was found guilty of murder; custody of the children was given to the husband's brother. A year or two later, the decision was overturned because the woman hadn't had access to effective expert testimony. This time my sister was called in and the woman was acquitted—but her brother-in-law kept custody of her kids.

"Battered women wind up in a no-win position," my sister says. "Most prosecutors say, 'The guy never killed you before. Why did you think he would kill you now?' Thus the only way a battered woman in fear for her life is credible is if she's dead." Lynne compared women who are abused to women who were prosecuted for witchcraft: "If they held your head underwater and you drowned, that proved you weren't a witch. If you didn't drown, you must have been a witch—so they burned you at the stake. You might be vindicated, but you were still dead."

While a growing number of states specifically mention domestic violence as a factor to be considered in child custody, most allow wide discretion to judges and don't give this situation special weight. Did he hit his kids? a judge often asks. And if the answer's no—even if the man threatened to, even if he increased the chances that his son would express himself with his fists and that his daughter would end up with an abuser—by golly, the judge considers him a father with rights. As of 1998, only thirteen states had adopted the Model Code of the Family Violence Project of the National Council of Juvenile and Family Court Judges. These statutes specify that there is a "rebuttable presumption" that it is not in the best interest of the child to be placed in sole custody, joint legal custody, or joint physical custody with the perpetrator of family violence. Too often battered women are deemed "uncooperative" when they resist coparenting arrangements. They may be charged with parental alientation or child abduction if they flee with the kids—or child abandonment if they flee alone.[19]

And then there are women who become pregnant as a result of a rape—a staggering sixty to eighty a day in the United States, many by someone they know. Too often these women are ordered to allow child visitation for the rapist. One woman told me how agonizing it was to hear the judge's ruling: "He said, 'I don't care what he did, he's still the natural father.'"

Reality: Abuse Is All Too Common

While the case of the major's wife is extreme, violence against women is all too common. Consider these facts: One-third of adult women will endure at least one physical assault from an intimate. Nearly three in ten high school and college students experience dating violence at some point.[20] Unlike any other crime, rape continues to be a source of shame for the victim. According to the U.S. Department of Justice, every two and a half minutes, someone—most likely female—is sexually assaulted, often by an acquaintance or intimate. A character in *Girls Town*, a movie about high school friends dealing with the aftermath of sexual assault, has this to say about date rape: "If men want to have sex and you don't want to have sex, they're going to fuck you anyway."[21] Marital rape may be illegal, but try proving it in a court of law.

These are inconvenient realities for the Big Boys. So they minimize them, relegating the problem of violence to a few bad apples, hauling up examples of a female batterer here and there and insisting we talk about "domestic abuse" rather than woman abuse. (When it comes to inappropriate behavior, the Big Boys love gender neutral.) They also demonize women for having "provoked" the problems—or feminists for overstating them. Be grateful, they tell women, that the majority of men aren't batterers or rapists—as if not being assaulted were the appropriate gauge of a good relationship.

Marriage Matters: The Case for Marriage Equality

According to the popular song, "Love and marriage go together like a horse and carriage." Piled in that carriage are a heap of rights, benefits, and responsibilities—1,138 to be exact. They allow married couples to buy joint insurance policies, inherit each other's pension or social security, give each other an unlimited amount of gifts without being taxed for them, and enjoy creditor protection for their marital home. Many employers offer health insurance coverage to an employee's spouse, and sick leave and bereavement leave to the employee should the spouse fall ill or die. If you're an immigrant, marrying a U.S. citizen can help you gain a green card. Have to move because of your spouse? You're likely entitled to unemployment compensation. And let's not forget the right to adopt as a couple, to visit each other in the hospital, and make medical decisions in case of one partner's illness or disability.

Ask Ray Vahey of Milwaukee what being denied the right to marry costs him and Richard Taylor, his partner for half a century. "We've been taxed higher for fifty years because we can't file jointly," Vahey told me. "Richard was not able to get medical, dental, long-term care, or a pension option from my last job. If I were to go first, he would lose a substantial amount of money

[Social Security payments] that has been coming in to the household. We're beneficiaries of each other's IRAs but not able to take ownership of them as a spouse could. Our estate will be taxed at a higher rate."[22]

At the time of the interview, Taylor was hospitalized with cancer. "We have directed in our living wills not to take heroic measures," Vahey said. "If we hadn't done that, some relative who might have a completely different set of principles could make the decision. I know of cases where [the same-sex partner] couldn't even go in the hospital room. You're really exposed."

Vahey and Taylor don't have children, but Debbie Knepke and her partner Candy Hackbarth do, a toddler and an infant. "We live under a black cloud for all the things that could happen," Knepke said. She especially worries what she'd do if one of the kids had to be hospitalized, since she's not the birth mother. "It's feasible to imagine that I wouldn't be allowed into an intensive care unit," Knepke explained, "because I am not considered a mother by the state of Wisconsin."[23]

These couples were among many fighting to stop additional discrimination—a proposed amendment in Wisconsin that would ban not only same-sex marriage but civil unions as well.[24] During World War II, Richard Taylor enlisted in the Navy at the age of seventeen. "It's ironic that this guy voluntarily put himself in harm's way for the people of that time and all the generations that followed," said Vahey, "and now there's a move to deny him equal rights under the law."

The Big Boys talk about marriage as if it were the solution to all problems. That's why their opposition to marriage for same-sex partners is so hypocritical. Any heterosexual who thinks the love and commitment of two men or two women is the reason their own marriage fell apart needs a cold shower or a new pair of glasses. As for those who point to the Bible to defend their denunciation of gays (or the submission of women), ask if they also believe people may possess slaves, both male and female, provided they are purchased from neighboring nations (Leviticus 25:44), or that men who work on the Sabbath should be put to death (Exodus 35:2), or that those with a vision defect may not approach the altar of God (Leviticus 21:20).

Once marriage was a business transaction; procreation was part of the deal in order to pass on property. The creation of democracy in the United States changed that notion—the "pursuit of happiness" included the joy of marrying for love.[25] Over the last 200 years, we've seen a movement toward equality in marriage. Ending discrimination against same-sex couples is the logical next step in that process.

On the Home Front

As marriage has evolved, so has dividing up the care of children and work in the home. Few men in the United States today would argue that changing babies or preparing meals is strictly women's work. Practically speaking, how are we doing?

Myth: Sharing the Second Shift

From the boardroom to the courtroom, the Big Boys point to examples of men running off to a soccer game or helping around the house as proof that men are sharing the load. Ads for diapers, talcum powder, baby food today often feature a proud and competent dad. Besides, we're told, more and more people simply hire someone else to do their dirty work. Women have never had it better.

Reality: Men Doing More but Not Nearly Enough

When I wrote the book *The Job/Family Challenge* (1995), I did a twelve-city book tour and talked on dozens of radio shows. I'd cited a study in the book showing that couples share the work in 19 percent of the cases, and in 61 percent, the men do virtually nothing. On the road, I heard from all of those men's wives—or at least, that's how it felt. "I can't get my husband to pick up his socks!" many would moan. I'd point out how insulting it is to men to assume they can't master this kind of task. Just think how many males in their fifties have learned to navigate the web. "If they can manipulate a computer mouse," I'd say, "they can certainly learn to put away those socks."

Ten years later, both women and men are doing less housework. Fathers' share increased for a while—and then went right back down.[26] Wives in the United States do 70 to 80 percent of the housework—regardless of their employment status.[27] A study of dual-earner couples found that after marriage, "the amount of time that a woman spends doing housework increases by approximately 17 percent, while a man's decreases by 33 percent."[28] In fact, many women feel their husbands create more work around the house than they perform. As for childcare, children under the age of twelve increase housework time for mothers at a rate three times greater than for fathers.[29] Even when married men become unemployed, their share of housework and childcare almost never exceeds 30 percent.[30]

In households where men and women share the work, women still tend to provide most of the arranging for childcare, appointments, and the like, most of the juggling, and most of the care for sick kids. They also do most of the remembering—what size shoes each kid wears, who has which laundry, who needs a clean shirt or signed permission slip. I encourage women in relationships with men to try the "hidden pictures" test: After a party, ask your male partner to look around the room and say how many dirty glasses there are. Women often tell me the glasses are the only things they notice—while their mate can't find even one.

Not all women are neat or organized, of course, nor are most men slobs. But the imbalance in most relationships is part of a bigger issue. A couple can assert that both parties are equal. But if one spends a lot more time after work—the "second shift"[31]—on daily maintenance, their *time* is not equally valued. "What lands in my lap are all those tasks no one notices," one friend told me, "the ones that have to be done over and over. My husband, God love him, gets to have after-work hours. He gets holidays and vacations. I'm always on duty, always on call."

I used to have a poster that summed this up: "Women's work is never done—or appreciated, or paid what it's worth."

And how much is it worth? Salary.com, which advises companies on compensation, calculated the annual value of the work performed by a full-time mom with two-school age children. The tab: $131,471. Researchers categorized the typical work under seven main job descriptions: daycare center teacher, van driver, housekeeper, cook, CEO, nurse, and general maintenance worker. They assumed a 100-hour workweek of six 15-hour days and one 10-hour day.

What's Love Got to Do With It

The Big Boys like to trivialize the conversation about who does what to keep the home "sparkling clean." In fact, we're talking about nothing less than equality between intimates. The majority of men have a lot of changing to do before they can claim to be in an equal relationship. Still, there's good news for those men: Whatever position of dominance you give up, you have infinitely more to gain from being a genuine companion to your mate.

I had a friend who began her marriage with traditional assumptions about gender roles. Julie did all the housework and cooking. Among her duties was bringing her husband a glass of orange juice every morning in bed. I wouldn't say Julie resented this particular chore, but she told me she usually brought the glass on automatic pilot, equating the orange juice delivery with brushing her teeth or other daily routines. Then Julie began attending a women's consciousness-raising group. The old assumptions didn't make sense anymore. Her husband acknowledged that the current arrangement conflicted with their general views about equality; everything changed.

"I no longer had to bring that glass of orange juice," Julie said. "But I found myself doing it anyway several times a week. I did it as a gift, a sign of love. And because I did it freely, and not out of duty, it meant a lot more to my husband as well."

Here's a story about the opposite kind of arrangement. My friend Chris told me about conversations he had as a teenager with Danny, the guy who drove a lunch wagon to a spot near Chris's school. One day, when things were slow, Chris confided in Danny about a crush he had on the smartest girl in his class. "Don't worry about her," Danny said. "There are plenty of fish in the sea." Chris was leaning into the little window where Danny handed out lunch orders. "But she's the one I really like talking to," Chris said. "What?" Danny replied. "Talk to the woman you fuck?"

Whenever I've told that story to men I respect, their reaction is similar to the one my husband Larry gave: "It may sound like a great deal to be waited on and sexually serviced. But nothing's more satisfying than a lover who's really a partner."

Reality: Men Still Assumed to Be Head of Household

No matter who does what work, one thing hasn't changed: which party is presumed to be in charge. In my family, I handle the bills and prepare the taxes. Every year the IRS sends me a tax form listing "You" and "Your spouse." I'm the one answering the questions, my name comes first alphabetically, and for many years, I earned more money. Nevertheless, "You" means my husband; I am "Your spouse." Once I had an error on my form and called the IRS to correct it. They couldn't find any record of Ellen Bravo. "Look under my husband's name," I suggested. Bingo—there I was.

In the scheme of things, this is a minor issue. I mention it not because it annoys me (although it does), but because language reflects culture. Our government, like most corporations, still assumes men are the "head of household." (So do all those credit card companies that ask for your mother's maiden name.)

And just why *do* women change their names—a habit that's increased in recent years?[32] "Tradition," my students tell me. I remind them of other traditions they're not so eager to hold on to. The root of this particular custom is that law I mentioned earlier, the one requiring a wife to suspend her identity or "consolidate" it with her husband's.

People sometimes complain about the burden on children if parents have different names. Ask my kids and others who grew up this way—it was simply no big deal. As for what last name to give the kids, parents have lots of choices and can decide what works best for them. My kids are Millers, like their dad; at the time, it was odd enough that he and I had different names and we didn't want to isolate ourselves from our neighbors. But when my sons were five and eight, I suddenly longed to have a name bond with them and broached the idea of their taking Bravo as a second middle name. "I understand about your name," Nat, the older one, told me. We'd discussed this issue several times. "That's who you are. But now this is my identity. I don't think I can change it."

Craig said nothing at the time. A few months later, on my birthday, he announced he had a surprise for me: "I'm going to do it! I'm changing my name to Ellen!" It took another year for him to figure it all out. "I know why you and Daddy have different names," he told me. "When you were a little girl, Daddy wasn't your brother." Too bad so many adults don't grasp what's obvious to a six-year-old.

On their own, names are small matters. But like the anachronistic laws and persistence of violence, these legacies symbolize the continuing undervaluation of women.

Why Should Boys Want to Grow Up to Do What Women Do?

My boys took the equivalent of home ec and learned a little cooking and sewing. Most girls (I hope) no longer have textbooks like the one commonly used in 1955 that included this information under "The Good Wife's Guide":[33] "His boring day may need a lift and one of your duties is to provide it. . . . [H]is topics of conversation are more important than yours. A good wife always knows her place." Progress—but the core expectations haven't changed. For a man, having a job and a family is normal; people feel sorry for him if one or the other is missing. For a woman, wanting both a job and a family is wanting too much. As the media reminds us frequently, a "working mother" will need to juggle and sacrifice (unless she's poor, in which case she better find employment, any job will do). It's up to her to make it all work. Her husband (no need to call him a "working father"—the word *husband* implies that he both procreates and provides) may "pitch in" and "help," but she's the conductor who orchestrates the arrangements. It's still her job to help her husband deal with the stress-filled battlefield of work—never mind that she may be mired in her own.

We can never forget that underlying this juggling image is the long, shameful, and violent history of women's subordination (see Chapter 1). "Real work" became equated with men's work; the work women performed was of lesser value. Women had to be "provided for" and "taken care of." They were therefore deemed to be less capable. Not only were women considered unfit to be decision-makers, they needed to be kept under control—including by force.

I once read about an essay assignment given to nine-year-old girls and boys, asking them to describe how they'd feel if they woke up the next morning as the opposite sex. Boys said things like "nightmare," "horror," and "I'd rather be dead." Admittedly, nine is an age when most kids hang out with their own gender and have little good to say about the opposite sex. But the girls' essays were very different from the boys. Many wrote things like, "I'd have more power, more opportunities." Said one, "My daddy would love me."

Are we surprised? Why would boys want to grow up to do what women do, when that work is held in such low esteem?

Reality: What Women Really Opt Out Of

And yet, if you follow the print media, you may think the majority of women want nothing more than to be housewives. We're told that women being groomed to take high-powered jobs are "opting out" instead, seeing work and family as conflicting choices and preferring to stay at home.[34] Louise Story, a 2003 Yale graduate, surveyed women at her alma mater and announced that 60 percent had already decided to "suspend or end their careers when they have children." The *New York Times* put her story on the front page in September 2005 with the title, "Many Women at Elite Colleges Set Career Path to Motherhood." The author claimed her research had turned up something new: "[W]hile many of their mothers expected to have hard-charging careers, then scaled back their professional plans only after having children, the women of this generation expect their careers to take second place to child rearing."[35] In Louise Story's view, the women were influenced by the experiences of their mothers, three-fifths of whom "did not work at all" or took several years off.

Research debunks the "opting out" myth (see Chapter 3). Here are the facts: According to economist Heather Boushey, there has been a consistent *decline* in the effect of children on women's participation in the workforce since the 1980s.[36] The employment rate of new mothers has fallen in recent years, but that's because the employment rate of women as a whole has fallen, thanks to the economic downturn of the early 2000s. Even among the ranks of the elite, there has been no statistically significant change over time in employment rates of mothers compared to nonmothers. Letters to the *Times* pointed out how skewed the "Set Career Path to Motherhood" headline was, given that 70 percent of the respondents actually said they planned to work full or part time once they had children. Women who preferred to remain childless were apparently weeded out of the author's interviews.[37]

Ask the majority of women what they think of this so-called trend of choosing home over career, and they'll answer much the same as Unita Blackwell. The first black woman mayor of Mayersville, Mississippi, Blackwell started working when she was six-years-old. "I never knew I had a choice," she said. Most women, like most men, work because they need to earn a living. As for the women who do express a desire to subordinate career to children, we shouldn't confuse their motives. Most don't yearn for the lives of their mothers and grandmothers so much as they reject the lives of their fathers and grandfathers, men they saw working maniac hours and having little or no time for their kids.

Costs for Men and Kids

I gained insight into career women taking time for kids after being invited to speak to several chapters of a group called Mothers and More. These are professional women who devote themselves to childrearing while their children are young, with the intention of returning to their careers when the kids reach a certain age. Some continue to freelance or hold part-time jobs. What they wanted from me were tips about how to describe this time and how best to get back into the workforce. I was happy to share ways they could summarize the skills and accomplishments they've developed during these years.[38] I gave ideas on how to stay connected to their field through freelancing, volunteer work, or membership in a professional association, and how to network and find out about openings when they're ready to go back full time.

Typically when I arrived, the women seemed defensive. I knew what was going on: They assumed I was critical of their choice and they were poised to argue its merits. It didn't take long for them to see I make no judgments about them, only about the workplace which is so inflexible and which fails to value the relational skills they've honed. As the women loosened up, they began to speak about the downside of their situation. To compensate for the lost income, their husbands often work even longer hours. Not only are the men not around for the kids, there's little time for the marital relationship, not much pitching in around the house—and certainly no time for moms to be sick.

"A couple weeks ago, I woke up with the flu," one woman said as the others around the table nodded in recognition. "I told my husband he'd have to call in sick. 'I can't do that,' he insisted, ticking off all the important meetings and calls he had. I tried to impress on him that I couldn't lift my head off the pillow, but he kept reciting those responsibilities. Finally I pointed to our eighteen-month-old daughter. 'All right,' I told him, 'as long as you know that Kyla will be on her own today.' That finally got his attention."

Sometimes over coffee, one or more of the women would talk about even more complex issues. "We both decided we wanted this and value my work in the home," another woman said. "But it's hard to feel equal when you have to ask for money."

The women love their bonds with their small children. But they worry their husbands won't know the kids well and the children will suffer as a result. It reminded me of a story about a guy who traveled a lot for his job. One day, as he was packing for yet another trip, his son asked him to play catch. "I'm sorry, Timmy, but I have to get ready," the man said. He put his arm around the boy. "You know how much I hate it when I miss your games. And I know how much you and Mommy miss me as well." "I do, Daddy," Timmy said, "but I miss you most when you're home."

What Men Want

The Big Boys think the current setup is just fine, though few will say so out loud. The conservative columnist quoted at the start of this chapter summed up the view that governs much of the corporate hierarchy. Women want those kids and well-kept homes—let them deal with them. We'll be glad to employ women, the author declares, as long as they function like men and are willing to work the long hours. But to hire women with caregiving responsibilities for the best jobs—that'll drive a company out of business.[39]

I'm happy to say, the Big Boys are out of step with male employees at all levels below them. Especially after September 11, more and more men are clamoring for jobs that allow them time to have a life and to be involved with their kids. A 2005 survey by *Fortune* magazine of male executives found that a whopping 84 percent agreed or strongly agreed with the statement, "I would like job options that let me realize my professional aspirations while having more time for family, community, religious activities, friends, and hobbies." For most of these men, average age just over fifty, more time took precedence over money or career advancement.[40]

Clearly many more men would be better fathers, sons, and husbands if they weren't punished for it at work. And far fewer kids would be missing their dads at home.

My husband once made an eloquent statement about this on TV. In 1983, less than a year after I helped found the 9to5 chapter in Milwaukee, someone from a public television station called to see if I'd debate a woman who'd written an op-ed blaming all problems in the family on mothers who work outside the home (see page 66). This woman agreed to appear on the show only if her husband joined her, so the station wanted to know if my husband would come as well. Larry was glad to do it. He and the other guy didn't get to say much; the woman and I were sparring from the moment we sat down. When Larry finally got a turn, this is what he said: "Men should be so grateful to the women's movement, because they've given us parenting. It's a lot of work, but it's such a joy—we should just say, 'Thanks.'"

Men like Larry enrich their children's lives by their involvement, and also by the model they represent. Larry's role in our family had already made an impact on Nat, then age five. Because this show aired live at 7 P.M. on a weeknight, we had arranged for a babysitter. "Why aren't there any boy babysitters?" Nat asked me as we were waiting for her to arrive. "There are boy babysitters," I assured him, "and you can babysit when you're older. But you're right, most babysitters are girls because most families aren't like ours—most dads don't share taking care of the kids." Nat looked up at me. "That's what you and Dad are going to talk about on the TV show, right?"

I wasn't able to gloat for long about my son's advanced consciousness. Turns out our program was on at the same time as "Greatest American Hero," and that's what my children watched. "But we turned on your show during commercials!" Nat declared when we returned home. I asked what he liked best about the parts he saw. "When the words came over your faces at the end," Nat replied. "That was really cool."

What Kids Want

Kids may not know everything. But when we listen to the children, we gain important insight into what should be driving the discussion about integrating work and family life.

Work-life expert Ellen Galinsky interviewed a nationally representative sample of more than a thousand children of employed parents to find out what they think about their parents' lives.[41] She asked adults to guess how their children would answer this question: "If you were granted one wish that could change the way your mother's or your father's work affects your life, what would that be?" The majority of adults thought the kids would wish for more time together. Children do care about time, especially wanting their parents not to miss important events. But above all, they wish their parents would be "less stressed and less tired." Only 2 percent of parents had figured that out.

For some people, the most surprising finding of Galinsky's research was that kids didn't resent their mothers for having jobs. Not one time throughout the study did children's having an employed mother predict how they assessed her parenting skills. When asked what they'd like to tell working parents, only 2 percent of the children answered, "Stay home." (This response might be more common among low-income children, who face fewer options for alternative care. A friend, then a single mother, told me her three-year-old daughter begged her not to go to work. "I have to work so we can eat," my friend told the girl. "I don't need to eat that much," her daughter replied.)

Many people believe that no one will love their children as much as they do—and therefore no one can really care for the kids as well as they can. But the Big Boys have seized on these feelings, using compartmentalization to promote "mommy wars" between mothers who "stay home" (as if taking care of children didn't involve massive amounts of running around) and those who leave their children with "strangers" because they "work." Typically, a media outlet will run some childcare horror tale, followed by stories that dwell on—and reinforce—mothers' feelings of guilt and fear.

Childcare is an area long studied, however, and studies confirm that what matters most isn't whether or not the mother works outside home but rather the issue of *quality*: the quality of parental care; the quality of outside care; and the quality of the parent's job—including how flexible it is and how supportive of the whole person. One writer compared childcare to a car. The issue is not whether you own a car but whether or not it's safe, whether or not there's a good driver.[42] Good care providers cease being strangers within hours. A parent can be home full time but be distracted, unhappy, and tense.

Like many people, Larry and I had a positive experience with child-care. Our children thrived there. They learned skills we didn't know how to teach them. Above all, they learned that they're special, but so are other children. Our neighborhood was diverse, but their childcare centers were even more diverse. Even when our finances were strained, we were lucky to find quality care we could afford. Larry's factory and then school schedule allowed him to be home in the late afternoon most of the time our kids were young. After I started working at 9to5, I was able to be home when they were sick. Larry and I certainly have had our share of stress on the job, but our kids grew up watching us do work we love. To me, these wonderful young men are the best confirmation of the research.

Who's Doing the Dirty Work?

The Big Boys are right about one thing: More people are hiring outside help to clean their houses and watch their children. But this doesn't guarantee a solution to the issue of equity within the family (women are usually the ones who line up and manage the workers)—and often adds to inequity in the community.

Nickel and Dimed, Barbara Ehrenreich's account of her "undercover" experiences in low-wage jobs, holds some important lessons about hiring someone else to clean up after you.[43] When working as a maid, Ehrenreich was surprised to find herself on her knees, virtually invisible to her employers. Hours can be long and unpredictable, usually with low pay and no job security, benefits, or pension. When domestic workers live in, the work may in fact be unending.

To find a maid's job, Ehrenreich traveled to Maine, where the majority of housecleaners are white. In other parts of the country, they're more like-ly to be immigrant workers—Pacific Islanders on the west coast, Chicanas in the Southwest, Caribbean islanders in New York. In some cases, these workers are like indentured servants, forced to work long days without any regular pay and with little recourse, thanks to language and cultural (and often immigration) barriers. The case of Hilda Rosa Dos Santos from Brazil, while extreme, serves as a cautionary tale. Dos Santos was trapped for twenty years performing unpaid work for her employers without ever going out on her own. They told her blacks were so disliked in the United States she'd be raped or killed if she did.[44]

While free to leave, Ehrenreich's crew also faced routine exploitation—docked if they didn't have perfect attendance, forced to work "off the clock" without pay. Like shunned outsiders, "nothing was to touch their lips" in a customer's house.

People often describe their domestic help as being "just like one of the family." But in a story with that name written by Alice Childress, a domestic worker named Mildred sets the record straight.[45] "I eat in the kitchen . . . your puppy sleeps on your satin spread," she tells her employers. If they like her work, Mildred urges them to show it with a raise, "but stop talkin' about me like I was a *cocker spaniel*. . . . I am not just like one of the family." The employer may consider it a "compliment" to say, "'We don't think of her as a servant" but in Childress's words, "after I have worked myself into a sweat cleaning the bathroom and the kitchen . . . making the beds . . . cooking the lunch . . . washing the dishes and ironing Carol's pinafores . . . I do not feel like no weekend houseguest. I feel like a servant."

And what message do our children receive from the way we treat our hired help? Feminist writer Audre Lorde, who's African American, recounts being in the grocery store with her two-year-old. A young white girl pointed at the toddler and said, "Oh, look, Mommy, a baby maid."[46]

Parents struggling to sort out issues of childcare and chores often feel torn between various inadequate options. Feminism gives us a better way to manage work outside work.

FEMINIST SOLUTIONS

Feminism both depends on and fosters genuine equality in intimate relationships. Our goal is simple: It should be normal for women as well as men to have work they care about—paid or unpaid—and to have a family, defined as people who love and commit to each other. To reach that goal, we need to change the way we work outside the home—but also the ways we (or others) work inside the home.

Feminist solutions for sharing childcare and housework start with the premise that a relationship between equals (a nonnegotiable) must place equal value on both parties' *time*. That means putting into practice this statement: Housework is work to be done by those who live in the house—it's not "Mom's work" that others do or don't "help" her with.

Children should participate as soon as they can clasp something and put it away. (Little children actually think this work is fun—get them in the habit right away.) There are a variety of ways to divide up the work. Some families rotate chores, others create some fair division of labor. In my case, for example, Larry loves to cook, I like doing laundry and dishes, and we always do those tasks. One friend with five kids kept a list of chores on the fridge. Whoever got up first on Saturday chose what task they wanted; whoever got up last, took what was left; no one could leave the house until they had satisfactorily completed their chore.

Three elements are key to sharing the work: First, there have to be objective standards. We can all agree, for instance, that plates left lying around with congealed food take much longer to clean than plates washed right away. Dirty bathrooms and dust-filled shelves aren't just unpleasant—they breed germs. Once we've agreed on the standards, we need an objective evaluation system and a way to review each family member's work. Otherwise Mom becomes the cop who has to nag, cajole, or do it all herself. Finally, failing to follow through has to result in *consequences*. With children, you can take away some privilege. With a mate, you can take away other things—whatever works in your setup. Don't rely only on punishment, though. Celebrate progress. Appreciate work well done. Make housework fun. My family discovered we cleaned best when someone was coming over, so we began to make up imaginary visits from famous people to inspire us. We'd put on loud music and each of the four of us would grab some cleaning implement and dig in until we were done.

For couples where one partner spends more hours at home caring for children or another family member, the plan will take that into account—but will also ensure that this partner has time off as well, and that tasks when both are home are shared as much as possible. Our goal is the model described in Chapter 3, where each partner is able to work a reasonable workweek and participate equally in family care.

Old habits can take a long time to transform. But even small changes can make a big difference in the quality of women's lives—and in children's expectations for their own futures.

Public Policies

Valuing relationships and women's work outside work requires other changes as well, including the following:

* End the exploitation of hired domestic help: A society that really

values families would make more community services available
to help working families, along with a shorter work week, quality
dependent care arrangements, and genuinely flexible work arrangements (see Chapter 3). To the extent that families hire others, that
relationship should include a contract listing job duties, reasonable
terms of employment, and an affirmation of basic employment rights,
including set hours and decent pay, safe working conditions, and
"time to rest."[47] Fair treatment of migrant workers goes hand in hand
with ending poverty in their home countries, so that women don't
have to leave their own children behind in order to take care of ours.

- Maintain Social Security and reform it to better reflect the contribution of caregivers in the home. One solution is adding a "caregiver's
  credit," an annual amount for up to five years to a parent who's
  focused on raising kids.[48] Proposed privatization of Social Security, however, would harm women, by replacing reliable payments
  with the unpredictable stock market, and especially by eliminating
  payments to children whose income-producing parent has died or
  become disabled.

- Change marriage laws so that they enshrine the principle of equality.
  Same-sex partners should have the same rights, benefits, and responsibilities as those of the opposite gender.

- Change divorce laws so that they enshrine the principle of equality. That means valuing caregiving as work deserving compensation,
  rather than seeing maintenance as charity from the higher-earning
  spouse. Marital property laws should follow the model of the few
  states that require fifty-fifty distribution. Where one partner has
  cared more for dependent children, future earnings should count as
  part of the property, with the goal of equalizing the parties' post-
  divorce standard of living. All states should be required to recognize
  the impact on earning if one partner has taken time out to be the
  primary caregiver—and judges should be required to know and follow the law. Divorce must take into account any evidence of violence
  and follow recommended guidelines of the Family Violence Project
  of the National Council of Juvenile and Family Court Judges. These
  include no single or joint custody if a risk of violence exists, and
  visitation rights to the perpetrator only if adequate safety provisions
  can be made for the child and the adult victim.

- Eliminate conditions that foster rape and all forms of violence against women and "non-manly" men. We need immediate reforms that guarantee sensitive and culturally appropriate treatment for victims of rape and other forms of violence, fully funded shelters and transition programs, more effective consequences for perpetrators, and a firm realization that shame belongs only to those who violate others. But the focus must be on prevention. That means significant changes in school curriculum to educate kids early about valuing themselves and others. Schools should adapt model programs that involve teachers, students, and administrators in zero tolerance for bullying. Sex education curriculum needs to promote equality in relationships and a dating culture where intimacy happens only when both parties consciously choose it. Together schools, media, and civic groups need to root out gender stereotypes that deny men access to the full range of emotions or that equate loving a person of the same gender with transgressing a universal norm. Eliminating violence against women means eliminating all notions that men need to be in control, or that any group has the right to dominate any other.

- Guarantee reproductive rights. We can't talk about women's rights without ensuring that women are able to determine whether and when to have children. That requires access to safe and affordable contraception, meaningful sex education, an end to involuntary sterilization, and a guarantee that every child born can be well cared for. It also requires access to safe and legal abortions regardless of income. Since religions vary on when life begins, criminalizing abortion amounts to an imposition of one religious view over another—a violation of a fundamental American value. Our country also is based on a deep appreciation of privacy; government simply doesn't belong in the bedroom. Whatever one's personal beliefs, outlawing abortion won't get rid of it—it will just make it unsafe. In an equitable relationship, partners would make this decision together, but as long as women bear the risk from pregnancy, they must have the legal right to the final decision. We should work to reduce the need for abortion by making it easier to prevent pregnancy. That means no more political tricks that block access to emergency contraception (as the Food and Drug Administration did for years)[49] or to other medical advances. We should also raise girls with dignity and hope for their own futures so that having babies isn't the only way they find value in their lives.

TAKING ON THE BIG BOYS

The Workplace Project

Much of the organizing to change work in the home happens in the private sphere. But some groups have taken on the Big Boys' exploitation of domestic workers. One of the best examples is the Workplace Project, founded in 1992 to address problems of low-wage immigrant workers on Long Island.

A big difficulty in organizing domestic workers has been their isolation from each other and the fact that each has a separate employer. Imagine how much harder the task when the workers are Latino immigrants with limited English and no cars in a sprawling area like Long Island. Staff at the Workplace Project knew they couldn't just train the domestic workers in Negotiations 101. They needed a collective and public solution to problems of low or unpaid wages, harassment, and lack of job security.

According to Jennifer Gordon, founder of the Workplace Project, the group decided to focus on the one point "where employers and workers came together in any numbers: the employment agency."[50] These intermediary groups often advertised services to homeowners for what amounted to below-minimum wage—then turned around and charged the domestic workers double or triple the usual fee for arranging the placement. In 1996, organizer Esly Umanzor began organizing domestic workers in the project's Fuerza Laboral Femenina (Female Labor Force) committee. After months of research and debate, they drafted the Workplace Project Domestic Worker Bill of Rights, which required agencies to charge no more than 10 percent of the first month's wages, to place workers only in jobs that pay at least minimum wage, and to use a detailed contract to be signed by the agency, the employer, and the worker at the time of hire.

In order to launch their campaign, the group decided to spotlight two of the biggest offenders. For weeks, they got allies to picket, call, and fax these agencies. After interviews with media outlets such as the *New York Times* and *Village Voice*, they organized a public meeting in February 1997 with the heads of the two agencies. Speakers included a local elected official and a group of homeowners who pledged to do business only with agencies that signed the bill of rights. Within a week the two agency heads signed on. Three months later, five of the six agencies in Nassau County displayed signs announcing, "We respect the Workplace Project Domestic Bill of Rights."

For most of the people involved, this was a "first-time experience," said Nadia Marin-Molina, current director of the Workplace Project.[51] "They were surprised that a local elected official was willing to meet and support the group. People liked having those agency heads on the hot seat—the tables were turned." The domestic workers involved realized that what they did "would affect not just them, but a much larger group of women who couldn't be present. By organizing with a relatively small group, they were able to pressure these agencies and feel like they were creating a change."

Stopping Unpaid Wages

The problem, says Marin-Molina, was how to monitor those agreements: "The fact is that domestic workers are very isolated. It's hard to build a large, stable group. Although a small group of committed workers was able to pressure the agencies, you'd need a lot more people to know what the Bill of Rights is and be willing to help report violations." As a next step, the group decided to back statewide legislation that would crack down on employers who violated current wage law. The result was the Unpaid Wages Prohibition Act, which would increase eightfold the penalty for violators—from a fine of 25 percent to 200 percent of the unpaid wages. The measure also raised the seriousness of the violation from a misdemeanor with a maximum $10,000 penalty, to a felony with maximum penalty $20,000.

Never shy about its tactics, the Workplace Project decided to start the campaign by lining up the most outspoken opponent of immigrant workers, state senator Dean Skelos. This Long Island Republican had voted to keep undocumented immigrants out of public hospitals and their children out of public schools. He also supported an "English only" measure, prohibiting local businesses from using bilingual materials.

"At the time everyone in the State Senate was Republican," Marin-Molina explained. "The campaign had to pick a target not in terms of who was most sympathetic, but who was the most important player." Later Skelos said two things won him over. Sitting down with the group of immigrant workers reminded him of his own family who had come here from Greece. Also, like most people, he was repelled by the idea that people would do the work and not be paid.

In six months, the Workplace Project had won the backing of not only Skelos, but nine of his Republican colleagues as well as Long Island business associations, labor, religious, and community groups. The Unpaid Wages Prohibition bill passed in June 1997; ten weeks later the Republican governor signed it into law—the strongest wage-enforcement law in the United States.

A wage enforcement bill is only as good as its actual enforcement, however—and that's been a harder fight. Still, the domestic workers scored a significant victory. They have protection against the situation that Yanira Juarez and others found themselves in. Juarez cared for the home and two children of a family in Suffolk County who told her they'd set up a "savings account" where her wages were being deposited. After six months of unpaid labor, Juarez was fired. She had no money and no recourse. Now, thanks to the efforts of the members of Fuerza Laboral Femenina, immigrant workers on Long Island have some power of their own.

Developing Leaders

The Project also launched a small domestic workers' cooperative called UNITY Housecleaners. Bypassing the agencies, UNITY arranges its own placements at $15 an hour, encouraging employers to avoid exploitation by hiring the co-op. Women who join take four classes, including one on domestic workers' rights—what they are and what they should be. Marin-Molina described a woman who on her own went back to her employer after this class and said she realized she was being paid much too little. "The woman got fired," Marin-Molina said. "She came back and told us about it. 'I don't care,' she said. 'I know I can get another job. I know at this place I was getting exploited.'"

According to Marin-Molina, some women participate in UNITY "not because they need a job the next day, but because they want a sense of community." She described women who came to the organization who had never spoken in public and had no experience with organizing. "Now, through the different activities of the cooperative, these women have been able to participate in protests, have done presentations, have really taken leadership in the organization," Marin-Molina said. "Some are even on the board of directors of the Workplace Project. It's a process that takes years, but it provides that opportunity." The women also give each other support in making changes on the home front on issues such as domestic violence.

The UNITY co-op participates in a statewide network called Domestic Workers United (DWU), working to raise the minimum wage for domestic workers. Marin-Molina said a survey her organization conducted found the average rate right now is $4.03 an hour. To improve the situation, a member group of DWU in Manhattan created citywide legislation focusing on a

Domestic Worker Bill of Rights, a document that includes the right to a minimum wage. The bill doesn't require payment of minimum wage, but it does require both agencies and individual employers to inform workers about the bill of rights and to make a record of their wage agreement, then file it in a central place. A local legislator has agreed to introduce the same bill on Long Island.

"It's not as much as we'd like," says Marin-Molina, "but it's a step in that direction. We're informing people that domestic workers do have rights."

FINAL THOUGHTS: NAMING THE FATHER

Programs to step up collection of child support provide crucial income to many parents, mostly women. But some government units have implemented harsh measures requiring women to name the father of their child or be denied access to childcare or other forms of assistance. Such measures ignore the reality of violence. "They go after the father," one woman told me, "he goes after me." Yes, we need to increase support from parents who do not have custody. But in the process, we can't endanger women's lives or interfere with their right to privacy. Naming the father must remain voluntary.

10. HOW YOU CAN HELP GET THERE

"I don't think I can call myself a feminist, because I haven't been an activist." That's how one of my students began her final paper last year. She went on to list three things she did do during the semester—took on a doctor who'd minimized her concerns about a lump in her breast; encouraged a friend to leave an abusive relationship; complained about a racist incident at her daughter's school.

"Oh, yes, you can call yourself a feminist!" I wrote back. "You stood up, you spoke out." Being a feminist does mean taking action—but that word encompasses an enormous range of behaviors, both individual and collective.

Say the word *activist* and women envision Norma Rae, Rosa Parks, Karen Silkwood—someone superbrave, willing to risk jail, maybe a relationship, maybe even her life. They admire these women but can't imagine themselves in their shoes. I see this over and over. At a workshop on work and family, participants discuss what needs to change in the workplace, in public policy, and in the home. I ask small groups to choose one of those areas to brainstorm how we get the change we need. The most frequent choice? The home front. When I probe, they tell me why. These women don't believe employers or politicians are capable of change and they don't see themselves as the agents of change. The one area where they can imagine some movement is at home.

I'm not surprised. The Big Boys have a huge stake in making us think the status quo is inevitable, immutable. They minimize both the need for and the existence of opposition, characterizing people as satisfied or apathetic. Some people are apathetic, it's true, too absorbed in their own advancement or partying to think about anyone else. But more typical are people who simply feel disheartened, disempowered, disenfranchised, overwhelmed—or afraid. What they lack isn't belief in the need for change, but a sense of how to accomplish it.

This book has shown we can take on the Big Boys, especially if we understand how they operate. Most of the examples I've cited are ordinary women, members of groups most people haven't heard of before. What enabled them to get involved wasn't extraordinary courage or superhuman strength. Above all, like Rosa Parks and Karen Silkwood, they had an opportunity and an organizational vehicle to make themselves heard.[1]

What It Takes

Many people would like to do something about the problems that concern them, but aren't clear where to start. There's certainly no shortage of experts eager to offer advice. A friend told me she was driving home when a radio psychologist proclaimed the solution to all her stress. "Worried about your kids, your job, your love life, your bills?" the radio shrink asked. My friend gripped the steering wheel and nodded vigorously. The radio doc was ready with advice: "Here's what you do. Just shove all those worries aside. Each day designate a Worry Hour. Whenever you find yourself fretting about your boss or your misbehaving child, say, 'I'll just think about that later, during my Worry Hour.'" My friend nearly drove off the road. "I scarcely have time to pee, much less take a bath," she said. "Where am I going to find an hour a day to worry?"

Then there's the woman who called her doctor in a panic. She described alarming symptoms—terrible insomnia and a persistent, excruciating headache. The woman really feared she had a brain tumor. "I can see why you're concerned," the doctor said. "Tell me some things about your life. How's your job? Your family?"

The woman groaned. "My job sucks. Every day as I'm about to leave, they find one more project I have to finish before I can get out the door. I'm never home before 6:30 or 7 P.M. And my family—as soon as I walk in, they start to whine, 'Why are you so late? What's for dinner?'"

The doctor cleared her throat. "Listen carefully," she said. "You don't need an appointment. I know what's wrong with you—you're under stress. I want you to try something experimental: Run ten miles a day for ten days, and then give me a call." The woman was dumbfounded, but she was so desperate, she was willing to try anything. Exactly ten days later, she phoned the doctor. "I can't believe it—I feel fabulous!" she shouted. "My headaches are gone, I'm sleeping through the night. It's a miracle."

The doctor expressed her delight. "And how's your job? Your family?"

"Who knows?" the woman told her. "They're 100 miles away."

Let me hasten to add, this is not the solution I subscribe to.

Dare to DREAM

Instead, I'd like to offer a multistep action plan, known by the shorthand DREAM:

Dare to imagine the world as it should be and work to make it happen. Even if we don't see it all, each change gets us closer to what we need.

Reach out. You don't need to do this alone. Look for one or two friends or family who feel the same way you do, and make this journey together.

Educate yourself. As we've seen, the Big Boys seek to control our view of reality. Happily, we now have a host of Web sites and alternative media, along with a number of trustworthy voices in the mainstream media. See Appendix B for a partial list of these resources. If you don't have a computer with Internet access, most libraries have them free of charge. You can turn an outing with children into a trip to the library—storytime or book selection for them, at least a few minutes online for you. Check our list of progressive resources with your library's collection and encourage them to add a few that are missing. Join an organization that works on the issues you care most about in order to get a steady flow of information and action alerts (more on this later).

Act. As my student came to realize, there are many things you can do as an individual even with little time and few if any resources—and all these actions matter. These include:

- Share information. As you learn new facts, pass them on to as many friends, relatives, and coworkers as you can.
- Speak up. Give support to a friend or critical feedback to a teacher or doctor—we hire these people, after all, and should have some say over their performance. Join in if you hear people discussing an issue of the day, or initiate the topic yourself. My friend Amy Stear, Wisconsin

Organizing Director for 9to5, starts up political conversations with whoever's standing beside her in line at the grocery or department store, first asking about the person's experience with the topic. Speaking up also means intervening when you hear someone else making a sexist or racist or homophobic joke. Even if you don't want to start a whole conversation, you might say, "That's not funny to me and many other people. I hope you won't repeat it." If you observe offensive behavior from someone in a position of authority—a store manager, a police officer, a supervisor at work—see if there's a way to challenge it or at least provide support to the person being targeted, and then report it to someone higher up. This really helps change the climate. Offenders count on the silence of those around them.

- Post domestic violence and other hotline numbers wherever you can—at work, in public restrooms, on community bulletin boards.
- Speak out. The section of the newspaper many people like best is letters to the editor. You can share your own views and experience on an issue; in the process, you help validate those who agree with you and perhaps open the mind of someone who doesn't. Many organizations provide sample letters with facts and talking points that you can use to get started, but nothing's as persuasive as your own story. You can also call in to radio shows to express your view. Do this with a buddy—you can practice on each other while you're waiting your turn.
- Contact elected officials. Progressive politicians tell us they always hear from the other side, which is quite well organized and well financed. Don't underestimate the importance of your call or letter or email, especially if you share a personal story—your own or that of someone you know. Even elected officials who agree with you value these contacts for two reasons: They can refer to them in explaining their own position, and they can use the examples to help win over colleagues. If the person has taken a good stand on some issue, be sure to thank him or her.
- Vote and help educate and then turn out those you know. You've heard stories of elections that were determined by one or a few votes. But your vote counts even if the candidate you want wins by a huge margin. At 9to5, we encouraged members to send a message with their ballot, providing a form they could fill out and mail to each candidate they voted for. The form went something like this: "I voted for you

because of your position on this-and-that. But my vote is not a blank check. I want you to know I'm concerned about your stand on such-and-such. My vote is my promise to stay involved on these issues."

- Support a progressive candidate. Campaigns always need volunteers. If you don't have lots of time, offer to make calls from home or take a stack of flyers to fold or distribute on your block.

- Encourage good candidates to run. Let people know that you want more women of all races and more men of color in office, but only if they take progressive stands.

- Support groups you care about. If you have any disposable income, donate, especially to groups organizing for systemic change. As someone who spent many years fundraising, I can assure you that even a small amount helps. Always give as generously as you can. Subsidize scholarships and resources for those who can't afford to join or to attend specialized training. If you own a business, offer space for a group to meet and some in-kind donations, such as copies and postage.

- Attend public hearings. This may be a good way to gather information. Just showing up and registering on the progressive side of an issue can help. Let the organizers know you're there and why. Even better, sign up to testify. See below for doing this as part of a group.

- Walk a picket line. Strikers really welcome any sign of support, including someone who'll join them for a while and help spread the word. Bring snacks, take photos, grab literature to hand out. Take some kids along.

- Help a group under siege. If right-wing protesters are ganging up on some group—a reproductive health clinic, say—offer to escort people who have to pass through their gauntlet.

- If you're a business owner, adopt family friendly policies. Even if you have a small operation, become a model for other companies. Speak in favor of public policies that would help level the playing field.

- Be a mentor. Don't underestimate what you have to offer. Whether you're a woman who's been on welfare and knows how the system works or a woman running a department or company, chances are your experiences—positive and negative—have taught you a lot that can be useful to someone else.

- Attend rallies. Public actions serve many functions. If well organized, they're a great way to draw attention to a problem and proposed solution. They help build morale and demonstrate support. The more people feel part of a movement, the greater their ability to believe in the possibility of change—and to see themselves as part of the process.

- Participate in national demonstrations. There may be times when groups need you to march side by side with people from all over the country. If you support such an action but can't attend, see if you can help in some other way: Pay for someone to go if you're able, write a letter supporting the march, offer to supply some food, come to a meeting to make signs, show up (with kids if you can) to help send people off.

- Help create progressive culture. Social justice is both reflected in and promoted by culture. Theater, music, zines, art, writing of all kinds can help change consciousness of what is and what needs to be. Find ways to support or participate in progressive cultural outlets.

- Help prepare the next generation. Every part of children's lives—from playing to sharing chores to dealing with hurtful remarks and thinking about future careers—offers opportunities to pass on lessons of social justice. You can have a huge impact on the next generation as a parent, loving relative, neighbor, friend, or volunteer. Each time you take one of the actions listed above, use the opportunity to educate a child about the importance of getting involved. Know what your kids are being taught and encourage them to get involved if the school curriculum or activities need to change.

- Be an informed consumer. Find out what you can about which stores don't rely on sweatshop labor. Support local businesses run by women and by men of color. Avoid companies engaging in antiunion activities—the AFL-CIO Web site maintains a list. Be aware of the content of any video games or music your children ask for.

- Appreciate workers. Always know who your server is. When someone does a good job, say so. Don't blame telemarketers for doing their job. If you're angry about a product or policy, explain to the clerk handling your complaint that you're not angry with him or her personally.

- Strive to meet the standards of the person you most admire. Live a life you're proud of every day. Take responsibility for your actions, admit your mistakes. Focus not on regret, but on changing step by step.

- Practice positive talk. If your best friend said, "I'm so fat/stupid/ugly," what would you respond? Be your own best friend.

Multiply. Take action as part of a group and help it grow. Over four decades of activism, I've learned that you don't always win if you stand up for yourself, but you never win if you don't. And the best way to make that stand, to get what you need for yourself, is to work with others on behalf of everyone. When our action is collective and intentional, we multiply our effectiveness.

It helps to have a realistic picture of the group you'd like to join. Often when I invited someone to a 9to5 meeting, I'd ask her what she expected. "A group of women who are best friends," she'd reply. "People who are really smart and know how to do everything. People who would expect me to spend massive amounts of time." Typically grassroots groups are just a bunch of people like you who've gotten together to try to make something happen. They welcome another pair of hands—and usually they appreciate whatever boundaries you set for your time. If you don't have time for many meetings, you can write a letter, make some calls.

I've met people who said, "I went to a meeting of XYZ group and didn't go back because it was boring/the people talked too much/no one talked to me/everyone descended on me/I didn't see what I could add/I felt overwhelmed by how much there was to do." If I can make one generalization about how to handle social justice groups, it's this: Don't generalize. Groups vary enormously, from each other and even from themselves over time. Go with a friend. Tell yourselves and the group's leaders that you're checking it out. And then do just that. If the issue really matters to you, remember that you can have an influence on what this group does and even on who its leaders are. If it's closed up tight and won't allow that, if it doesn't appreciate your time and isn't responsive to your reality or concerns—find another organization.

If you work in a unionized workplace, be sure to join the union. If you're already a member, attend meetings or find other ways to stay informed and get involved. If the union steward or president is not attentive to issues that matter to you, go as high as you need to until someone listens.

To locate groups in your area, you can start by contacting the public library reference desk; they often keep a list of grassroots organizations. You can also try a local women's studies office or the phone book, or look for a branch of an organization you've heard of nationally, such as the AFL-CIO, 9to5, or Planned Parenthood. Many congregations have social justice or social action committees—you can check with the denomination you feel most comfortable with. If you're looking for faith-based work, see if there's an interfaith alliance with a focus on social justice issues.

If there doesn't seem to be a group paying attention to the area you're most interested in, consider starting your own with a few friends or acquaintances. Seek advice from a relevant national group, such as those listed in Appendix A. Some organizations have starter kits for just this purpose. Few have national or state organizers who can fly in and help you—but sometimes if you can demonstrate interest and initiative, they'll be able to offer a range of technical assistance.

What You Can Do as a Group

Once you realize you're not alone, you can explore various kinds of collective action. Your group can organize an educational program or speak-out; get a school to introduce a course on women's studies or review its compliance with Title IX; work on a political campaign; mobilize people to vote; arrange a meeting with one or more elected officials; develop a women's radio or cable TV show; oppose the nomination of a racist judge; get a campus to provide access to emergency contraception; start a union organizing drive; identify policymakers willing to address job training needs; petition for more public contracts to women-owned businesses; support the rights of immigrant workers. You might convince some people to run for office—and then make sure they stay connected to the grassroots base that helps elect them. The list is endless.

Here are some examples of what organizations can do more effectively than individuals:

- Analyze who holds power in the situation you're concerned about, and decide who to target and how.
- Move from a onetime action to a campaign with all its components: outreach, education, meeting with elected officials, finding allies, working with the media, holding rallies, or other direct action.
- Develop a message and a framework of analysis, creating fact sheets and key talking points that supporters can use in a variety of ways to educate the public and policymakers.
- Help people tell their stories. At 9to5, women gather and share their experiences; someone on staff then types them up. The women give each other support and advice. "Start with that story—that was great," someone might say. "Make that last point shorter—it makes it more powerful."

- Keep reaching out to new people and deepen their understanding and leadership skills.
- Find allies with a common interest in this issue and develop a coalition.
- Above all, organizations help build a *movement* that can continue to grow and work for long-lasting, systemic change. And that movement within the United States can reach across borders to create a transnational, global women's movement capable of eliminating poverty and violence, of cherishing diverse cultures, of nurturing the environment.[2]

Whether you're trying to change public policy or win change at an individual workplace, it's wise to follow what I call the 6 R's:

Reach out. It's unlikely you're the only one who feels this way. Make a list of all the people around you and rank them in order of their concern about the issue at hand and their willingness to speak up. Note those who might not be likely to take the lead but might be willing to join in once others have taken the first step. Start with one or two of those at the top of your list. If someone says no, move on to the next person.

Research. As a group, track down best practices in other locations or workplaces. Identify in detail what policy would make a difference. That might include surveying those in your group and others you know to see where the need is greatest. Then determine who the decisionmakers are and what's the best way to get their attention. Figure out who might go to bat for you. Some higher-ups may be willing to give you advice, even if they don't have the power to make this decision themselves.

Rehearse. As part of preparing your case, think of every argument that might be made against you and decide how to address it. Once in the meeting, it's extremely empowering to hear points you've already anticipated and are ready to answer.

Request. Schedule a time to make your request, rather than having an impromptu discussion in the hall of the legislature or at the water cooler at work.

Rejoice. I once went with a 9to5 member to a meeting with funders. After only a few minutes, I knew we weren't going to get the money; one of the board members was a corporate executive who signaled his dislike for our group. I left with a heavy heart. The 9to5 member turned to me with a triumphant grin. "I can't believe it—I didn't throw up!" she said. Even if you don't win your key demand, the very fact that you've organized as a group and secured the meeting are reasons to celebrate.

Regroup. Whatever the outcome, stay together as a group. If you win step one, think about what should come next. If you don't succeed, brainstorm what steps you can take to maximize your own power and minimize that of the person(s) in charge. Regrouping means reaching out to new people—and going through the other steps as well.

Reproducing

Once involved, you can work to recruit others. Every additional leader represents that much more your group can accomplish—or that much less time the core members have to put in. Each person has skills to learn or refine as she becomes involved. But an important part of the growth process is helping people recognize leadership they already possess. Here's how Carmen Perez described such a moment of recognition. Carmen had traveled from Brooklyn to a 9to5 leadership conference in Washington, DC. She told me later the women she met there awed her. "They were so smart and outspoken and determined," she said. "At first I was intimidated. And then I realized, really they were just like me. If they could do this, so could I."

The best leaders, of course, are those who facilitate this process for others. Becoming active isn't about becoming a star. If you do have access to media coverage or speaking offers, be sure to share them. The strongest groups are those in which each member is special but no one is indispensable, and day-to-day leadership reflects the racial and class makeup of organization's desired constituency.

The groups I support are those that take a stand against all forms of oppression—what I've described as social justice feminism. They do so not out of pity for the downtrodden, but from an understanding of what it takes to build power. A saying by Lila Watson, an aboriginal activist, expresses this well: "If you have come to help me, please go away. But if you have come because your liberation is bound up with mine, let us work together." Putting at the center of our work those who have been most affected by oppression means the solutions we fashion will reach deep, all the way down to the roots of the problem. Removing barriers for those at the bottom is the greatest guarantee of removing them for all women.

Taking on the Big Boys can be exhausting. We have to make sure we walk our talk about integrating work and personal life, and always remember why we do what we do. Kirsten Downey, a *Washington Post* reporter who spent weeks investigating reports of sexual harassment at Mitsubishi, once asked me how I handle listening to stories of women's pain. In the three weeks she spent in Normal, Illinois, she'd had horrible nightmares and kept hearing echoes of the women's words. Here's how I do it, I told her. By focusing on all the women who stand up when so few win because they're reclaiming their power, because they want to make it harder for the Big Boys to do it to anyone else. I think of all the women I know who turned their lives around, used their anger over a personal injustice to try to change an unjust system. They give me inspiration. And they give me hope.

Are You a Feminist?

People often say things like this: "I'd like to be feminist but I wear make-up/I changed my name when I got married/I'm taking time to raise kids/I like perfume/I like pornography/I'm into guys/I am a guy/I shop at Wal-Mart."

The Big Boys don't have a secret handshake, and neither do we. There are no superficial criteria required to belong to the Feminists. Really, the best guidelines to aim for are simply these:

- Don't participate in the oppression of anyone.
- Look for opportunities to speak out against oppression of any kind.
- Look for opportunities to work with others to end all forms of oppression.
- Above all, embrace the notion that our founding fathers were right to want a nation built on justice and equality. This time around, everyone will be included.

FINAL THOUGHTS: THAT VISION THING

Together the chapters in this book lay out a vision of the kind of society we need—a society that genuinely values women and work associated with women, one that rejects all forms of domination. The society I envision reflects the best of our nation's ideals of fairness, liberty, opportunity, and prosperity, but goes much further. In this feminist future, no one's success depends on anyone else's failure. Rather than signifying the freedom to exploit, freedom will encompass the absence of fear and of want. Health care and education and having enough to eat will not be privileges, but rights belonging to all. The prosperity of the United States will become a force for eliminating, not perpetuating or profiting from, poverty in the developing world. Our government will resolve conflicts not with preemptive military strikes, but as an equal partner in a global community.

Each semester, I tell my students I'm handing them each a magic wand and ask them to describe the world they want. They offer only tentative plans. Wait, I remind them, you have that wand. We need to think big, imagine the real changes we need, even as we work for one small step or another.

Whatever you do, don't let go of that magic wand. Dream the world you want—and let the Big Boys know we won't settle for anything less.

1. OVERVIEW

1. Peggy Reeves Sanday, professor of anthropology at the University of Pennsylvania, describes the Minangkabau of West Sumatra, a group she studied for 18 years who call themselves matriarchal. In this case, Sanday says, "*Adat matriarchaat* constitutes an ethos and worldview grounded in an egalitarian social system backed by custom and tradition in which neither sex rules as a class over the other" ("Matriarchy and Islam Post 9/11: The Case of the Mimangkubau of Indonesia." Asia Social Issues Program, April 2003, www.ciaonet.org/wps/repol. See also *Women at the Center: Life in a Modern Matriarchy* [Ithaca, NY, and London: Cornell University Press, 2002]).

2. Clara Sue Kidwell describes the situation in North America when the Europeans arrived, where 7 million indigenous people of more than 1,000 nations lived ("Native American Women," in *Sisterhood is Forever*, ed. Robin Morgan [New York: Washington Square Press, 2003] 165–75). Most of these tribes offered a much more egalitarian society than the new conquerors had ever experienced. In the Iroquois tradition, for example, men operated as leaders but their powers often came from women. Clan mothers made many important decisions, including when and whether to wage war. Carolyn Foreman, author of *Indian Women Chiefs*, quotes John Adair in the late eighteenth century deploring the "petticoat government" of the Cherokee and praising their recent emergence "like all of the Iroquoian Indians, from the matriarchal period" (cited in Kidwell, 169).

3. This theory was developed by Gerda Lerner in *The Creation of Patriarchy* (New York: Oxford University Press, 1986), a fascinating and thorough analysis of relevant studies and theories. Lerner explains, for example, why it would have been much harder to exchange men—you couldn't ensure their loyalty to the tribe to which they were traded. Women, on the other hand were less likely to rebel because of their attachment to the children they produced, now identified with the new tribe.

4. He said this in 1776 regarding laws of inheritance (James Boswell, *Life of Johnson 1740–1793* [Oxford: Oxford University Press, 1953], 702).

5. Similarly, Europeans justified their domination of indigenous people and slaves with an ideology of white superiority.

6. See Robin Morgan's excellent introduction to *Sisterhood Is Forever*, ed. Robin Morgan (New York: Washington Square Press, 2003), for a wide range of examples of feminist rebellion, writing, and activism going back to the twelfth century. Just as history looks very different when we look at women, so women's history looks very different when we look at all women, not just white middle-class women in the United States—although even they were speaking up early on. In 1776, Abigail Adams had warned her husband John, who was attending the Continental Congress in Philadelphia, to "remember the ladies" and "not put such unlimited power into the hands of the husbands." She reminded the future president that "arbitrary power is . . . very liable to be broken."

7. "Declaration of Sentiments," The Seneca Falls Women's Rights Convention, Seneca Falls, New York (July 10 and 20, 1948).

8. See, for example, Angela Davis, *Women Race and Class* (New York: Random House, 1981) and Eleanor Flexner, *Century of Struggle: The Women's Rights Movement in the U.S.* (New York: Atheneum, 1972). On page 144, Flexner cites Elizabeth Cady Stanton's derogatory references to "Sambo" and the enfranchisement of "Africans, Chinese, and all the ignorant foreigners the moment they touch our shores." She and Susan B. Anthony opposed allowing black men to vote if white women could not, and argued that suffrage for men "creates an antagonism between black men and all women that will culminate in fearful outrages on womanhood, especially in the Southern states."

9. Inspired by a letter from Jennifer S. Macleod to the Harvard Business Review (May/June 1989), 206–7, responding to an earlier article by Felice Schwartz entitled "Management Women and the Facts of Life" (January/February 1989): 65–76.

10. Horace Bushnell, *Women's Suffrage—the Reform Against Nature* (New York: C. Scribners and Co., 1870). Cited in Michael S. Kimmel, "Misogynists, Masculinist Mentors, and Male Supporters: Men's Responses to Feminism," in *Women: A Feminist Perspective*, ed. Jo Freeman (Mountain View, California: Mayfield Publishing Company, 1995), 562–63.

11. Edward O'Donnell, "Women as Bread Winners—The Error of the Age," *The American Federationist* (October 1897).

12. Mr. and Mrs. John Martin, who coauthored a book in 1916 critiquing feminism, compared voting to ordering coal as one of those "ordinary, humdrum" male tasks. "Somebody has to vote," they wrote, because, unfortunately, we have to have a government, just as, in our climate, we have to have fires, and therefore have to order fuel. But there is nothing joyous, nothing exhilarating, nothing elevating about either act, nothing that confers an atom of weight or a spark of glory on those who perform it" (*Feminism: Its Fallacies and Follies*. [New York: Dodd, Mead & Co., 1916], 312).

13. C.H. Freedman, *Manhood Redux: Standing Up to Feminism* (New York: Samson Publishers, 1985), 109.

14. Phyllis Schlafly, a leading antifeminist who headed the right-wing Eagle Forum, called feminists "a bunch of bitter women seeking a constitutional cure for their personal problems" (Susan J. Douglas, *Where the Girls Are: Growing Up Female With the Mass Media* [New York: Times Books, 1994], 221).

15. Susan Douglas describes how in 1970 ABC anchorman Howard K. Smith began a newscast on the fiftieth anniversary of women's suffrage—a day marked by women's demonstrations around the country—by quoting Vice President Spiro Agnew: "Three things have been difficult to tame. The ocean, fools, and women. We may soon be able to tame the ocean, but fools and women will take a little longer." Smith ended the segment with a quote from West Virginia senator Jennings Randolph, who characterized the women's movement as "a small band of bra-less bubbleheads." (*Where the Girls Are: Growing Up Female With the Mass Media* [New York: Times Books, 1994], 163.)

16. Gloria Steinem, "The Media and the Movement," in *Sisterhood Is Forever*, ed. Robin Morgan (New York: Washington Square Press, 2003), 111.

17. See Susan J. Douglas, *Where the Girls Are: Growing Up Female With the Mass Media* (New York: Times Books, 1994) for a thorough discussion of the catfight and of the media's depiction of feminists.

18. Susan Faludi, *Backlash* (New York: Crown Publishers, Inc., 1991), xi.

2. WHY SOCIAL WORKERS EARN LESS THAN ACCOUNTANTS: PAY EQUITY

1. Jane Fonda knew Karen Nussbaum, one of the founders of 9to5, and wanted to create a movie that highlighted the group's issues. Karen told me the original plot involved murdering the boss. "That's not really our agenda," she told Fonda. Hence the kidnapping (also not part of the agenda). The fantasies about how to off the boss did flow from conversations Fonda had with forty 9to5 members in Cleveland.

2. A survey done by the Industry Standard among its 2,600 subscribers found a 27 percent compensation gap among women and men in the Internet economy when bonuses were considered along with pay. "Still a Man's World," *The Industry Standard* (January 1–8, 2001): 80–81.

3. National Committee on Pay Equity (NCPE). That group attributes the slight rise in these 2005 figures from the numbers in 2004 (76 cents overall, 66 cents for African American women, 56 cents for Latinas, and 80 cents for women of Asian descent) to the fact that men's earnings fell more than women's. Women's earnings were $31,858, a drop of 1.3 percent, while men's earnings were $41,386, a drop of 1.8 percent from the previous year.

4. See the study done by Steven J. Rose and Heidi Hartmann, "Still a Man's Labor Market: The Long Term Earnings Gap" (Washington, DC: Institute for Women's Policy Research, 2004), which looked at a random sample of women and men over a 15-year period.

5. See the study done by Steven J. Rose and Heidi Hartmann, "Still a Man's Labor Market: The Long Term Earnings Gap" (Washington, DC: Institute for Women's Policy Research, 2004). Another study by Sylvia Hewlitt of 2,443 highly qualified women (graduate degrees and high honors undergraduate) found more than a third stopped working for some period of time, usually to care for children, 24 percent for elders. The average time of this "off-ramping," as Hewlitt calls it, was 2.2 years. The leave cost women 18 percent of their earning power—37 percent if they took three or more years off. See Hewlitt, "The New Have-It-All Myth," *More* magazine (June 2005).

6. "Laura," Electronic testimony to the Economic Sufficiency Task Force of Wisconsin

Women Equal Prosperity, a statewide project to raise the status of women in Wisconsin (May 2004): http://wiwep.org/EconomicSufficiency/homepage.

7. Abby Ellin, "When It Comes to Salary, Many Women Don't Push," *New York Times*, February 29, 2004.

8. U.S. Census Bureau, median earnings of women 25 years or older working full time, year round as a percentage of men's annual earnings in 2003. See http://www.census.gov/hhes/income/histinc/p24/html.

9. Hilary M. Lips, "The Gender Wage Gap: Debunking the Rationalizations," WomensMedia.com: http://www.womensmedia.com/new/Lips-Hilary-gender-wage-gap shtml. In 2001, women's pay compared to men's overall was 76 percent. The figures were 72 percent for those with masters degrees, 75 percent for those with doctorates, and 60 percent for those with professional degrees. Jane Waldfogel found that the "mommy wage gap"—the gap between earnings of mothers and nonmothers—grew from 10 percent in 1980, when nonmothers earned 66 percent and mothers 56 percent of the pay of their male counterparts, to 17.5 percent in 1991, when nonmothers earned 90.1 percent but mothers only 72.6 percent of men's pay. "Understanding the 'Family Gap' in Pay for Women with Children," Journal of Economic Perspectives 12, no. 1 (1998): 137–56.

10. Steven J. Rose and Heidi Hartmann, "Still a Man's Labor Market: The Long Term Earnings Gap" (Washington, DC: Institute for Women's Policy Research, 2004). See also Hilary M. Lips, "The Gender Wage Gap: Debunking the Rationalizations," WomensMedia.com, http://www.womensmedia.com/new/Lips-Hilary-gender-wage-gap.shtml.

11. Adapted from remarks by Steve Lerner, then head of the AFL-CIO Organizing Institute, at a conference in Washington, DC, entitled "Low-Wage Workers in the New Economy: Strategies for Opportunity and Advancement," May 24, 2000.

12. As the first major purchaser of typewriters, the government created the category "Female Clerk" (later called "Typist") and set the annual pay at $600; "Male Clerks" (whose job involved filing, rewriting certain documents, and reception) earned $1,200 per year (Paul Van Riper, *History of the United States Civil Service* [Evanston, IL: Row, Peterson, 1958], 479).

13. Donald J. Treiman and Heidi I. Hartmann, *Women, Work and Wages: Equal Pay for Jobs of Equal Value* (Washington, DC: National Academy Press, 1981): 62-71.

14. Social psychologists have demonstrated repeatedly that occupations associated with women or requiring stereotypically feminine skills are rated as less prestigious and deserving of less pay than occupations associated with men and masculine skills. As more and more women enter an occupation, there may be a tendency to value (and reward) that occupation less and less. See Donald Tomaskovic-Devey, *Gender and Racial Inequality at Work: The Sources and Consequences of Job Segregation* (Ithaca, NY: ILR Press, 1993).

15. Daniel H. Weinberg's "Evidence from Census 2000 about Earnings by Detailed Occupation for Men and Women," shows men earning more than women in all 20 of the highest-paid occupations for both sexes as well as in all 20 of the lowest-paid (*Census Bureau Report* [June 2004]: http://purl.access.apo.gov/gpo/lps64752). Steven Rose and Heidi Hartmann ("Still a Man's Labor Market: The Long Term Earnings Gap" [Washington, DC: Institute for Women's Policy Research, 2004]) divided jobs into three categories—elite, good, and less skilled. In each tier, male-dominated categories pay

more than those held primarily by women, even though the educational requirements are similar. The Center for Gender Studies found only four occupational categories for which comparison data were available in which women earned even a little more than men: special education teachers, order clerks, electrical and electronic engineers, and miscellaneous food preparation occupations.

16. National Institute for Early Education Research, "Massive National Study Finds Many Prekindergarten Teachers Underpaid; Others Lacking Required Credentials," press release (May 3, 2005): http://nieer.org/mediacenter/index.php?PressID=44.

17. Heidi Hartmann et al., "Equal Pay for Working Families: National and State Data on Pay Gap and Its Costs" (Washington, DC: Institute for Women's Policy Research, June 1999).

18. Ronnie Steinberg, speech at Emory University, "Ronnie Steinberg discusses future efforts in pay equity reform" (April 29, 1996).

19. Lorraine Adams, "The Hazards of Elder Care," *The Washington Post* (October 31, 1999): http://pqasb.pqarchiver.com/washingtonpost/access.

20. *County of Washington v. Gunther*, 452 U.S. 161 (1981).

21. This provision is known as the Bennett Amendment.

22. Kimberly Bayard et al., "New Evidence on Sex Segregation and Sex Differences in Wages from Matched Employer-Employee Data," Working Paper No. 7003 (Cambridge, MA: National Bureau of Economic Research, 1999).

23. According to Sara Evans and Barbara Nelson, the base salary for a Clerk I working for the state of Minnesota in 1983 was $11,922, only 17 percent above the poverty line of $10,178 (*Wage Justice* [Chicago: University of Chicago Press, 1989], 99–100). Over the next four years, without the state's pay equity initiative, the base salary would have risen to $13,675, 22 percent above the then-current poverty line. However, as a result of pay equity, that Clerk I took home $15,931, 42 percent above the poverty line. Contrary to critics who said the state would have to cut jobs and that women's share of state jobs would decline, the total number of state employees increased from 32,383 in January 1982 to 35,643 in January of 1986. Women's representation in state employment increased from 42 percent of employees in 1982 to 44 percent in 1986.

24. Michael Lowery, in-person testimony at an open forum of the Wisconsin Women Equal Prosperity project in Milwaukee, February 25, 2004.

25. Clarence M. Pendleton Jr., appointed by President Reagan to chair the U.S. Commission on Civil Rights, made this statement in 1984 (see "On Comparable Pay for Comparable Work," *New York Times*, November 17, 1984.)

26. Memo to White House Counsel Fred F. Fielding on February 20, 1984. Roberts, then-associate White House counsel, also wrote, "It is difficult to exaggerate the perniciousness of the 'comparable worth' theory. It mandates nothing less than the central planning of the economy by judges" ("Memorandum re Nancy Risque Request for Guidance on Letter from Congresswoman Snowe et al." [see http://www.savethecourt.org]).

27. Governor Earl created the Task Force as a compromise with the union, Council 24 of the American Federation of State, County, and Municipal Workers. AFSCME had lodged a complaint with the EEOC and State Personnel Commission after state administrators balked at implementing a provision of the Omnibus Civil Service Reform Act of

November 1977 to end the practice of paying traditionally female jobs less than similar jobs held by men. That provision was grounded in a comprehensive review of the civil service system under Governor Patrick J. Lucey earlier that year. Examples cited included barbers and cosmetologists, bakers and cooks, and stock clerks and typists. For a more detailed background, see Dennis Dresang, "Gender and Pay: The Politics of Pay Equity in Wisconsin," in *The Politics and Practice of Pay Equity*, ed. Ronnie Steinberg (Nashville: Vanderbilt Press, forthcoming).

28. Dennis Dresang, ibid. See also my article, "From the Grassroots: Developing an Effective Political Strategy" in the same volume.

29. The hearing was held in Milwaukee December 10, 1984.

30. Attorney Barry Chaet. The debate took place in 1985 on WISN radio in Milwaukee on "Nighttalk" with Dave Begel.

31. See Ray Kenny, "Keen Wit Serves Bravo Well in Fight Over Women's Pay," July 16, 1985.

32. Phone interview, June 28, 2005.

3. CAN YOU HAVE A JOB *AND* A LIFE?

1. Cited in "10 Things that Could Happen to You if You Didn't Have Paid Sick Leave," Milwaukee's 9to5 National Association of Working Women (November 2004): 4.

2. In 2005, nearly two-thirds of all mothers of children under five were employed outside the home, 55 percent of mothers of infants under the age of one, and 78 percent of mothers whose children are 18 or under (see http://www.bls.gov).

3. The Family and Medical Leave Act passed Congress in 1991 and 1992 but was vetoed both times by then-president George H.W. Bush. It was finally passed again and signed into law as the first act of the Clinton administration in February 1993.

4. On December 7, 1976, the Supreme Court ruled that treating "pregnant people" differently wasn't gender discrimination since not all women are pregnant. Congress may not always know much, but they did understand that pregnancy had something to do with sex and passed the Pregnancy Discrimination Act two years later (*General Electric Co. v. Gilbert*, 429 U.S. 125: www.civilrights.orf/research_center/permanent_coalition/resources/mainlibrary.html).

5. This is the language of the New Jersey Temporary Disability Insurance fund, created in 1946.

6. When the Commission on Leave studied who took leave, researchers found that half of those who are both covered and eligible for FMLA had to forgo caring for a seriously ill family member or newborn child. Some didn't take time off even for their own serious health conditions—mainly because they couldn't afford to lose their wages. Commission on Family and Medical Leave (U.S.), *A Workable Balance: Report to Congress on Family and Medical Leave Policies* (Washington, DC: Commission on Leave; Women's Bureau, U.S. Department of Labor, 1995).

7. *Moore v. Alabama State University*, 980 F. Supp. 426 (M.D. Ala. 1997). The court ruled favorably for the plaintiff in a case challenging the university's failure to promote her. The vice-president for Academic Affairs told the plaintiff that he would not consider her for the promotion because she was married with a child, that he believed a woman

should stay at home with her family, and that the new job entailed too much travel for a married mother. Cited in "The New Glass Ceiling," a report by Joan Williams and Nancy Segal (American University, Washington College of Law, 2002).

8. Theo Emery, "Maternity Leave Company Sued by Woman Fired While Pregnant," AP (June 27, 2003).

9. The teachers were interviewed as part of a project called Across the Boundaries, conducted jointly by 9to5 and the Radcliffe Public Policy Institute in 2000 and 2001. The findings were written up in a report that I cowrote with Lisa Dodson and Tiffany Manuel entitled, "Keeping Jobs and Raising Families in Low-Income America: It Just Doesn't Work" (Boston: Harvard University, 2002).

10. In-person interview, Eau Claire, Wisconsin, September 24, 2003.

11. July Amparano Lopez, "The Enforcers," *Wall Street Journal*, (June 21, 1993), R7.

12. When Linda K. Stroh and Karen S. Kush surveyed how many companies had formal, permanent flextime programs available to a significant portion of work force, only 14 percent said yes. Ninety-two percent of the remainder said it was "unlikely" or "very unlikely" that they would adopt (Summarized in "Flextime: The Imaginary Innovation," *The New York Times*, November 27, 1994).

13. Jack Welch, *Winning* (New York: HarperCollins, 2005).

14. Elliott Lehman, then CEO of Fel-Pro in Chicago, told the Commission on Family and Medical Leave about the costs of "control turnover, the loss of somebody who has left you who you would like to keep." In addition to administrative costs of finding a replacement, he said, "it takes a year and a half for a person you have replaced to get up to the speed of the person who has left" (Commission Public Hearing, Chicago, May 8, 1995).

15. Kenneth Weaver, verbal testimony at the Commission on Family and Medical Leave Public Hearing, May 8, 1995, Chicago.

16. Governor Thomas H. Kean, *The Politics of Inclusion* (New York: Free Press, 1988), 336 and 338.

17. Unlike the United States, 163 countries around the world offer guaranteed paid leave to women in connection with childbirth; 45 ensure paid leave for men (Jody Heymann, "The Work, Family and Equity Index: Where Does the United States Stand Globally?" *The Project on Global Working Families* (Boston, MA: Harvard School of Public Health, 2004).

18. Enron, for example, received $382 million in refund checks from the federal government in just four years, according to Mark Zepezauer (*Take the Rich Off Welfare* [Cambridge, MA: South End Press, 2004]). Zepezauer estimates the total amount of corporate welfare to be $815 billion a year.

19. Janet C. Gornick and Marcia K. Meyers, *Families That Work: Policies for Reconciling Parenthood and Employment* (New York: Russell Sage Foundation, 2003).

20. The GDP, according to the government's Bureau of Economic Activity, was 10987.9 billion dollars for 2003. Mark Zepezauer's estimate of corporate welfare as $815 billion puts it at 7.4 percent of the total GDP (*Take the Rich Off Welfare* [Cambridge, MA: South End Press, 2004]).

21. Rhona Rapoport and Lotte Bailyn, "Relinking Life and Work: Toward a Better Future" (New York: Ford Foundation, 1996).

22. Quoted in Erik Gunn, "Medical Leave Debated," in the *Milwaukee Journal*, September 23, 1987.

23. William J. Gainer, "Estimated Costs of HR 925, the Family and Medical Leave Act of 1987" (Washington, DC: Government Accounting Office, November 10, 1987).

24. The Institute for Women's Policy Research in Washington, DC, produced an excellent report in 1990 called "Unnecessary Losses: Costs to Americans of the Lack of Family and Medical Leave" (see www.iwpr.org)

25. Statement at a press conference at the National Press Club in Washington, DC, January 13, 2004, sponsored by the Take Care Net, whose steering committee I sit on.

26. Bill Hurley, *Milwaukee Sentinel*. February 25, 1988. The *Milwaukee Journal*, ran the AP story with the headline, "Children Win Support for Family-Leave Bill." The subhead read, "Official Can't Deny Young Lobbyists' Plea."

27. Cited in Nathan Seppe, "Family Leave under Attack," *Wisconsin State Journal*, June 9, 1991.

28. Hearing on "The Family and Medical Leave Act: Present Impact and Possible Next Steps," Subcommittee on Children and Family, Senate Committee on Health, Education, Labor and Pensions, July 14, 1999 in Washington, DC. I testified again at a roundtable of the same committee on June 23, 2005 against efforts to change the regulations covering FMLA in ways that would make it much harder to use.

29. Prepared Statement of Deanna R. Gelak, director of governmental affairs for the Society for Human Resource Management, for the July 14, 1999, hearing.

30. The hearing was before the Subcommittee on Worker Protection of the House Committee on Education and the Workforce.

31. July 14, 1999, Hearing transcript, U.S. Printing Office, Serial No. 108–7, 32–3.

32. More and more women entered the workforce because they wanted to and because they had to as a result of falling male wages and of marriages that ended or never began. Between 1963 and 1997, the percentage of women who were never married nearly tripled (from 6 to 17 percent) and the percentage previously married (mostly divorced) doubled from 10 to 19 percent. The share of married couples in which both partners were employed grew from 36 to 60 percent between 1970 and 1997. By the year 2000, 74 percent of single mothers were employed. (Janet C. Gornick and Marcia K. Meyers, *Families that Work: Policies for Reconciling Parenthood and Employment* [New York: Russell Sage Foundation, 2003], 29–32).

33. Phone interview, May 16, 2005.

4. CAN A WOMAN DO A MAN'S JOB?

1. Lisa Belkin, "The Opt-Out Revolution," *New York Times* magazine, October 26, 2003.

2. Louise Bernikow, WeNews, November 30, 2004, www.womensnews.org.

3. Phone interview, August 15, 2005.

4. Joan Williams and Nancy Segal, "The New Glass Ceiling: Mothers and Fathers Sue for Discrimination" (Washington, DC: American University, Washington College of Law, November 2002).

5. *Trezza v. The Hartford, Inc.*, No. 98 Civ. 2205, 1998 WL 912101 (S.D.N.Y. Dec. 30,

1998). Cited in Joan Williams and Nancy Segal, "The New Glass Ceiling: Mothers and Fathers Sue for Discrimination" (Washington, DC: American University, Washington College of Law, November 2002).

6. Phone interview, July 12, 2004. For research on mothers, see Daniel Aloi, "Mothers Face Disadvantages in Getting Hired," Cornell University News Service, August 4, 2005, http://www.news.cornell.edu/stories/Aug05/soc.mothers.dea.html

7. Phone interview, April 6, 2005.

8. You can read all about it in Susan Antilla's *Tales from the Boom-Boom Room: Women Vs. Wall Street* (Princeton, NJ: Bloomberg Press, Princeton, 2002).

9. Statement of Allison Schieffelin, *EEOC v. Morgan Stanley and Schieffelin v. Morgan Stanley*, No. 01 Civ. 8421 (RMB)(RLB), September 10, 2001.

10. Patrick McGeehan, "What Merrill's Women Want," *New York Times*, August 22, 2004.

11. Ibid.

12. Phone interview, April 8, 2005.

13. "A Career in the Courtroom: A Different Model for the Success of Women Who Try Cases," 2005 Survey by the Chicago-based Defense Research Institute, cited in Dave Simanoff, "Law Firms Address Harassment Issues," *Tampa Tribune*, April 6, 2005.

14. "Women Present Evidence of Widespread Discrimination at Wal-Mart," April 28, 2003. http://www.walmartclass.com/staticdata/press_releases/wmcc.html

15. Sara Rimer, "For Women in Sciences, the Pace of Progress in Academia is Slow," *New York Times*, April 15, 2005.

16. In-person testimony, Wisconsin Women Equal Prosperity Open Forum, Platteville, Wisconsin, February 20, 2004.

17. Martha Burk details the problems with these "best lists," including how many employers buy their way on by making large donations to the organization, in a chapter called "Diversity Dodge" in *Cult of Power: Sex Discrimination in Corporate America and What Can Be Done About It* (New York: Scribner, 2005).

18. "A Century for Women, Part I, Work and Family," Turner Broadcasting System (TBS), June 7, 1994.

19. Ibid.

20. "Women Present Evidence of Widespread Discrimination at Wal-Mart," April 28, 2003. http://www.walmartclass.com/staticdata/press_releases/wmcc.html

21. The IRS requires that the employee pay income tax on the "fair market value" of the premium paid by the employer for the domestic partner coverage. "Fair market value" is generally interpreted as the difference between the cost for single coverage and the amount for domestic partner coverage, minus any contribution paid by the employee. See T. Santora, "What's Good for the Goose: A Critical Review of Unions as Employers and the Continuing Struggle Toward Equal Benefits in the Marketplace," Pride @ Work (Washington, DC: AFL-CIO, 2000).

22. See, for example, *Simonton v. Runyon* (232 F.3d 33, 35 2d Circuit 2000). That case involved a New York postal worker who was subjected to vulgar and degrading behavior for being gay. While the Second Circuit Court of Appeals found the behavior "morally reprehensible," the judges concluded that Title VII's protection against sex discrimina-

tion did not extend to discrimination based on sexual orientation. However, the judges noted that a plaintiff might prevail by arguing that the harassment was based on failure to conform to gender norms. Earlier, in *Price Waterhouse v. Hopkins*, 490 U.S. 228 (1989), the Supreme Court ruled that harassment directed at a person who doesn't conform to traditional sex stereotypes is covered under Title VII.

23. Minnesota, Rhode Island, New Mexico, California, Illinois, and Maine.

24. Walter Brasch, "State Sanctioned Sexism," March 2002, www.walterbrasch.com/state/htm.

25. Ibid.

26. See Rannveig Traustadottir, "Obstacles to Equality: The Double Discrimination of Women with Disabilities Overview Article," July 1990, www.dawn.thot.net/disability.html.

27. Women with physical disabilities earn a median of $25,201 per year, compared to $32,345 for men with physical disabilities and $28,164 for women without disabilities ("Employment and Earnings by Disability Status for Civilian Noninstitutionalized Women 21 to 64 Years: 2000," U.S. Census Bureau, Census 2000, http://www.census. gov/hhes/www/disability/cps/cps104.html). Not surprisingly, poverty rates for women with physical challenges are greater than those for men in the same situation, and more than two and a half times greater than for women with no disability. See sex by age by disability status by poverty status for the civilian noninstitutionalized population five years and over ("2003 American Community Survey Summary Tables," http://factfinder. census.gov/servlet/DTTable?_bm=y&-geo_id=04000US03&-ds_name=ACS_2003_ EST_G00_&-redoLog=false&-mt_name=ACS_2003_EST_G2000_P060).

28. "Economics and People with Disabilities," The Center for an Accessible Society, www.accessiblesociety.org/topics/economics-employment/.

29. Interview by her daughter, Claudia White Harreld, January 1952, reprinted in *Black Women in White America: A Documentary History*, ed. Gerda Lerner (New York: Vintage Books, 1992).

30. President Bill Clinton signed an executive order to this effect, known as the "responsible contractor rule," shortly before leaving office. His successor, George W. Bush, repealed the rule on December 27, 2001 (Craig Aaron, "A Timeline of Failure," *In These Times*, October 28, 2004, http://www.inthesetimes.com/site/main/article/1539).

31. 9to5 Newsline, March 1998.

32. It's hard to swallow the hypocrisy of our current president on this front. George W. Bush had his Justice Department side against affirmative action at the University of Michigan in a 2003 Supreme Court case. A C student with undistinguished SAT scores, Bush nevertheless made it into Yale the year the university decided to give special consideration to the size of the applicant's family contributions. In 2004, both Harvard and Princeton admitted legacy applicants at a rate more than triple that of applicants whose parents had not attended (Daniel Golden, "Family Ties: Preference for Alumni Children in College Admissions Draws Fire" *Wall Street Journal*, January 15, 2003).

33. Diana Roose, "Revitalizing the EEOC: Survey Results and Recommendations" (Cleveland, OH, 9to5: 1994).

34. Georgia Pabst, "Possible changes in filing EEOC complaints draw concern," *Milwaukee Journal Sentinel*, July 1, 2003.

35. In-person interview, Cleveland, Ohio, April 20, 2005.

5. YOU WANT TO SEE MY *WHAT?* SEXUAL HARASSMENT

1. Speaking to the author on *Crossfire*, January 15, 1992.

2. The first documented use of the term was a 1975 conference at Cornell University that included a "Speak-Out on Sexual Harassment." Lin Farley and Catharine A. MacKinnon popularized the phrase in the titles of their books, Farley's *Sexual Shakedown: The Sexual Harassment of Women on the Job* (McGraw Hill, 1978), and MacKinnon's *Sexual Harassment of Working Women: A Case of Sex Discrimination* (New Haven: Yale University Press, 1979). Finally in 1980, after a number of public hearings, speak-outs, court cases, and media articles about the subject, the Equal Employment Opportunity Commission (EEOC) developed a definition. See Ellen Bravo and Ellen Cassedy, *The 9to5 Guide to Combating Sexual Harassment* (Milwaukee: 9to5 Working Woman Education Fund, 1999).

3. Statements during the hearing by Sens. Arlen Specter (R-PA), Alan Simpson (R-WY), and Orrin Hatch (R-UT), respectively ("The Thomas Nomination: Excerpts from Sentate's Hearing on the Thomas Nomination," *New York Times*, October 12, 1991.

4. Phone interview, January 19, 2005.

5. In-person meeting, February 8, 2005.

6. Barbara Gutek and R. Done, "Sexual Harassment," in *Handbook of the Psychology of Women and Gender*, ed. R. K. Unger (New York: Wiley, 2001).

7. Testimony from Thomas Garthwaite, Veterans Affairs deputy undersecretary, before the house Veterans Affairs subcommittee, April 23, 1998. According to Garthwaite, nearly one in five female veterans seeking services from the department report that they've been sexually assaulted in the military (http://www.va.gov/OCA/testimony/hvac/sh/23AP98TG.asp). Reports of assault increased 20 percent in 1997. According to a *60 Minutes* report of February 20, 2005 entitled "Rape in the Military," women in the military are ten times as likely to say they've experienced sexual assault as civilian women—three out of 100 compared to three out of 1,000. The Miles Foundation, a nonprofit dedicated to stopping violence against women in the military, refers to a recent survey that found more than one in three women raped while on active duty said they'd been raped more than once; 14 percent reported having been gang raped (http://hometown.aol.com/milesfdn/myhomepage/).

8. Sadler, Booth, Cook, and Doebbling, "Factors Associated With Women's Risk of Rape in the Military Environment," *American Journal of Industrial Medicine*, March 2003, 43(3), 262–73.

9. February 20, 2005.

10. Anita Hill, among others, describes the way slaveholders justified the rape of slave women to continue and enlarge their holdings by casting them as "wanton, perverse, and animalistic . . . unchaste and eagerly available." *Speaking Truth to Power* (New York: Doubleday, 1997), 280. Hill quotes a prize-winning 1925 essay by Marita O. Bonner, "On Being Young—a Woman—and Colored," which asked, "Why do they see a colored woman only as a gross collection of desires, all uncontrolled reaching out for their Apollos and Quasimodos with avid indiscrimination?" (*The Crisis* [December 1925], cited in Hill 1997, 281).

11. Cited in Ellen Bravo and Ellen Cassedy, *The 9to5 Guide to Combating Sexual Harassment* (Milwaukee: 9to5 Working Women Education Fund, 1999), 70–71.

12. *Zabkowicz v. West Bend Co.*, 589 F Supp. 780 (ED Wis. 1984).

13. *Oncale v. Sundowner Offshore Services, Inc.*, 523 US 75 (1998).

14. *Tompkins v. Public Service Electric & Gas Company*, 422 F Supp 553 (USDC E. Dist. of NJ 1976).

15. *Corne v. Bausch & Lomb, Inc.*, 390 F Supp. 161 (1975).

16. Ann C. Wendt and William M. Stonaker, "Sexual Harassment and Retaliation: A Double-Edged Sword," in *Advanced Management Journal* 67, no. 4 (Autumn 2002): 54.

17. Cited in Melanie Howard, "Surviving Sexual Harassment," *American Health* 18, no. 7 (July/August 1999): 24–25. This is the case dramatized in the 2005 movie *North Country*, starring Charlize Theron, Frances McDormand, and Sissy Spacek.

18. Timothy Lynch of the Cato Institute, quoted in Alexandra Alger and William Flanagan, "Sexual Politics," *Forbes Magazine* 157, no. 9 (May 6, 1996): 110.

19. Freada Klein came up with this figure after surveying 160 large manufacturing and service corporations for *Working Woman* magazine (Klein Associates, "The 1988 Working Woman Sexual Harassment Survey Executive Report" (Cambridge: Klein Associates, 1988).

20. Tom Helds, "$24.7 million verdict in 'Seinfeld case' reversed," *The Milwaukee Journal Sentinel*, February 23, 2000.

21. For more on the Mitsubishi case, see Ellen Bravo and Ellen Cassedy, *The 9to5 Guide to Combating Sexual Harassment* (Milwaukee: 9to5 Working Women Education Fund, 1999), 127–29, 127–38.

22. *Crossfire*, November 24, 1992. The diaries, which came to light in October 1993, revealed liaisons with staffers and lobbyists going back to 1969. More damaging were Packwood's tales of leaning on lobbyists for retainers for his ex-wife as a way of avoiding paying alimony—and reputed tampering with the diaries to erase presumably worse revelations. Facing possible expulsion, the senator resigned. Many commentators who had supported Packwood stopped doing so when the diaries appeared. But not all. Listen to this comment from Charles Paparella: "This does not excuse Packwood, but we believe it does explain him. He is guilty of being a lecher, perhaps . . . a cad, a boor, an unattractive and oversexed American man, granted. But if all organizations were to expel all men who could reasonably be found to possess similar undesirable characteristics, there would be no police departments, no fire departments, no airlines, and no armed forces. There would likely be no organization that is predominantly male" (untitled article, *The Shore Journal: Delmarva's Original Electronic Magazine* (1995): www.intercom.net/local/shore_journal/cfp10910.html).

23. In 1988, the *Seattle Times* revealed that Adams had been charged the previous year with sexually assaulting a friend of his daughter's. He denied the charge and continued to campaign for reelection. Two weeks later the *Seattle Times* reported that eight other women were accusing Adams of sexual molestation over a period of two decades, describing a history of drugging and subsequent rape. Later that day, while still proclaiming his innocence, Adams ended his campaign. See Michael Janofsky, "Brock Adams, 77, Senator and Cabinet Member, Dies," *New York Times*, September 11, 2004.

24. Phone interview with the author, March 21, 2005.

25. Justice Steven Breyer, writing for eight of the justices in *Burlington Northern Santa Fe Railway v. White*, 05-259.

26. Phone interview, August 17, 2005.

27. For additional information relative to Miles and subsequent military court decisions see Michael F. Noone and Mary Jo Wiley, "Sticks, Stones and Broken Bones: Military Law's Criteria for Aggravated Assault," in *Feminist Issues*, 14, no 1 (Spring 1994): 67-93.

28. Secretary Rumsfield made this comment in a memorandum on zero tolerance on February 2004. That memorandum and subsequent policy directives issued by the Department of Defense may be found at http://www.sapr.mil The press conference conducted on January 4, 2005, by Dr. David Chu is also available via this Web site.

29. Formally known as the Ronald Reagan Defense Authorization Act for Fiscal Year 2005.

30. For more on this, see Suzanne Pharr, *Homophobia: A Weapon of Sexism* (Inverness, California: Chardon Press, 1988).

6. NINE TO FIVE: NOT JUST A MOVIE—THE RIGHT TO ORGANIZE

1. Martin Jay Levitt with Terry Conroy, *Confessions of a Union Buster* (New York: Crown Publishers, 1993), 17.

2. T. S. Arthur, *The Lady at Home: or, Leaves from the Every-Day Book of an American Woman* (New York: Alden, 1844), 177–78, cited in Philip S. Foner, *Women and the American Labor Movement* (New York: The Free Press, 1982), 2.

3. September 5, 2005, phone interview with Candace Owley, president of the Wisconsin Federation of Nurses and Health Professionals, about comments from G. Edwin Howe. On June 23, a group of union nurses donned wedding gowns and went to Howe's office with a sign reading, "Marry us, Ed Howe." Turns out his 2003 compensation included a whopping $1.3 million for his pension—and his employer, Aurora Health Care, paid the taxes on the amount to boot.

4. Juliet H. Mofford, "Women in the Workplace: Labor Unions," *Women's History Magazine* (Spring/Summer 1996).

5. Sarah Bagley in letter to a friend, quoted in "Documents from the Lowell Mills": http://womenshistory.about.com/od/worklowellmill/index.htm.

6. See the 1905 case known as *Lockner v. New York*, 198 US 45, when the Supreme Court overruled a New York law to limit bakery workers to a ten-hour day, six-day week because it violated the "freedom to contract."

7. Juliet H. Mofford, "Women in the Workplace: Labor Unions," in *Women's History Magazine*, (Spring/Summer 1996).

8. For more detailed information, see Ruth Milkman, *Women, Work and Protest: A Century of U.S. Women's Labor History* (Boston: Routledge and Kegan Paul, 1985).

9. Sarah Jane Deutsch, "From Ballots to Breadlines," in *No Small Courage: A History of Women in the United States*, ed. Nancy F. Cott (New York: Oxford University Press, 2000), 466.

10. For a fascinating account of women in the labor movement from the 1930s to the

1970s and their impact on public and workplace policy, see Dorothy Cobble, *The Other Women's Movement: Workplace Justice and Social Rights in Modern America* (Princeton, NJ: Princeton University Press, 2004).

11. Ibid., 21.

12. From a letter to employees drafted by (former) union buster Martin Levitt, quoted in his memoir with Terry Conroy, *Confessions of a Union Buster* (New York: Crown Publishers, 1993), 110.

13. Ibid., 178.

14. Ibid., 194.

15. Phone interview, August 26, 2005.

16. Email interview, September 23, 2005.

17. Frieda Miller, quoted in Dorothy Cobble, *The Other Women's Movement: Workplace Justice and Social Rights in Modern America* (Princeton, NJ: Princeton University Press, 2004), 128.

18. Ibid., 215–19.

19. E. Galinsky, *The 1997 National Study of the Changing Workforce*, Families and Work Institute (1997): www.familiesandwork.org/nationalstudy.html

20. Dorothy Cobble, *The Other Women's Movement: Workplace Justice and Social Rights in Modern America* (Princeton, NJ: Princeton University Press, 2004), 138.

21. Speech on introducing the Fair Pay Act and Paycheck Fairness Act, April 19, 2005.

22. Cited in Linda Housch Kwanza Collins, "To Hell With You, Charlie," in *Building on Diversity: The New Unionism*, ed. Lisa Oppenheim (Chicago: Midwest Center for Labor Research, 1993), 72.

23. Phone interview with the author, July 14, 2006.

24. Phone interview, November 6, 2005.

25. Steven Greenhouse, "Why Can't Wal-Mart, a Retailing Behemoth, Pay More?" *New York Times*, May 4, 2005.

26. According to Ralph Nader, the ratio between executive and worker pay in Europe is close to 25 to one. Compare that to the United States, where the figure is 525 to one. See "How to Curb Corporate Power," in *The Nation*, October 10, 2005.

27. S. Homes and W. Zellner, "The Costco Way," *BusinessWeek*, April 12, 2004, 76–77.

28. The percentage of union members who were women increased slowly at first (up to 24 percent in 1970) and then much faster (43 percent today). The biggest gains were among women of color, who are unionized at a higher rate than white women. Partly this growth resulted from a changed focus for unions beginning in the 1960s, as they turned to public sector and service jobs and to victories by the civil rights movement against Jim Crow laws and practices (Ruth Milkman, "Labor Unions," in *The Reader's Companion to U.S. Women's History*, eds. Wilma Mankiller and others [Boston: Houghton Mifflin, 1999]: 302–4). In 2005, 15.6 percent of African American, 12.7 percent of Asian women, and 11.5 percent of Latina women were represented by unions, compared with 12 percent of white women workers. The underrepresentation of women of color earlier in the century reflected racism among employers as well as among unions; for example, according to

Cobble, the phone company didn't hire black women until the 1960s (Dorothy Cobble, *The Other Women's Movement: Workplace Justice and Social Rights in Modern America* [Princeton, NJ: Princeton University Press, 2004], 46.

29. "Union Membership in America," *Union Free America* (2004): http://www.union freeamerica.com/union_membership.htm

30. Ibid.

31. Kate Bronfenbrenner, "Uneasy Terrain: The Impact of Capital Mobility on Workers, Wages, and Union Organizing," testimony submitted to the U.S. Trade Deficit Review Commission, September 6, 2000: http://www.attac.org/fra/toil/doc/cornell.htm

32. From transcript of Fred Long, president of the consulting firm WCIRA, recorded by Joel D. Smith and cited in John Logan, "Consultants, Lawyers and the Union Free Movement in the USA Since the 1970s," London School of Economics, *Industrial Relations Journal* 3, no. 3 (2002): http://www.americanrightsatwork.org/resources/studies.cfm.

33. "The Employer War: Employer Interference by the Numbers," *AFL-CIO Fact Sheet* (2005): http://www.aflcio.org/joinaunion/why/uniondifference/upload/this_is_america .pdf.

34. Martin Levitt and Terry Conroy, *Confessions of a Union Buster* (New York: Crown Publishers, 1993), 184.

35. Kenneth Roth, "Unfair Advantage: Workers' Freedom of Association in the United States Under International Human Rights Standards" (New York; Washington; London; Brussels: Human Rights Watch 2000): http://hrw.org/reports/pdfs/u/us/uslbr008.pdf.

36. Martin Levitt and Terry Conroy, *Confessions of a Union Buster* (New York: Crown Publishers, 1993), 203.

37. Gordon Lafer, "Free and Fair? How Labor Law Fails U.S. Democratic Standards" (Washington, DC: American Rights at Work, 2005), 27.

38. See Pamela Roby and Lynet Utal, "Putting It All Together: The Dilemmas of Rank-and-File Union Leaders," in *Women and Unions: Forging a Partnership*, Dorothy Cobble, ed. (Ithaca, NY: Cornell University Press, 1993), 363–77.

39. Ruth Needleman, "Comments," in Pamela Roby and Lynet Utal, "Putting It All Together: The Dilemmas of Rank-and-File Union Leaders," in *Women and Unions: Forging a Partnership*, Dorothy Cobble, ed. (Ithaca, NY: Cornell University Press, 1993), 409.

40. See Ruth Needleman, "Space and Opportunities: Developing new leaders to meet labor's future," in *Building on Diversity: The New Unionism*, ed. Lisa Oppenheim (Chicago: Midwest Center for Labor Research, 1993), 15–19.

41. Cited in T. Santora, "What's Good for the Goose: A Critical Review of Unions as Employers and the Continuing Struggle Toward Equal Benefits in the Marketplace," Pride @ Work (Washington, DC: AFL-CIO, 2000), 2. Santora cites a great example of the mutual benefits of partnerships between oppressed groups. In 1984, the Teamsters in San Francisco promoted their boycott of Coors beer in the gay community. As part of its efforts to keep out the union, Coors administered lie detector tests to prospective employees. Applicants had to field questions about their support for a union—and their sexual orientation. Gay activists agreed to support the boycott provided the Teamsters promote hiring openly gay truck drivers. The Teamsters agreed, the boycott grew, and the offensive questions were removed.

42. Bill Fletcher, "Debate Over the Future of the AFL-CIO: More Heat Than Light," *Monthly Review* (June 2005): http://www.monthlyreview.org/0605fletcher.htm.

43. Lea Grundy and Netsy Firestein, "Work and Family and Labor/Management Collaboration," A Work in America Institute National Policy Study (2000): http://www.laborproject.org/publications/pdf/wp2.pdf.

44. In 2003, District 925 locals in Boston, Cleveland and Cincinnati merged into other SEIU locals. Only the Seattle local, itself an amalgamated group, retained the 925 name.

45. Lois Blinkhorn, "Working 9 to 5: They just want to earn a living with rights, respect," *Milwaukee Journal*, October 1, 1982.

46. "Managers hold morning seminar on 9to5 group," *Milwaukee Journal*, December 16, 1982.

47. Phone interview, September 19, 2005.

48. "It's Your Business," August 17, 1993. The Chamber no longer has this show. The other panelists that day were Richard Lescher, president of the U.S. Chamber of Commerce, Edward Merlis, senior vice president of External Affairs for the Air Transport Association, and Thomas Higginbotham, of the International Association of Machinists.

49. Phone Interview, September 22, 2005.

7. WORKING OTHER THAN NINE TO FIVE: PART-TIME AND TEMPORARY JOBS

1. Told to me in 1999 by a reporter about the newspaper she works for. She asked me to keep the name confidential.

2. The other two are treating people differently because of actual or perceived sexual orientation or because of marital or family status (see Chapter 4).

3. Quotes taken from descriptions of "Featured Staffing Employees" on the Web site of the American Staffing Association (2006): http://www.americanstaffing.net.

4. "Staffing FAQs," http://www.americanstaffing.net/staffingcustomers/faq.cfm.

5. Kaiser Family Foundation/Health Research and Educational Trust, *Employer Health Benefits, 2004 Annual Survey*, Exhibits 2.5 and 2.6 (September 2004): 40–41, at http://www.kff.org/insurance/7148/sections/ehbs04-2-5.cfm and http://www.kff.org/insurance/7148/sections/ehbs04-2-6.cfm.

6. According to a 1997 report by the Economic Policy Institute, 28.1 percent of women employed by temporary help agencies earned less than $5.95 an hour. So did 36.7 percent of female part-timers. Fewer than one of ten women temps and two in ten part-timers received health insurance from their employer. Arne Kalleberg et al., *Nonstandard Work, Substandard Jobs* (Washington, DC: Economic Policy Institute, 1997).

7. Gilbert Nicholson, "Manage Temp Benefits Without Turning into the Next Microsoft Debacle" (September 1, 2000): http://www.workforce.com.

8. The findings were written up in a report entitled "Illegal and Unfair: Milwaukee Temp Agencies Fail Employment Testing" (Milwaukee: 9to5 Women's Education Fund, May 2000). Wisconsin is a "one-party consent state"—one party to a conversation may tape it without the other's knowledge.

9. Day Labor/Contingent Work Committee, National Campaign on Jobs and Income Support, "Permanent Struggle, Temporary Solutions: Contracting Out America," report

(Washington, DC: unpublished, February 26, 2002).

10. Interview for "Contingent Workers Fight for Fairness," a report by the North American Alliance for Employment (NAFFE) (2000): http://www.fairjobs.org/fairjobs/contingent/cwffe.php.

11. Quoted in Jacquelyn Lynn et al., "50 Ways to Save Money in Your Business," Entrepreneur.com (June 18, 2004): http://www.entrepreneur.com/article/0,4621,316002,00.html.

12. Cynthia Costello and Anne J. Stone, eds., *The American Woman 2001–2002: Getting to the Tip* (New York: Norton, 2001). Women were more than 70 percent of the increase in moonlighters from 1978–98.

13. Chris Tilly, *Half a Job: Bad and Good Part-Time Jobs in a Changing Labor Market* (Philadelphia: Temple University Press, 1996).

14. Joe Barry, "Contingent Higher Education Faculty and Their Unions in the USA: A Very Brief Summary," Report to the Conference on Contingent Academic Labor (CO-CAL), August 2004.

15. Interview for "Contingent Workers Fight for Fairness" (2000): http://www.fairjobs.org/fairjobs/contingent/cwffe.php.

16. Steven Greenhouse and Michael Barbaro, "Wal-Mart Memo Suggests Ways to Cut Employee Benefit Costs," *New York Times*, October 26, 2005.

17. Jeffrey Wenger, briefing paper for the Economic Policy Institute (April 2003): http://www.epinet.org/epinews/epinews200306.html.

18. Ibid.

19. In *Lovell v. BBNT Solutions LLC*, 295 F. Supp. 2d 611 (ED Va 2003), a federal court ruled that the Equal Pay Act may be violated when a female part-time worker is paid less per hour than full-time employees—but only if you can prove the part-timers are predominantly female and the full-timers predominantly male. See "The Network News: A Work-Family News Publication," *Sloan Work and Family Research Network* 7, no. 4 (April 2005): 2.

20. Phone interview, August 11, 2004.

21. See Daniel Pink, *Free Agent Nation: How America's New Independent Workers Are Transforming the Way We Live* (New York: Warner Books, 2001).

22. Ellen Bravo, "Recommendations of the U.S. Study Team for Achieving Equity and Fairness in Contingent Work," report for the Philippine American Foundation, 1996.

23. Eileen Appelbaum and Kimetha Firpo, "Company Practices: A Barrier to Good-quality Part-time Employment in the U.S.," *Economic Bulletin* 40, no. 10 (Berlin: DIW [German Institute for Economic Analysis]): 336.

24. "Contingent Workers Fight for Fairness" (2000): http://www.fairjobs.org/fairjobs/contingent/cwffe.php.

25. Phone interview, September 29, 2004.

26. Proposed legislation in New York is a good model, listing nine criteria for independent contractors, all of which must be in place for the classification to hold. These include maintaining a separate business with their own office, equipment, materials, and other facilities; holding a federal employer identification number; operating under contracts to perform specific services or work for specific amounts of money, controlling the means

of performing the services or work; and succeeding or failing depending on the relationship of business receipts to expenditures. If any other person, corporation, partnership, association, or other entity "maintains substantial control over the manner in which such individual performs his or her assigned duties and retains a significant financial stake in such individual's earnings," the status of independent contractor would be denied (http://assembly.state.ny.us/leg/?bn=A3347).

27. 9to5 issued a report in 1986 called "Working at the Margins" on problems of part-time and temp work (Cleveland, OH, National Association of Working Women: 1986). We cosponsored a conference in Washington, DC, with SEIU in 1987 on "Solutions for the New Workforce," in which contingent work issues played a big part. Afterward Karen Nussbaum, then-director of 9to5, and then-SEIU president John Sweeney published a book entitled *Solutions for the New Work Force: Policies for a New Social Contract* (Cabin John, Maryland: Seven Locks Press, 1989).

28. The Legal Assistance Foundation began employment testing in 1993, under the direction of Leann Lodder. She and her staff helped Linda Garcia design 9to5's temp testing.

29. *Kyles v. J.K. Guardian Security Service Inc.*, United States Court of Appeals for the Seventh Circuit, No. 98-3652 (2000). Earlier, a federal district court ruled against the employment testers because they were not really interested in the jobs for which they applied. In July 2000, the Seventh Circuit reversed that decision, ruling that employment testers serve the public interest by "provid[ing] evidence that is frequently valuable, if not indispensable."

30. Speech at a rally at QPS on March 27, 2003.

31. The survey of 1,000 adults was done for NAFFE by Lake, Snell, Perry & Associates in January 2000. Results were published in "Contigent Workers Fight for Fairness" (2000): http://www.fairjobs.org/fairjobs/contingent/cwffe.php.

32. Mary Diebel, "Despite a Booming Economy, Some Still Have Only Temporary Jobs," *Scripps-Howard News Service*, May 23, 2000.

33. Lake Snell Perry and Associates, "Contingent Workers Fight for Fairness" (2000): http://www.fairjobs.org/fairjobs/contingent/cwffe.php.

34. *M.B. Sturgis*, 331 NLRB 1298 (2000). For decades, the NLRB had held that separate employing entities could not be required to negotiate in a "multiemployer" unit unless the employers specifically agreed to negotiate through a joint bargaining agent or else agreed to bargain as a group. The *Sturgis* decision changed that, ruling that temporary employees supplied by a staffing agency could be included in a single bargaining unit with regular employees of the contracting employer. The staffing agency and the contracting employer did not have to consent; all that was required was for the temps and the regular workers to share a sufficient community of interest. In *H.S. Care L.L.C.*, 343 NLRB No. 76 (2004), a board majority overruled *Sturgis*, finding that the 2000 decision was "misguided both as a matter of statutory interpretation and sound national labor policy."

35. Sarah Henry, "Labor and Lace," *Los Angeles Times*, August 1, 1993.

36. Phone interview, November 14, 2005.

37. Cited in Gary Delgado, "How the Empress Lost Her Clothes: Asian Immigrant Women Fight Jessica McClintock," in *Beyond Identity Politics: Emerging Social Justice Movements in Communities of Color*, ed. John Anner (Boston: South End Press, 1996).

38. Ibid.

8. WHAT THIS NATION REALLY THINKS OF MOTHERHOOD: WELFARE REFORM

1. Richard J. Herrnstein and Charles Murray, *The Bell Curve: Intelligence and Class Structure in American Life* (New York: The Free Press 1994), 548.

2. Three exceptions come to mind—Cong. Lynn Woolsey, Cong. Barbara Leigh, and Sen. Patti Murray had each been on welfare at some point. They voted against the bill, known as the Personal Responsibility and Work Opportunity Reconciliation Act, or PRWORA.

3. Letter to then-archbishop Rembert Weakland, who had expressed concerns about W-2. See "Governor Tells Bishop to 'Read His Bible,'" *Christian Century*, Oracle Publishing Co. (July 17, 1996): 711.

4. 1935 Senate Finance Committee Report on the President's Economic Security Bill, *Social Security Online*: http://www.ssa.gov/history/reports/35senatereport.html. Cited in Jason DeParle, *American Dream: Three Women, Ten Kids, and a Nation's Drive to End Welfare* (New York: Viking Press, 2004), 86.

5. According to Jason DeParle, AFDC tried to make a national program out of a hodgepodge of Mothers' Pensions established in the states to keep poor children out of orphanages. Like those programs, it was intended for "fit" parents—meaning white and widowed. Congress allowed states to set payments as low as they wanted and to determine their own eligibility rules, eliminating language seen as prohibiting racial discrimination (*American Dream: Three Women, Ten Kids, and a Nation's Drive to End Welfare* [New York: Viking Press, 2004], 86).

6. Ibid., 92.

7. The racial breakdown for AFDC recipients in 1994 was as follows: White 37 percent, Black 36 percent, Hispanic 20 percent, Asian 3 percent, Native American 1 percent, and Unknown 2 percent. U.S. Department of Health and Human Services, Office of Family Assistance, 2004. Cited in Sanford F. Schram, "Contextualizing Racial Disparities in American Welfare Reform: Toward a New Poverty Research," in *Perspectives on Politics* 3, no. 2 (June 2005): 258.

8. "Welfare Myths: Fact of Fiction? Exploring the Truth about Welfare," National Center for Law and Economic Justice (Formerly the Welfare Law Center) (1986): http://www.welfarelaw.org/myths.html.

9. Roberta Spalter-Roth et al., *Welfare That Works: The Working Lives of AFDC Recipients* (Washington, DC: Institute for Women's Policy Research, 1995).

10. Paul Kleppner and Nikolas Theodore, *Work After Welfare: Is the Midwest's Booming Economy Creating Enough Jobs?* (Dekalb, IL: Midwest Job Gap Project, 1997).

11. Ibid.

12. Jason DeParle, *American Dream: Three Women, Ten Kids, and a Nation's Drive to End Welfare* (New York: Viking Press, 2004), 92.

13. Steve Kangas, "Poverty and Welfare," *Liberalism Resurgent* (1994): www.huppi.com/kangaroo/7Welfare.htm.

14. Heinz Kerry, who made the remark during the 2004 presidential campaign, quickly apologized. See "Teresa Heinz Kerry apologizes for Laura Bush comment," *USA Today* (October 20, 2004).

15. Quoted in Juan Williams, "A Question of Fairness," *Atlantic Monthly*, February 1987.

16. For two years, 9to5 and the Radcliffe Public Policy Center conducted research on low-wage workers in Boston, Denver, and Milwaukee to see how they "crossed the boundaries" between work, family, and community. Of the scores of women interviewed who had experience with welfare, not one wanted to be on assistance. See Lisa Dodson and Ellen Bravo, "Keeping Jobs and Raising Families in Low-Income America: It Just Doesn't Work" (Boston: Harvard University, 2002), http://www.radcliffe.edu/research/pubpol/boundaries.pdf.

17. Research shows that about 20 percent of women receiving cash assistance are current victims of domestic violence, while about 50 to 60 percent have experienced domestic violence during their adulthood. Nisha Patel and Vicki Turetsky, "Safety in the Safety Net: TANF Reauthorization Provisions Relevant to Domestic Violence" Pub No. 04-48 (Washington, DC: Center on Law and Social Policy, October 22, 2004). DeParle notes that Newt Gingrich argued to end welfare by pointing to "twelve-year-olds having babies." Hattie Mae Crenshaw, the mother of one of the three women DeParle followed for several years, was "the rare woman who really did get pregnant at twelve"—after being raped. Hattie Mae did go on AFDC, and as a result, was able to move and get away from her rapist (Jason DeParle, *American Dream: Three Women, Ten Kids, and a Nation's Drive to End Welfare* [New York: Viking Press, 2004], 35).

18. Testimony October 2, 2003, at a public meeting of the Good Jobs and Livable Neighborhoods Coalition, a network of more than 30 organizations in Milwaukee working to secure a Community Benefits Agreement in the development of an area known as Park East.

19. Robert Scott, "U.S.-China Trade, 1989–2003: Impact on Jobs and Industries, Nationally and State-by-State" (Washington, DC: Economic Policy Institute, January 2005).

20. In-person interview May 22, 2003.

21. Ibid, 26. Cheating is another common accusation leveled at women on welfare. They were all blamed for it, and some of them did, in fact, have jobs they didn't report while receiving a check. Given how little income welfare provided, this shouldn't surprise us. But abuse of the welfare system pales in comparison to the long history of cheating poor blacks. DeParle cites a 1939 work by anthropologist Hortense Powdermaker, who traveled extensively, examining the living conditions of blacks in the South. "She was startled at how openly planters talked of cheating," DeParle writes. "They justified it by arguing that 'the Negro is congenitally lazy and must be kept in debt in order to be made to work'" (Powdermaker, *After Freedom* [1939; repr., Madison: University of Wisconsin Press, 1993]: 22–23, cited in Jason DeParle).

22. Ibid.

23. One third have severely limited cognitive abilities, 13 percent near-daily bouts of depression, 10 percent medical disabilities, and 9 percent problems from cocaine use. Ibid., 93, citing Krista K. Olson and LaDonna Pavetti, "Personal and Family Challenges to the Successful Transition from Welfare to Work," The Urban Institute, May 17, 1996.

24. "Remarks by HHS Secretary Tommy G. Thompson: Presentation of The President's Fiscal Year 2003 Budget for the U.S. Department of Health and Human Services,"

United States Department of Health and Human Services, press release (February 4, 2002): http://www.hhs.gov/news/press/2002pres/20020204b.html.

25. Jason DeParle, *American Dream: Three Women, Ten Kids, and a Nation's Drive to End Welfare* (New York: Viking Press, 2004), 162 ff.

26. Ibid.

27. Forum on W-2 at the Italian Community Center in Milwaukee, sponsored by the Interfaith Conference of Greater Milwaukee, October 1, 2004.

28. Conversation with the head of Wisconsin's Workforce Solutions program, January 13, 2005.

29. Ibid.

30. Phone interview, June 15, 2001.

31. Department of Workforce Development is now working with advocates to develop accountability guidelines, but problems of discouraging applicants remain.

32. See Lisa Dodson and Ellen Bravo, "Keeping Jobs and Raising Families in Low-Income America: It Just Doesn't Work" (Boston: Harvard University, 2002), http://www.radcliffe.edu/research/pubpol/boundaries.pdf.

33. In-person interview, January 20, 2002.

34. Gregory Acs and Pamela Loprest, "Final Synthesis Report of Findings from ASPE 'Leavers' Grants" (Washington, DC: The Urban Institute, November 27, 2001). A 2005 report by the Legislative Audit Bureau in Wisconsin found that only 42.1 percent of those who left W-2 in 1999 earned more than the poverty level in 2003—and that's only when you count the state and federal earned income tax credits. During the first year after leaving the program, only one in five earned more than the poverty level (www.legis.state.wi.us/LAB/reports/05-6Highlights.htm).

35. Gretchen Wright, "American After 3PM: First-Ever National Household Survey On How Kids Spend the After School Hours to be Released," *Afterschool Alliance*, news release (May 19, 2004): http://www.afterschoolalliance.org/press_archives/America_3pm.pdf. The group found that 25 percent of African American students from kindergarten through twelfth grade take care of themselves after the school day ends. See Gretchen Wright, "One in Four African American Students Care for Themselves After the School Day Ends, Study Finds," *Afterschool Alliance*, news release (June 15, 2004): pdhttp://www.afterschoolalliance.org/press_archives/america_3pm/african_american_pr.pdf

36. Racism has been a problem in some programs to deal with "deadbeat dads." In Dane County, Wisconsin, for example, arrest rates for African Americans for nonpayment of child support have been shown to be 35 times those of white residents. Nearly one in two of those arrested for this reason were African Americans in a county whose 2000 African American population was 4 percent of the total county population. (Rebecca May and Marguerite Roulet, "A Look at Arrests of Low-Income Fathers for Child Support Nonpayment," *Center for Family Policy and Practice* [January 2005]), http://www.cffpp.org/publications/pdfs/noncompliance.pdf.

37. Despite the arguments of opponents, studies show past increases had no measurable negative impact on employment. According to the Economic Policy Institute and Fiscal Policy Institute, new economic models explain why: Employers absorb some of the costs of an increase through higher productivity, lower costs associated with turnover,

decreased absenteeism, and increased worker morale.Fiscal Policy Institute, "States with Minimum Wages above the Federal Level have had Faster Small Business and Retail Job Growth," March 30, 2006, www.fiscalpolicy.org/FPISmallBusinessMinWage.pdf.

38. A government employee named Molly Orshansky developed the poverty level in 1963–64 by assuming that food constituted one-third of a family's budget. She based the official level on what was actually a substandard diet, and then multiplied that by three. The poverty levels were never adjusted to take into account that the cost of housing has risen at a much higher rate than food. See Sara M. Evans and Barbara J. Nelson, *Wage Justice, Comparable Worth and the Paradox of Technocratic Reform* (Chicago: University of Chicago Press, 1989), 99.

39. This concept was first created by Dr. Diana Pearce at the organization Wider Opportunities for Women (WOW) in Washington, DC, in 1992.

40. Don Behm, "Lawsuit seeks to block payment to Cabela's," *Milwaukee Journal Sentinel*, September 30, 2005.

41. "The Bush Record on Shipping Jobs Overseas," *AFL-CIO Issue Brief*, August 2004. Consider this example cited by Alan Sloan in *Newsweek* ("Tax Holiday," January 24, 2006): Ford Motors got a $250 million tax break from a 2004 bill known as the American Jobs Creation Act. The law allowed Ford and other corporations to pay only 5.25 percent tax—rather than the usual 35 percent—on profits made overseas and brought back to the U.S., allegedly in order to create jobs. Just one problem: rather than creating jobs, Ford cut 10,000 of them and announced its intention to cut up to 30,000 more.

42. Cited in Jason DeParle, *American Dream: Three Women, Ten Kids, and a Nation's Drive to End Welfare* (New York: Viking Press, 2004), 89.

43. See Teresa Funicello's powerful essay, "Poverty Wears a Female Face," in *Sisterhood Is Forever*, ed. Robin Morgan (New York: Washington Square Press, 2003).

44. Jason DeParle, *American Dream: Three Women, Ten Kids, and a Nation's Drive to End Welfare* (New York: Viking Press, 2004), 75–76.

45. Ibid., 113.

46. Ibid., 102.

47. The debate took place September 25, 1997, at Harry W. Schwartz Book Store in Milwaukee.

48. In-person interview, January 19, 2005.

49. When the EEOC investigated, Maximus claimed the lower pay rate was part of a training program for women on W-2. Yet Tracy Jones wasn't on W-2; neither she nor the other women involved in the complaint, who had been on W-2, ever received any special training. Despite efforts by Senator Moore and a finding of a pattern of discrimination by the EEOC, the agency's contract was unaffected by Jones's case. Maximus also received only minimal fines for the financial shenanigans, which administrators blamed on a "junior bookkeeper." See "Working for Change—Maximizing profits and multiplying miscues," www.workingforchange.com/article.cfm?ItemID=11320.

50. Lisa Dodson and Ellen Bravo, "Keeping Jobs and Raising Families in Low-Income America: It Just Doesn't Work" (Boston: Harvard University, 2002), http://www.radcliffe.edu/research/pubpol/boundaries.pdf.

51. "Welfare as We Know It: The Case for Reforming TANF" (Milwaukee, WI: 9to5, National Association of Working Women, 2002).

52. President Bush proposed taking $300 million a year from TANF funds for marriage promotion initiatives, including advertising campaigns as well as counseling sessions. See www.jeanhardisty.com/essay_challengingmarriageasacureforpoverty.html.

53. Barbara Ehrenreich, "Prodding the Poor to the Altar," *The Progressive*, August 2001, 65 (8):14–15.

54. Phone interview, June 28, 2005.

55. Phone interview, April 28, 2005.

9. REVALUING WOMEN'S WORK OUTSIDE OF WORK

1. Marty Nemko, "Why Women Earn Less," *The American Conservative Union Foundation* (2004): http://acuf.org/issues/issue21/040929gov.asp.

2. William Blackstone, "Commentaries on the Laws of England." A Facsimile of the First Edition of 1765–1769, Vol. I (Chicago: University of Chicago Press, 1979).

3. Demie Kurz, *For Richer, for Poorer* (New York: Routledge, 1995). Some experts put this figure even higher. See Stephen Rose, *On Shaky Ground: Rising Fears About Incomes and Learning* (National Commission for Employment Policy Research Report No. 94–02, 1994), who says it's 70 percent. Cited in Joan Williams, *Unbending Gender: Why Family and Work Conflict and What to Do About It* (New York: Oxford University Press, 2000), a thorough resource on the laws and court cases regarding marriage, divorce, and custody.

4. "Maryland Gender Bias Report," *Gender Bias in the Courts* (Maryland Special Joint Committee, 1989), 59–62. Cited in Joan Williams, *Unbending Gender: Why Family and Work Conflict and What to Do About It* (New York: Oxford University Press, 2000).

5. Cited in Joan Williams, *Unbending Gender: Why Family and Work Conflict and What to Do About It* (New York: Oxford University Press, 2000), 126. Ann Crittenden, *The Price of Motherhood*, notes that women who remarry on average enjoy a living standard five years after the divorce that is 125 percent of what they had in the year before the divorce. Divorced men average 130 percent five years later—whether or not they remarry New York: Metropolitan, 2001, 147.

6. Cited in Ann Crittenden, *The Price of Motherhood* (New York: Metropolitan, 2001), 155. This book is an excellent discussion of the Mommy Tax and the inequities remaining in divorce and child support.

7. Ibid., 155–56.

8. Phone interview, November 10, 2005.

9. Phone interview, November 14, 2005.

10. Susan Dominus, "The Father's Crusade," *New York Times Magazine*, May 8, 2005.

11. Ibid.

12. Cited in Joan Williams, *Unbending Gender: Why Family and Work Conflict and What to Do About It* (New York: Oxford University Press, 2000), 139. See Susan Estrich, "Marcia Clark Deserves Better," *USA Today*, March 9, 1998.

13. Cited in Joan Williams, *Unbending Gender*, 139. A year later Prost quit her job and took another that allowed her to be home at three o'clock; she was then awarded joint custody.

14. Joseph E. Cordell, J.D., *Civil War: A Dad's Guide to Custody*, excerpted on www.dadsdivorce.com/resources/guides/custody/index.php.

15. "Achieving Equal Justice for Men and Women in the Courts—the Draft Report of the Judicial Council Advisory Committee on Gender Bias in the Courts" (The California Gender Bias Report, 1990).

16. Susan Dominus, "The Father's Crusade," *New York Times Magazine*, May 8, 2005.

17. Phone interview, November 11, 2005.

18. M. A. Straus, "Ordinary Violence, Child Abuse, and Wife Beating: What Do They Have in Common?" In *The Dark Side of Families: Current Family Violence Research*, eds D. Finkelhor, R. J. Gelles, G. T. Hotaling, and M. A. Straus (Newbury Park, CA: Sage, 1983), 213–34.

19. Daniel G. Saunders, "Child Custody and Visitations Decision in Domestic Violence Cases: Legal Trends, Research Findings and Recommendations," (1998): http://www.ssw.umich.edu/research/saunddan/CustodySaundersVAW-net.pdf. According to a 2004 Massachusetts survey by Harvard professor Jay Silverman, alleged batterers fighting for child custody won in an astonishing 54 percent of cases, almost all using the argument of "parental alienation." Cited in Sarah Childress, "Fighting Over the Kids," *Newsweek*, September 25, 2006, 35.

20. S. Brustin, "Legal Response to Teen Dating Violence," *Family Law Quarterly* 29, no. 2, 331 (Summer 1995): 333 (citing Barrie Levy, *In Love & In Danger: A Teen's Guide to Breaking Free of an Abusive Relationship* [Seattle, WA: Seal Books, 1993]).

21. Statement by Patti, played by Lili Taylor, in *Girls Town*, October Films, directed by Jim McKay, 1996.

22. Phone interview, July 14, 2006.

23. Phone interview, July 18, 2006.

24. The amendment passed on November 7, 2006.

25. See Stephanie Coontz, "The Heterosexual Revolution," *New York Times*, July 5, 2005.

26. Suzanne M. Bianchi, Melissa A. Milkie, Liana C. Sayer, and John P. Robinson, "Is Anyone Doing the Housework? Trends in the Gender Division of Household Labor," *Social Forces*, 79, no. 1 (2000): 191–228.

27. Xiaole Xu, "Convergence or Divergence: The Transformation of Marriage and Relationships in Urban America and Urban China," *Journal of Asian and African Studies* (August 1, 1998), http://www.highbeam.com.library.doc3asp?docid=IGI:70980086.

28. Phyllis Moen and Patricia Roehling, *Career Mystique: Cracks in the American Dream* (Maryland: Rowman & Littlefield, 2005).

29. Bianchi et al., "Is Anyone Doing the Housework?"

30. George Akerloff and Rachel Kranton, "Economics and Identity," *Quarterly Journal of Economics*, 115(3) (2000):715–53; cited in Ann Crittenden, *The Price of Motherhood* (New York: Metropolitan, 2001), 24.

31. See Arlie Hochschild with Anne Machung, *The Second Shift: Working Parents and the Revolution at Home* (New York: Viking, 1989).

32. A 2004 study by Harvard economic professor Claudia Goldin found that 44 percent of women in the 1980 Harvard class who married within a decade after graduation kept their birth names. The percentage fell to 32 percent for the class of 1990. By 2003, more than three in four college-educated women were taking their husband's name ("A

New Comfort Zone? Fewer Women Keeping Names on Marriage," *Harvard University Gazette*, August 26, 2004. Also cited in Maureen Dowd, "What's a Modern Girl to Do?" *New York Times* magazine, October 30, 2005).

33. *Housekeeping Monthly*, May 13, 1955: http://j-walk.com/other/goodwife/index.htm.

34. Lisa Belkin, "The Opt Out Revolution," *New York Times* magazine, October 26, 2003.

35. Louise Story, "Many Women at Elite Colleges Set Career Path to Motherhood," *New York Times*, September 20, 2005.

36. Heather Boushey, "Women Opting Out? Debunking the Myth" (Center for Economic and Policy Research, November 2005). According to this report, the rate of women with children employed outside the home in 2004 lagged behind the rate for women without kids by 8.2 percent—down from 9.9 percent in 2000, and 20.7 percent in 1984.

37. For an excellent rebuttal of the story survey, see Katha Pollitt, "Desperate Housewives of the Ivy League?," *Nation*, October 17, 2005.

38. Ann Crittenden summarizes the value of these relational skills in *If You've Raised Kids, You Can Manage Anything: Leadership Begins at Home* (New York: Gotham Books, 2004).

39. Marty Nemko, "Why Women Earn Less," *The American Conservative Union Foundation* (2004): http://acuf.org/issues/issue21/040929gov.asp.

40. Jody Miller and Matt Miller, "Get a Life," *Fortune*, November 28, 2005.

41. Ellen Galinsky and Judy David, *Ask the Children: The Breakthrough Study that Reveals How to Succeed at Work and Parenting* (New York: Quill, 1999).

42. Sue Shellenbarger, "It's the Type of Job You Have That Affects the Kids, Studies Say," in *Work and Family: Essays from the "Work and Family" Column of the Wall Street Journal.* (New York: Ballantine Books, 1999).

43. Barbara Ehrenreich, *Nickel and Dimed: On (Not) Getting by in America* (New York: Metropolitan, 2001).

44. Joy M. Zaremka, "America's Dirty Work: Migrant Maids and Modern-Day Slavery," in *Global Woman: Nannies, Maids and Sex Workers in the New Economy*, eds. Barbara Ehrenreich and Arlie Hochschild (New York: Metropolitan Books, 2002), 149.

45. Alice Childress, *Like One of the Family: Conversations from a Domestic's Life* (Boston: Beacon Press, 1956).

46. Cited in Barbara Ehrenreich and Arlie Russell Hochschild, "Maid to Order," in *Global Woman: Nannies, Maids, and Sex Workers in the New Economy*, (New York: Metropolitan Books, 2003), 92.

47. See Childress, "Hands," and "We Need a Union," in *Like One of the Family: Conversations from a Domestic's Life* (Boston: Beacon Press, 1956).

48. A number of groups, including the Institute for Women's Policy Research and the National Women's Law Center, have examined this issue and made suggestions for further research to identify the most effective reforms (see www.ipr.org and www.nwlc.org for more information).

49. Susan Wood, the FDA's assistant commissioner for women's health and director of the Office of Women's Health, resigned August 31, 2005, to protest the agency's delay in approving the "morning-after pill" known as Plan B. "I can no longer serve as staff when

scientific and clinical evidence, fully evaluated and recommended for approval by the professional staff here, has been overruled," she wrote in an email to FDA staff. Marc Kauffman, "FDA Official Quits Over Delay on Plan B," *Washington Post*, September 1, 2005.

50. Jennifer Gordon, *Suburban Sweatshops: The Fight for Immigrant Rights* (Cambridge: Belknap Press of Harvard University Press), 2005.

51. Phone interview, December 2, 2005.

10. HOW YOU CAN HELP GET THERE

1. See Juan Williams, "The Long History of a Bus Ride," *New York Times*, October 31, 2005. Williams points out that Parks, a leader of the local NAACP chapter in the late 1940s, had refused to enter the back of the bus as early as 1943.

2. Adapted from a statement entitled "Building a 21st Century Transnational Women's Movement: A Collective Statement of Shared Vision," written by a group of women activists from around the world who met at Sarah Lawrence College in New York September 10–14, 2005 (text available at the *Women of Color Resource Center*, www.coloredgirls.org/programs/documents/finalglobal.htm).

ORGANIZATIONS DESCRIBED IN THE BOOK

9to5, National Association of Working Women
207 East Buffalo, Suite 211
Milwaukee, WI 53202
Phone: 414-274-0925
Fax: 414-272-2870
9to5@9to5.org
www.9to5.org

Asian Immigrant Women Advocates (AIWA)
310 8th Street, Suite 301
Oakland, CA 94607
Phone: 510-268-0192
Fax: 510-268-0194
info@aiwa.org
www.aiwa.org

Center for Community Change
1000 Wisconsin Avenue NW
Washington, DC 20007
Phone: 202-342-0567
Fax: 202-333-5462
info@communitychange.org
www.communitychange.org

Direct Action for Rights and Equality (DARE)
340 Lockwood Street
Providence, RI 02907
Phone: 401-351-6960
Fax: 401-351-6977
DARE@ids.net

Hard Hatted Women
3043 Superior Avenue
Cleveland, OH 44114
Phone: 216-881-8550
Fax: 216-861-7204
info@hardhattedwomen.org
www.hardhattedwomen.org

Miles Foundation
PO Box 423
Newtown, CT 06470-0423
Phone: 203-270-7861
Milesfdn@aol.com or milesfdn@yahoo.com

The Workplace Project
91 N. Franklin Street, Suite 207
Hempstead, New York 11550-3003
Phone: 516-565-5377 or 5372
Fax: 516-565-5470
workplace@igc.org
www.workplaceproject.org

A SAMPLING OF OTHER FEMINIST ORGANIZATIONS

American Association of University Women (AAUW)
1111 16th Street NW
Washington, DC 20036
Phone: 202-785-7720
Phone: 800-326-AAUW
Fax: 202-872-1425
TDD: 202-785-7777
info@aauw.org
www.aauw.org

Black Women's Health Imperative
600 Pennsylvania Ave SE, Suite 310
Washington, DC 20003
Phone: 202-548-4000
Fax: 202-543-9743
nbwhp@nbwhp.org
www.blackwomenshealth.org

Business and Professional Women/USA
1900 M Street NW, Suite 310
Washington, DC 20036
Phone: 202-293-1100
Fax: 202-861-0298
memberservices@bpwusa.org
www.bpwusa.org

Catalyst
120 Wall Street, Fifth Floor
New York, NY 10005
Phone: 212-514-7600
Fax: 212-514-8470
info@catalyst.org
www.catalystwomen.org

Center for the Advancement of Women
25 W. 43rd Street, Suite 1104
New York, NY 10036
Phone: 212-391-7718
Fax: 212-391-7720
info@advancewomen.org
www.advancewomen.org

Center for Research on Women
University of Memphis
339 Clement Hall
Memphis, TN 3815-23550
Phone: 901-678-2770
Fax: 901-678-3652
crow@memphis.edu
http://cas.memphis.edu/isc/crow/ind

Choice USA
1010 Wisconsin Avenue NW, Suite 410
Washington, DC 20007
Phone: 202-965-7700
Toll-free (888) 784-4494
Fax: 202-965-7701
info@choiceusa.org
www.choiceusa.org

Disabled Women on the Web
info@disabledwomen.net
www.disabledwomen.net

Equal Rights Advocates
1663 Mission Street, Suite 250
San Francisco, CA 94103
Phone: 415-621-0672
Fax: 415-621-6744
info@equalrights.org
www.equalrights.org

Esperanza Peace and Justice Center
922 San Pedro
San Antonio, TX 78212
Phone: 210-228-0201
Fax: 210-228-0000
esperanza@esperanzacenter.org
www.esperanzacenter.org

Family Violence Prevention Fund
383 Rhode Island Street, Suite 304
San Francisco, CA 94103
Phone: 415-252-8900
Fax: (415) 252-8991
TTY: (800) 595-4889
info@endabuse.org
www.fvpf.org

Feminist Majority Foundation
1600 Wilson Boulevard, Suite 801
Arlington, VA 22209
Phone: 703-522-2214
Fax: 703-522-2219
www.feminist.org

INCITE! Women of Color Against Violence
Incite_national@yahoo.org
www.incite-national.org

Indigenous Women's Network
Alma de Mujer 13621 FM 2769
Austin, TX 78726
Phone: 512-258-3880
Fax: 512-258-1858
iwn@indigenouswomen.org
www.indigenouswomen.org

Institute for Women's Policy Research
1707 L Street, NW, Suite 750
Washington, DC 20036
Phone: 202-785-5100
Fax: 202-833-4362
iwpr@iwpr.org
www.iwpr.org

Labor Project on Working Families
2521 Channing Way #5555
Berkeley, CA 94720
Phone: 510-643-6814
Fax: 510-642-6432
lpwf@berkeley.edu
www.laborproject.org

League of Women Voters
1730 M Street NW, Suite 1000
Washington, DC 20036-4508
Phone: 202-418-1965
Fax: 202-429-0854
lwv@lwv.org
www.lwv.org

Legal Momentum
395 Hudson Street
New York, NY 10014
Phone: 212-925-6635
Fax: 212-226-1066
www.legalmomentum.org

MADRE
121 W. 27th Street, Suite 301
New York, NY 10001
Phone: 212-627-0444
Fax: 212-675-3704
madre@madre.org
www.madre.org

NARAL Pro-Choice America
1156 15th Street NW, Suite 700
Washington, DC 20005
Phone: 202-973-3000
Fax: 202-973-3096
www.naral.org

National Asian Pacific American Women's Forum
1112 16th Street NW, Suite 110
Washington, DC 20036
Phone: 202-293-2688
Fax: 202-293-4507
www.napawf.org

National Center for Human Rights Education
PO Box 311020
Atlanta, GA 31131
Phone: 404-344-9629
Fax: 414-346-7517
info@nchre.org
www.nchre.org

National Center for Lesbian Rights
870 Market Street, Suite 370
San Francisco, CA 94102
Phone: 415-392-6257
Fax: 415-392-8442
info@nclrights.org
www.nclrights.org

National Coalition Against Domestic Violence
1120 Lincoln Street, Suite 1603
Denver, CO 80203
Hotline: 1-800-799-SAFE
Phone: 303-839-1852
Fax: 303-831-9251
TTY: 303-839-1681
mainoffice@ncadv.org
www.ncadv.org

National Committee on Pay Equity
C/O AFT
555 New Jersey Avenue NW
Washington, DC 20001-2079
Phone: 703-920-2010
Fax: 703-979-6372
fairpay@pay-equity.org
www.pay-equity.org

National Conference of Puerto Rican Women
5 Thomas Circle NW
Washington, DC 20005
Phone: 202-387-4716
Fax: 305-592-6601
chicotorre@aol.clom
www.nacoprw.org

National Council of Negro Women
633 Pennsylvania Avenue NW
Washington, DC 20004
Phone: 202-737-0120
Fax: 202-737-0476
www.ncnw.org

National Council of Women's Organizations
1050 17th Street NW, Suite 250
Washington, DC 20036
Phone: 202-393-7122
Fax: 202-293-4507
ncwo@ncwo-online.org
www.womensorganizations.org

National Network of Abortion Funds
42 Seaverns Avenue
Boston, MA 02130-2865
Phone: 617-524-6040
Fax: 617-524-6042
info@nnaf.org
www.nnaf.org

National Partnership for Women and Families
1875 Connecticut Avenue NW, Suite 710
Washington, DC 20009
Phone: 202-986-2600
Fax: 202-986-2539
info@nationalpartnership.org
www.nationalpartnership.org

National Organization for Women
1100 H Street NW, 3rd floor
Washington, DC 20005
Phone: 202-628-8669 x 120
Fax: 202-785-8576
www.now.org

National Welfare Rights Union
PO Box 3586
Highland Park, MI 48201
Phone: 313-832-0618
Fax: 313-832-1409
info@nationalwru.org
www.nationalwru.org

National Women's Alliance
1807 18th Street NW, 2nd floor
Washington DC 20009
Phone: 202-518-5411
www.nwaforchange.org

National Women's Law Center
11 Dupont Circle, NW, Suite 800
Washington, DC 20036
Phone: 202-588-5180

National Women's Studies Association (NWSA)
University of Maryland
7100 Baltimore Boulevard, Suite 500
College Park, MD 20740
Phone: 301-403-0525
Fax: 301-403-4137
nwsaoffice@nwsa.org
www.nwsa.org

Planned Parenthood Federation of America
434 W. 33rd Street
New York, NY 10001
Phone: 212-541-7800
Fax: 212-245-1845
1-800-230-PLAN (7526)
communications@ppfa.org
www.ppfa.org

Rape, Abuse and Incest National Network (RAINN)
635-B Pennsylvania Avenue SE
Washington, DC 20003
Phone: 202-544-1034
Fax 202-544-3556
800-656-HOPE (4673)
info@rainn.org
www.rainn.org

Refugee Women's Network
4151 Memorial Drive, Suite 103-F
Decatur, GA 30032
Phone: 404-299-0180 ext. 224
www.riwn.org

SAKHI for South Asian Women
PO Box 20208
Greeley Square Station
New York, NY 1001
Phone: 212-714-9153
Fax: 212-564-8745
sakhiny@aol.com
www.sakhi.com

Sisters on the Rise
Mothers on the Move
PO Box 740581
Bronx, NY 10474
Phone: 718-991-6003
www.sistasontherise.org

Sister Song: Women of Color Reproductive Health Collective
P.O. Box 311020
Atlanta, GA 31131
Phone: 404-344-9629l
www.nchre.org

Third Wave Foundation
511 W. 25th Street, Suite 301
New York, NY 10001
Phone: 212-675-0700
www.thirdwavefoundation.org

WAND (Women's Action for New Directions) Education Fund
691 Massachusetts Avenue
Arlington, MA 02476
Phone: 781-643-6740
Fax: 781-643-6744
info@wand.org
www.wand.org

The White House Project
110 Wall Street, 16th Floor
New York, NY 10005
Phone: 212-785-6001
Fax: 212-785-6007
admin@thewhitehouseproject.org
www.thewhitehouseproject.org

Wider Opportunities for Women (WOW)
1001 Connecticut Avenue, NW, Suite 930
Washington, DC 20036
Phone: 202-464-1596
Fax: 202-464-1660
info@wowonline.org
www.wowonline.org

Women of Color Resource Center
1611 Telegraph Avenue, Suite 303
Oakland, CA 94612
Phone: 510-444-2700
www.coloredgirls.org

Women Employed Institute
111 N. Wabash, Suite 1300
Chicago, IL 60602
Phone: 312-782-3902
Fax: 312-782-5249
www.womenemployed.org

Women's Edge Coalition
1825 Connecticut Avenue NW, Suite 800
Washington, DC 20009
Phone: 202-884-8396
Fax: 202-884-8366
edge@womensedge.org
www.womensedge.org

Women's Leadership Circles
672 S. LaFayette Park Place, Suite 27
Los Angeles, CA 90057
Phone: 213-388-3050
www.w-l-c.org

Women's Research & Education Institute (WREI)
3300 North Fairfax Drive, Suite 218
Arlington, VA 22201

Women's Rights Project
American Civil Liberties Union
125 Broad Street, 18th Floor
New York, NY 10004
Phone: 212-549-2668
Fax: 212-549-2580
www.aclu.org

APPENDIX B.
ALTERNATIVE SOURCES OF INFORMATION

Air America
641 6th Avenue, 4th Floor
New York, NY 10011
www.airamericaradio.com

AFL-CIO
(American Federation of Labor-Congress of Industrial Organizations)
815 16th Street NW
Washington, DC 20006
Phone: 202-638-5000
www.aflcio.org

Applied Resource Center
900 Alice Street, Suite 400
Oakland, CA 94607
Phone: 510-653-3415
Fax: 510-653-3427
www.arc.org

ColorLines Magazine
PMB 319
Oakland, CA 94611-5221
Phone: 510-653-3415
Fax: 510-653-3427
colorlines@arc.org
www.colorlines.com

Democracy Now!
87 Lafayette Street, Ground Floor
New York, NY 10013
Phone: 212-431-9090
Fax: 212-431-8858
mail@democracynow.org
www.democracynow.org

Green Stone Media
200 West Mercer Street, Suite 102
Seatlle, WA 98119
Phone: 877-854-6200
www.greenstonemedia.net

Mother Jones
222 Sutter Street, 6th Floor
San Francisco, CA 94108
Phone: 415-321-1700
Fax: 415-321-1701
backtalk@motherjones.org
www.motherjones.org

MoveOn
www.MoveOn.org

***Ms.* Magazine**
433 South Beverly Drive
Beverly Hills, CA 90212
Phone: 310-556-2515
Fax: 310-556-2514
www.msmagazine.com

The Nation
33 Irving Place
New York, NY 10003
Phone: 212-209-5400
Fax: 212-982-9000
www.thenation.com

The Progressive
409 East Main Street
Madison, WI 53703
Phone: 608-257-4626
Fax: 608-257-3373
www.progressive.org

SheSource
Sarah Bacon, Fenton Communications
Phone: 212-584-5000
sbacon@fenton.org
www.shesource.org

Sister to Sister
1611 Telegraph Avenue, Suite 303
Oakland, CA 94612
Phone: 510-444-2700
Fax: 510-444-2711
info@coloredgirls.org
www.coloredgirls.org
(3 times a year, publication of Women of Color Resource Center)

Women's E News
135 W. 29th Street, Suite 1005
New York NY 10001
Phone: 212-244-1720
Fax: 212-244-2320
www.womensenews.org

Women's Media Center
350 5th Avenue, Suite 901
New York, NY 10118
Phone: 212-563-0680
Fax: 212-563-0688
info@womensmediacenter.org
www.womensmediacenter.org

The Feminist Press at the City University of New York is a nonprofit literary and educational institution dedicated to publishing work by and about women. Our existence is grounded in the knowledge that women's writing has often been absent or underrepresented on bookstore and library shelves and in educational curricula—and that such absences contribute, in turn, to the exclusion of women from the literary canon, from the historical record, and from the public discourse.

The Feminist Press was founded in 1970. In its early decades, the Feminist Press launched the contemporary rediscovery of "lost" American women writers, and went on to diversify its list by publishing significant works by American women writers of color. More recently, the Press's publishing program has focused on international women writers, who remain far less likely to be translated than male writers, and on nonfiction works that explore issues affecting the lives of women around the world.

Founded in an activist spirit, the Feminist Press is currently undertaking initiatives that will bring its books and educational resources to underserved populations, including community colleges, public high schools and middle schools, literacy and ESL programs, and prison education programs. As we move forward into the twenty-first century, we continue to expand our work to respond to women's silences wherever they are found.

For information about events and for a complete catalog of the Press's 250 books, please refer to our Web site: www.feministpress.org.